The Education of Children with Medical Conditions

EDITED BY

ALISON CLOSS

David Fulton Publishers
London

David Fulton Publishers Ltd
Ormond House, 26–27 Boswell Street, London WC1N 3JD

First published in Great Britain by David Fulton Publishers 2000

Note: The right of Alison Closs to be identified as the editor of this work has been asserted by her in accordance with the Copyright, Designs and Patents Act 1988.

Copyright © David Fulton Publishers 2000

British Library Cataloguing in Publication Data
A catalogue record for this book is available from the British Library

ISBN 1–85346–569–0

Typeset by Elite Typesetting Techniques, Eastleigh, Hampshire
Printed in Great Britain by The Cromwell Press Ltd, Trowbridge, Wilts.

Contents

Foreword

The past decade has seen major developments (and expectations) in terms of the inclusion of children with a range of disabilities and medical conditions within the lives of their local communities. For most children (and families), access to education is a cornerstone of everyday living, offering important opportunities for personal achievements and friendships and helping to plan for adult life. But when a child has a chronic or serious shorter term medical condition, those expectations may be challenged. Schools and families may be alarmed at the implications of including children with special care needs. When a condition is degenerating or life-threatening, there may be fear and embarrassment about discussing the child's perception of that condition and his or her needs. Many schools feel anxious at the level of responsibility placed on them, particularly when a child's medical care and treatment may necessitate special and additional support in the classroom. Few mainstream schools will have direct experience of managing special health care needs, and in an increasingly litigious society, governors may fear legal action if a vulnerable child has an accident or if school staff fail to carry out a special medical procedure appropriately.

However, notwithstanding anxieties, the Government's commitment to developing a more inclusive education system (and the greatly improved life expectancy of many children with complex and challenging medical conditions) has created what the Warnock Committee described as a 'sea change' in thinking about the wider range of special needs which a school may encounter. This book is particularly timely in offering schools, education departments and health and social services an informed perspective on the experiences, policies, practices and development plans which can ensure that this group of children **can** enjoy the same educational opportunities as their peers.

The book gives powerful messages from children, siblings and parents about the emotional and physical impact of growing up with a serious medical condition. It also demonstrates the importance of asking families what **they** need in order to support their children's learning and physical and emotional well-being. It offers invaluable practical advice to those who will offer support on a daily basis to children who will often be atypical in that learning environment and where the teacher or learning support assistant may hesitate to ask questions which may appear intrusive or inappropriate.

A child's chronic medical condition affects the whole family. The impact will vary according to the child's age and stage of development. But for the majority of children, developmental progress will be affected by the restricted social experiences; periods of hospitalisation; the impact of particular treatments and family emotions around 'living with uncertainty'. Education services may find it challenging to develop positive partnerships with parents who are constantly anxious and whose lives have been dramatically affected by their child's condition. Attitudes to the child may be over-protective, or reflect low expectations and limited challenges. Managing medical conditions in educational settings cannot only be problem-focused. Understanding the condition, its likely impact on the child and his or her learning and on family life, will facilitate the development of coping strategies.

Very importantly, this book gives practical suggestions for communicating directly and honestly with the children themselves and building **their** wishes and feelings into their education programmes. Fully including a child with a medical condition in the life of a school (and minimising the risk of bullying and social exclusion for children who may be seen as very 'different') requires planning and action. The concept of social skills training for children themselves in managing their own condition in school settings is exciting and positive. There are also practical suggestions for preparing schools (including peer pupil groups) to receive a child with a special medical condition or health care need within the life of that educational community.

As one author notes, truancy and school exclusions excite considerable public debate, with a strong and united emphasis upon the importance of getting these children back into the school system. Children with medical conditions are often a silent minority within the access and inclusion debate. There may be doubts about how best to differentiate curriculum activities; what role the teachers should play in meeting specific healthcare needs and how the school can support inclusion when outcomes are uncertain.

But this group of children can, and wish to, achieve like their peers. Education may be a lifeline of opportunity and normality to children and families. Education will not only be school based. In many cases children will need a combination of flexible and school-based, hospital and home tuition. Health service staff will have a key role in understanding and supporting what the Court Committee on Child Health services described as 'educational medicine'. Social services will have an important role in supporting families and ensuring that any necessary aids, equipment or home adaptations are available. Education

Departments will have a crucial role in advising and supporting individual schools.

The Education of Children with Medical Conditions is an important and timely contribution to discussion and debate about how we achieve maximum inclusion for all children with special education or health care needs. It emphasises the need for strategic partnerships between education and health services, teachers, children and families in understanding the practical and emotional impact of a chronic medical condition on education and development. Most importantly it recognises the potential and the entitlements of this minority group of children to positive educational opportunities and, thereby, for higher expectations of a valued adult life in family and community.

Philippa Russell
Director, Council for Disabled Children
September 1999

Notes on authors

Angela Bolton was the Project Officer for the National Association for Sick Children's *Pupils' and Parents' Voice Project* and has since been Research Fellow in Social Policy and Social Work at Warwick University. Her research interests also include child employment, research methods with children and young people, the impact of welfare and penal policies on women prisoners.

Ann Burnett is the Senior Teacher in the City of Edinburgh's Hospital and Home Teaching Service. She taught in mainstream schools both as a class teacher and in learning support before entering the hospital service. She has particular interests in the use of counselling approaches within education and in information communication technology in the education of sick children.

Alison Closs is Senior Lecturer in the Department of Equity Studies and Special Education at Edinburgh University, and a Course Leader in the Master's Programme in SEN. Her research interests include the education of children and young people with medical conditions, refugee children, and equity in education for all potentially disadvantaged children.

Mairi Ann Cullen is an educational researcher at the National Foundation for Educational Research in Slough. She previously worked at the Scottish Council for Research in Education and at Moray House Institute of Education, both in Edinburgh. She has one son and it is as a mother that she has written for this book.

Richard Docherty is now 15 years old and completing his Standard Grade examinations. He hopes to go to university to study Sports Management eventually. He is a schoolboy international in both rugby and hockey and would like to complete a triple by representing Scotland in football as well. He has had diabetes since he was in his last year of primary school.

Sinead Douglas is 19 years old and currently enrolled in the first year of an Honours Degree in Health Studies. She has a wide range of interests from theatre and ballet to really loud modern music. She has a large circle of friends and an active social life, which she works hard to manage while coping with cystic fibrosis.

Christine Eiser is Director of the Child and Family Research Group in the School of Psychology, University of Exeter, and is funded by the Cancer Research Campaign. She has written several books concerned with the psychosocial implications of chronic and life-threatening disease for children and their families. She is currently attempting to develop measures that specifically reflect the child's perception of quality of life during treatment.

Peter Feeley has been the Co-ordinator of the Hospital Education and Home Tuition Service in the City of Glasgow since 1993. He was previously an Adviser in Special Educational Needs within Strathclyde Region for ten years and has taught in Primary and Special Schools in Glasgow.

Helen Hart is a counsellor and counselling supervisor with a background knowledge of education. She is a trustee of the Ataxia Telangiectasia (A-T) Society and has two adult sons with A-T. She is the Family Counsellor for the Society and also counsels for Cruse Bereavement Care. She is married and lives in Edinburgh.

Ronnie Hassard is one of three Vice-Principals in Grosvenor Grammar School, Belfast. His background is in English teaching, of which craft he is still a practitioner, and from which most of his recreational interests arise. His work now involves him in most areas of a lively and successful school.

Kathryn Hegarty left school recently and has applied for a Higher Education Access Course with a view to studying nursing at university. She is currently having a 'year out' undertaking voluntary and paid work and regaining her health on effective new medication for her asthma.

Patricia Jackson is a Consultant Paediatrician specialising in Community Paediatrics with particular interests in children with severe complex disability, the development of preschool multidisciplinary teams and parent-led organisations which facilitate better communication between parents and health professionals. She is a Medical Adviser to the Scottish Down's Syndrome Association and a Director of the Children's Hospice Association Scotland.

Bernadette Kelly, aged 18, is the second youngest in a family of five children. She is a sixth year pupil at St Andrew's High School in Kirkcaldy. She hopes to study theology at Edinburgh University. She is very much an activist, being involved at school and within her church and local community with organisations to do with human needs and rights.

Oliver Leaman teaches at Liverpool John Moores University, and has worked for many years in the School of Education. He writes on the treatment of death in the school curriculum, and is currently co-editing the *Encyclopaedia of Death and Dying* (with Glennys Howarth) for Routledge.

Tanya Lyke is 22. She edits *Young Arthritis News* and has spoken at several international conferences on arthritis. She left school in 1994 and still hopes to go to university some time, health permitting. Her main interests are reading, writing and friends (including her dogs). She is a keen car driver.

Sandra Mason is married with two boys (16 and 12), the elder of whom has a serious kidney disorder. As a result of this experience, she has been involved in coordinating a support group for parents of children with special needs and is undertaking a counselling course at college. Eventually, she would like to be a family counsellor.

Joy McFarlane taught in two primary schools before being appointed assistant head teacher at Balmalloch Primary, where she helped set up its new infant school, then, after having her family, she moved to Borestone Primary, Stirling, as assistant, deputy and then head teacher. Her chapter in this book is based on work carried out towards the end of eight very fulfilling years there. She recently became head teacher of Dunblane Primary School.

Jeremy Nelson is now 26. He graduated from Edinburgh University with an honours degree in artificial intelligence and computer science, staying on to work there for 18 months before moving to London to work as a computer software developer. His other interests include hill walking, reading and an active social life.

Claire Norris is a freelance researcher currently living in Abu Dhabi. She has worked as a researcher for the Scottish Office and in Moray House Institute of Education, Edinburgh. Her research and writing has covered housing issues, the education of Romany Traveller children, the education of children with medical conditions, and the rise of attention deficit disorder (ADD).

Amanda O'Sullivan gave up work as a Psychiatric Nurse in 1989 to start a family. She is now a full-time housewife and mother of two daughters, Amy and Emma. Her interests include swimming, dancing and do-it-yourself activities.

Tony O'Sullivan is Head of Research with Scottish Homes and an economist by training. He spent five years as a Lecturer at the University of Glasgow. Beyond work, his interests are his family, PCs and Manchester United.

Carolyn Skilling is an educator with experience in all sectors of education and in management. She introduced computer-assisted learning to special schools in Leicestershire and linked British and American schools via e-mail to develop the curriculum. As second Director of the National Association for the Education of Sick Children (NAESC/PRESENT), she is intent on developing new technologies to enable sick children to continue learning.

Kirsteen Tait is the Employment Training Policy Adviser for the Refugee Council. She was the founder Director of the National Association for the Education of Sick Children (NAESC/PRESENT) for five years. Before that, and since, she has worked as a consultant in education and social exclusion.

Introduction

Alison Closs

Health is an educational issue: it is not something which happens 'elsewhere' beyond school. Health, whether good or impaired, is an issue to be addressed by families, medical personnel and education staff, working together in real partnership in all schools and other educational provision.

Preamble

When we, as mature adults, are ill or have an impairment or medical condition, we want certain responses from other people or services:

- practical help or support to make us feel better and manage our lives better
- empathic understanding of the situation in which we find ourselves
- no 'fuss'.

Children are no different in these respects. This book is intended to help schools and other education services to provide enabling environments and employ the kind of staff who can provide effective education for children with medical conditions.

The use of the group term 'children with medical conditions' is explained and justified in the first chapter, but it includes children with physical or systemic conditions which may be subject to change for better or worse or which may fluctuate. Their education may be at risk through absence or through lowered ability to benefit from education while at school.

The omission of children with mental health difficulties reflects the need for more research and development in relation to the education and educational inclusion of children affected by these most complex difficulties. As a topic it needs and deserves its own book. The omission of more stable disabilities and of the everyday conditions which affect all children – common childhood ailments and short-term infectious diseases, routine surgery and minor accidents – is not to ignore either the inconvenience and potential educational disadvantage they may impose on individual children. It is rather to set manageable boundaries on the book and to prioritise effort where, so far, less has been written. This is also the reason for focusing on children of statutory school age rather than reaching out in depth to the preschool or post-school sectors, although some mention is made of these younger and older children (see Chapters 7 and 8).

The editor has tried to keep the book free from gender bias although nature is less equitable. Medical conditions affect more male than female children from birth onwards and the incidence of mortality is also higher in males.

The positive part that parents may play in their children's education is widely acknowledged, but nowhere should credit be given more fully than to parents of children with medical conditions. Throughout the book the term 'parents' is used to cover all those who assume parenting responsibilities including birth parents, guardians, adoptive and foster parents and carers.

Aims of this book

It is hoped that this book will be seen as a positive contribution to improving the knowledge, skills and understanding which should not only support the education of children with medical conditions but may also enhance more effective and inclusive education for *all* children. Acquiring understanding is a critical aspect of school and teacher preparation. Teachers should be, and are, more effective in differentiating curricula, improving physical and emotional environments and creating support systems in school than they are in changing 'in-child' or 'in-family' characteristics. However, unless they know and *understand* something of these 'internal' matters, their differentiation, improvements and support systems will be less efficient. They may even be grossly insensitive and ineffective, like shots in the dark.

- The first aim of the book is therefore to offer the reader the opportunity to develop empathy with those most affected by medical conditions by reading first-person accounts by young people, parents and siblings.
- The second aim is to allow readers to share the experiences, policies, practices and development plans of other 'ordinary' schools and of specialist services, and to compare them with those they themselves provide.
- The third aim is to discuss issues which education staff, parents and families all recognise as important, but also recognise as potentially problematic or even painful. In addition to discussion, the book offers illustrative examples and makes suggestions, based on existing good practice, which offer choices for constructive ways ahead.

- The fourth aim is to inform education staff and others about relevant legislation, guidance and children's educational entitlements, specialist services and resources to support pupils, families and staff.

The described context of the book is the UK and its four constituent countries. Despite significant differences in education legislation and guidance frameworks, however, it is striking that when young people with medical conditions, their parents or concerned professionals come together nationally and internationally, for example, within east and west Europe, north America, Australia and New Zealand, there is very substantial commonality in their concerns despite the different contexts. This book may also be useful to other professionals, to voluntary organisations, and to parents as well as those working in education – education officers, mainstream and special school managers, class, subject and guidance/pastoral care teachers, learning support staff/SENCOs (special educational needs coordinators), school auxiliary helpers, educational psychologists and welfare officers – and could help generate much needed wider educational debate, research and development.

Introduction to the following chapters

In Chapter 1 Alison Closs looks at the children and young people who are the focus of this book, the nature of their conditions and why their education may be at risk. She discusses whether or not they have special educational needs and if their needs should be statemented/recorded. Their educational entitlements, the legislative and guidance frameworks in which their education is shaped, and the importance of Individualised Educational Plans/Programmes (IEPs) are discussed. Finally, the vexed issue of school placement and the current state of inclusion for children with medical conditions is explored.

It is important that the reality of living and learning with a medical condition should be expressed as a first-person experience. Four young people reflect on their own school education and their lives in Chapter 2.

- Kathryn Hegarty describes her plans for a university course after a mainstream school career punctuated by absences and hospitalisation triggered by acute asthma attacks. Her school's Alternative Education Unit played a key part in maintaining her morale and educational aspirations.
- Tanya Lyke attended a special school and questions whether this would now have been necessary. Faced with continuing acute flare-ups of arthritis, the residual damage of previous episodes and frequent hospitalisation, she describes her struggle to remain in control of her life, social and vocational.

- Richard Docherty talks about his school life, his friends, sporting activities and possible future in sports management. He is a schoolboy international player in rugby and hockey. Despite his success he is aware of some inner resistance to some aspects of his diabetes regime.
- Sinead Douglas expresses appreciation of her two mainstream schools for enabling her to do and experience so much without any 'fuss'. Her future seems unclear as lung damage caused by cystic fibrosis disrupts her university course.

In Chapter 3 Christine Eiser discusses the psychological impact of chronic illness on the lives of children and their families, noting the extreme complexity of interplay between children's and families' individuality, the environments in which they function, children's ages and stages of development and the nature and extent of the condition. She makes a plea for more research to take children's own perspectives into account.

Research which specifically focuses on the education of children with medical conditions has been sparse until very recently. Angela Bolton, Alison Closs and Claire Norris reflect in Chapter 4 on two recent educational research projects in England and in Scotland respectively (Bolton 1997, Closs and Norris 1997) in which they sought the views of parents and children whose education was affected by medical conditions. They discuss the background to both studies, the priorities identified by families for the children's education, and the most effective and ethical means of accessing parents', children's and teachers' 'real' views.

While it is clear that parental and child views do not always coincide, in this field as in any other, parents of children with medical conditions are often their children's main advocates and supporters in education, on some occasions the only supporters. In Chapter 5 parents of three children give their views on their children's education, making plain how important is partnership with schools and other services, and how their own involvement has helped achieve quality education.

- Sandra Mason describes how her son Andrew's acute and recurring kidney condition changed the family members' lives and intermittently puts Andrew's mainstream education in jeopardy. She describes her appreciation of the home-visiting teacher service and how her son's secondary school has learned to accommodate Andrew's needs.
- Medical conditions do not respect children's other vulnerabilities. Amy has severe learning difficulties combined with a particularly aggressive form of eczema. Amanda and Tony O'Sullivan describe the care with which they selected a school for their daughter which would address all her needs, recognise and appreciate her strengths, and encourage her development. They explain how the special school they chose has fulfilled their hopes.

- Mairi Ann Cullen, with some help from her son Patrick who has multiple acute allergies, talks about the difficulties of finding a school which would be able to cope with Patrick's safety and medical needs. She describes the negotiations necessary for ensuring that he has as normal and stimulating an environment as possible and full access to the breadth of the curriculum. They recommend ways in which this can be achieved.

Voluntary organisations, including those for families or parents or those led by them, have played a critical role in the development of statutory services in the UK, through political lobbying, assembling and organising families and parents with shared interests, undertaking research and development work. In Chapter 6 Kirsteen Tait describes the work of the National Association for the Education of Sick Children (NAESC/PRESENT), a national 'umbrella' organisation, and Helen Hart talks about the role of a small condition-specific organisation, the Ataxia Telangiectasia (A-T) Society, in promoting the education of affected children by providing relevant information for schools and teachers. Both kinds of organisations have a vital part to play in developing greater equity in education.

Patricia Jackson, a consultant in paediatric community health, describes in Chapter 7 the roles and work undertaken by medical and paramedical services involved in supporting families and schools so that all children can access quality education while also having their health care needs met. In advocating close partnership with medical services, she also makes a plea for children's individuality and ordinary aspirations to be remembered at all times. Suggestions are made as to how medical services should develop and cooperate with education services to meet families' needs and to advance children's education and inclusion.

The following three chapters focus on the challenges faced by schools in providing effective education and a positive social experience in school for pupils with medical conditions. In Chapter 8 Alison Closs examines some matters of particular concern to mainstream and special school and unit staff: understanding and working with families, effective communication, educational continuity and support for learning, children's peer relationships, and working constructively with children who are regressing physically and/or cognitively. She makes constructive suggestions for schools based on existing good practice.

Mainstream primary schools, even those which have already developed good home–school systems and relationships and an overall positive ethos, may sometimes still be surprised by the emergence of previously unrecognised needs. In Chapter 9 a head teacher of a mainstream Scottish primary school – Joy McFarlane – describes how she and the school's medical officer carried out an audit of medical conditions in the pupils and how the resulting list led to a more systematic approach to managing children's health, and a more holistic approach to all pupils' education.

The large size and curricular and staffing complexity of mainstream secondary schools do not make the easiest environments for pupils whose needs are significantly different from the norm. The system may, all too readily, be prioritised over the individual. This may be particularly so within the kind of selective system which makes assumptions about ability and fitness. In Chapter 10 Ronnie Hassard, a deputy principal of a Northern Irish grammar school, describes in some detail how the educational system in Northern Ireland – unfamiliar to many UK readers – has only recently fully acknowledged and accommodated more effectively the special educational needs of pupils. The frameworks within which resources are allocated are explained, and found wanting, in relation to making desired improvements. Case studies and pupil perspectives are used to develop a constructive critique of the policies and practices of his traditionally academic and caring school in relation to pupils with medical conditions.

Out-of-school education is not yet an entitlement for every child absent longer term on the grounds of health in the UK, nor are there clear quality or quantity criteria for its provision. Peter Feeley, the head of a combined hospital and home teaching service, discusses in Chapter 11 ways towards ensuring quality out-of-school education for children. Carolyn Skilling addresses the same challenge, but from the perspectives of a former education authority officer and, more recently, as the second Director of NAESC/PRESENT. The need for imaginative and innovative approaches to education delivery is emphasised and the necessity of out-of-school services and children's 'home' schools collaborating to support children's learning and its continuity.

In Chapter 12 Ann Burnett takes a case-study approach to describing her work in hospital or at home with children with a poor prognosis. She talks of how the boundaries between the formal curriculum and a child-led curriculum, which respects both the individuality of each child and the constraints in which they find themselves, may become fluid. She describes how teaching may, in these circumstances, come to require the training and skills associated with child counselling as well as those of a teacher.

Although death and loss are inevitable facts of life, they are facts which schools have found hard to address within the curriculum and even harder to face when they affect school pupils and staff directly. In Chapter 13 Oliver Leaman suggests ways in which death and loss may usefully become part of the curriculum, how pupils with life-threatening conditions must be included academically and socially in the work of the class, and how teachers may handle questions about death. He goes on to list suggestions about how schools may cope with the death of a pupil in ways that are supportive to all concerned.

How siblings will be affected by their brothers' or sisters' illnesses or impairments depends on very many factors which will vary with each child, family, school, to mention only some of the key variables. Research indicates that there may be both positive and negative repercussions. Schools should be aware of both aspects. In Chapter 14 two young people set out their particular perspectives.

- Bernadette Kelly talks about how it felt and feels, both at home and at school, to be an elder sister of John, who has a very severe heart condition.
- Jeremy Nelson reflects on his siblings – Matthew and Miriam – and on how their lives, especially at school, and their deaths affected his life in practical ways but also, more significantly, in the ways he now responds to others and feels about life and death.

Education staff working with children with medical conditions now, or likely to encounter them professionally in the future, have only rarely had their need for knowledge, understanding and skills addressed adequately through their initial or subsequent in-service education. In Chapter 15 Alison Closs groups and lists resources – human, organisational, published and ideas – which could be supportive of education staff working to include pupils with medical difficulties and trying to establish mutually supportive and very necessary partnerships with families, non-educational services and voluntary organisations.

Acknowledgements

Warm thanks are due to David Fulton and his team at David Fulton Publishers for their advice and practical support, to my family and colleagues, including Kerstin Phillips, for continuing encouragement, and to Georgie Hunter, Janet Closs and Alison Bowers for expert assistance in checking drafts and references. I am very grateful to my former research colleague, Claire Norris, for sharing and nourishing my commitment to this topic.

Most of all, I would like to thank all the contributors, especially the parents and the young people who put so much time, thought and energy into their parts of the book, in the hope that it would advance educational opportunities for other young people and children with medical conditions. The book is dedicated to them and to all the other children with medical conditions who feature in the book or who were in the minds of the contributors.

CHAPTER 1

Introduction to the children and their educational frameworks

Alison Closs

This chapter is divided into two main sections. The first discusses which children are the focus of the book and establishes why their education is at risk. The second section discusses whether children with medical conditions have special educational needs, the possibility and desirability of a Statement/Record of Needs, what the children's educational entitlements are, the official guidance frameworks within which they are educated in the UK, the advisability of IEPs and children's educational placement.

The children and why their education is at risk

Which children?

The children with whom this book is concerned and who are grouped informally under the heading of 'having medical conditions' include the following:

- those who might, in conventional lay terminology, be considered as 'sick' or 'ill', sometimes to a life-threatening extent – as a result of genetic, infective or unknown causes, for example, children with cancers of various kinds, liver diseases, AIDS, acute rheumatic conditions, sickle cell anaemia;
- children with prolonged infective or viral conditions or responses to such conditions for whom a recovery may normally be expected at some unspecified time, such as tuberculosis, glandular fever, chronic fatigue syndrome (ME);

- those who are required to undergo prolonged or recurrent surgery or treatment for orthopaedic conditions, serious injuries, organ repair or transplant, burns;
- children with genetically determined conditions which cause physical and/or cognitive deterioration and which are currently life-threatening/life-shortening, such as cystic fibrosis, Duchenne's muscular dystrophy, mucopolysaccharide conditions such as Hurler's syndrome, and Friedreich's ataxia;
- children who experience a range of symptoms or needs which arise from organ or central nervous system impairment, damage or other dysfunction, such as diabetes, epilepsy, heart conditions, kidney failure;
- children with otherwise more stable impairments who are subject to periods of associated illness, for example children with spina bifida who have recurrent urinary tract infections, children with cerebral palsy who have intermittent epilepsy;
- those with allergic or other responses to environmental or ingested substances, for example children with eczema and other skin conditions, asthma, bowel irritation, migraine, those who experience anaphylactic responses.

This is very much a lay – non-medical – person's list of physical and systemic conditions, of which a medical practitioner might be rightly critical. There is overlap, particularly in the large grey areas between 'disabilty' and 'illness' and 'fitness' and 'sickness' (Barnes and Mercer 1996, Pinder 1996) and there are gaps. The list is illustrative and very far from comprehensive, even if at first reading it seems overwhelming. It is intended to give the reader a flavour of the range and diversity of children and young people whose educational needs are addressed within this book. It is likely that most readers can recognise some of the conditions listed.

Longer-term conditions result in longer-term effects, whether they are continuous or intermittent and accumulative. They therefore place education in greater jeopardy than shorter one-off experiences. Other than that, the book does not try to establish any kind of hierarchy of impact of conditions on children's lives and education. Hay fever is not a life-threatening condition, nor are affected people seriously ill. However, for children and young people who are badly affected, it can divide the school year into two, the learning part from late autumn to early spring and then the misery months of snuffling, sneezing and under-achieving. In contrast, a mother of two boys with a life-shortening physically degenerative condition, on being asked how they were, replied, 'They're weak, get the odd chest infection, but otherwise they're as fit as fleas'. The medical, physical, environmental, emotional and attitudinal variables that affect the experience of any condition are so numerous within the individual child, and the conditions themselves so numerous, that trying to list them comprehensively or to establish a prioritised order of conditions would not be a productive approach. It is perhaps in recognition of this that recent recommended changes to the Code of Practice include removing the illustrative list of conditions (DfE 1994, paragraph 3.89).

Recent research (Closs and Norris 1997) highlighted how education professionals had a very dichotomous view of illness and health. When urged to reflect, respondents sometimes remembered experiencing the rather unpleasant but usually short and not totally disabling 'in-between' experience of being neither really well nor really ill. What they found harder to grasp was that for many children, especially those with chronic disease, this 'in-between' state was their long-term norm.

There is no wish to create a new category of impairment nor is there any intention, despite the importance of medication and medical treatments in the lives of many of the youngsters we talk about in this book, of supporting a return to the medical model of disability or education. In the medical model, difficulties in learning and living were attributed only, or mainly, to impairments while educational solutions were perceived in terms of treating or 'fixing' the children concerned.

The social model of disabilty identifies discrimination and ignorance within socio-political and organisational systems and in society at large as the factors which turn impairments into disabilities (Oliver 1996). This model offers children with medical conditions, their families and education personnel an outward focus for their efforts to improve access to education and quality of education. It has been criticised as elevating collective disability pride but denying some individuals' experiences of physical or intellectual restrictions arising directly from impairments, of pain, and of facing and fearing death (Morris 1991, French 1993). Shakespeare and Watson (1998), however, suggest that it is possible to accommodate both the collective and individual identities and experiences, when they argue for, 'a balance between understanding disabled people as individuals and members of a disadvantaged group, and between realising the commonalities and respecting the differences' (p. 13).

The critical need is for a holistic and individual approach to the education of children with medical conditions while, at the same time, remembering the importance of including them with their peers socially and educationally.

Why is the education of children with medical conditions at risk?

Pupil, parent, teacher, researcher and other accounts – formal and informal – indicate that children with medical conditions have an increased likelihood of experiencing at some time, or frequently or constantly, a constellation of factors which may directly or indirectly place their education at risk. Some of these factors are not unique to this group of children; it is their duration, combination and complexity which are potentially, particularly educationally, disadvantageous. The factors are:

- substantial absence from school due to the condition without adequate out-of-school education;
- feeling under-par while attending school with the accompanying risk of under-achieving;
- requiring medication or medical/paramedical treatment while at school, leading to disruption of the school day and loss of socialising time with peers;
- having physical and other aspects of 'difference' arising from the condition or its treatment which may generate anxiety or rejection in peers and in education staff;
- living with uncertainty related to the course of the condition and to the response of others to it, leading to difficulties in planning ahead and general anxiety;
- possibly belonging to an already disadvantaged population.

In relation to the last point it is important to note that some kinds of illness and medical conditions are more prevalent in families at socio-economic disadvantage and in minority ethnic communities. In pointing this out, the Acheson Report (1998) criticised medical care itself for inequity. It is also important that assumptions of health and well-being are not made in relation to children perceived as educationally and socio-economically advantaged in school. Any ignorance or preconceived notions can lead to a lack of awareness and of timely and appropriate action.

If education is to be effective for children with medical conditions, education authorities, schools and staff must make positive educational responses to these issues. Despite evidence of some goodwill, good intentions and examples of individual teachers and some schools developing good practice, the overwhelming picture is that most establishments are ill-prepared in terms of experience and professional development – and therefore of knowledge, skills and attitudes – to take up and sustain the challenge in an in-depth way.

This situation is not brought about by malevolence, but is rather the outcome of ignorance and a lack of systems to ensure that all children receive appropriate education. *It is actually this lack of focused thought on the part of education providers and lack of preparedness to ensure quality education, rather than the actual medical conditions, that put children's education most at risk.* Research has clearly indicated that well-prepared 'ordinary' schools *can* cope very effectively with including children with very serious and complex conditions.

The educational frameworks of children with medical conditions

It would be very easy to allow this section of the book to become a book in its own right, detailing the minutae of the various UK countries' legislation and guidance. In order to avoid this, key documents only will be referred to for each country. Some of the documents are specific to children with medical conditions while others are more generic. The documents are detailed in the book's References. Some are available on the Internet. The most recent issue of the *Education for Sick Children: Directory of Current Provision* (NAESC/PRESENT 1998) also provides a referenced summary introduction to each country's provision for sick children by a representative of the relevant government department.

Do children with medical conditions have special educational needs?

It seems plain that the Government's and relevant Departments' views are that they certainly may have, but that this is not necessarily so in every case. The basic legislation in which the concept of special educational needs is set out is the Education Act 1993 (for England and Wales), the 1980 Education (Scotland) Act (as amended) and the Education and Libraries (Northern Ireland) Order 1986. The tantologous definition – that a child has special educational needs if he or she has a learning difficulty which calls for special provision to be made for him or her – is linked in all four countries to two factors. These are: that the child has greater difficulty in learning than the majority of his or her peers, and/or, that the child has a disability which prevents or impedes him or her from using the educational facilities of the kind provided for children of the same age within the same education authority.

In practice, however, it seems that, apart from children whose medical conditions plainly place them within the boundaries of overt cognitive or physical impairments, many children with medical conditions are *not* deemed to have special educational needs. As a result, they may not be able to access the kind of support that would most benefit their education. The key cause of confusion is in the varied understandings of 'learning difficulties', 'disabilities' and 'difficulties in learning'. The first is sometimes interpreted by professionals as meaning some degree of cognitive impairment resulting in globally and constantly lowered performance. Let us consider the child with acute eczema who is rarely absent but who is, for weeks or months on end, tired and irritable due to chronic lack of sleep and constant itching. In the mind of some professionals the lowered performance of the child with eczema would not qualify him or her as having special educational needs, even though the lack of sleep and constant itching plainly make it more difficult for this child to learn most of the time than many of his or her peers.

Similarly, conditions which affect the internal organs or systems such as irritable bowel syndrome, asthma or ME in children of normal ability may certainly make it more difficult for them to learn than many of their peers, but these conditions would not be seen by some educational professionals as physical disabilities because they do not affect movement and mobility.

The issues of duration and stability of the overt symptoms of the medical condition may also weigh in the debate over whether a child has special educational needs or not. Those who have long-term, constant or increasing overt symptoms are more likely to be perceived as having special educational needs than those with shorter-term or fluctuating symptoms.

In other words, some children with medical conditions may be less likely to be considered as having special education needs than children with constant or deteriorating and/or overt cognitive and/or physical impairments. This is because of widespread ignorance among education professionals about medical conditions and their impact on education. This is compounded by an unnecessarily narrow and rigid understanding of the concept of special educational needs and its associated terminology.

In an attempt to be fair to children with medical conditions and to assess whether they do indeed experience learning difficulties and have special educational needs, and in particular learning difficulties which might merit a statutory assesment, both the Codes of Practice of England and Wales (DfE/Welsh Office 1994, paragraphs 3.89–94) and Northern Ireland (DENI 1998, Appendix paragraphs 31–36) place considerable emphasis on gathering evidence of negative discrepancy in educational performance or behaviour/emotional affect in comparison with peers, noting the negative impact of absence, some conditions, and forms of treatment on education. Without such advice, children with medical conditions might not be considered eligible for the kind of facilitation and monitoring of education available to pupils perceived as having special educational needs, nor for a statutory assessment which might lead to a Statement or Record of Need.

The Scottish official guidance on learning difficulties is helpful (SOEID 1996, paragraph 9.2) when it offers the 'rule of thumb' that, 'it should be assumed that children or young people have a "learning difficulty" if additional arrangements need to be made to enable them properly to access the curriculum' (p. 3). This common-sense assumption clearly brings very many children with medical conditions within the ambit of special educational needs and facilitative and monitoring measures.

May children with medical conditions have a Statement/Record of Needs, and is it useful?

The issue of whether or not a child with a medical condition may have a Statement or Record of Needs depends, in the first instance, on their being recognised as having special educational needs, and thereafter on whether they meet the criteria for a statutory assessment on which the decision to open a Record or Statement will be based. The criteria in the various countries vary, particularly between Scotland and the other three countries. In Scotland, local authorities are required under section 60(2)(b) of the Education (Scotland) Act to open a Record of Needs for all children who, 'have pronounced, specific or complex special educational needs which are such as require continuing review'. The Scottish process is not driven by resources since school education must be, again by law (section 62(3) of the 1980 Act), 'adequate and efficient' for *all* pupils, including those with special educational needs. If additional resources are required to ensure that a child's education is adequate and efficient, then these must be provided whether or not the child has a Record of Need. It has to be said, however, that Scottish education authorities vary in their interpretation of the law relating to recording, and also in what 'adequate and efficient' education actually comprises.

In contrast, the main criterion for drawing up a Statement in England, Wales and Northern Ireland, as set out in the Codes of Practice (England and Wales 1994, paragraph 4.2 and Northern Ireland 1998, paragraph 4.1) is that the Local Education Authority or Board considers that the special educational provision required by the child cannot be met within the resources normally available to mainstream schools in its area. A Statement therefore accesses additional resources.

Plainly, some children with medical conditions would meet these criteria and benefit from the monitoring and regular reviewing and the additional placement request rights which a Record/Statement guarantees in all countries, and the additional resources which a Statement would facilitate in England, Wales and Northern Ireland. It has to be remembered, however, that opening a Record or drawing up a Statement is a cumbersome process and results in a relatively static document which cannot respond to frequent fluctuations in need. It has less immmediate impact on classroom practices than an IEP (see next section of this chapter).

Educational entitlements and official guidance

Before looking specifically at educational guidance, some mention should be made of the implications of the Children Act 1989 for England and Wales, the Children (Northern Ireland) Order 1995 and the Children (Scotland) Act 1995 for children with medical conditions. They come within the scope of the legislation since, without services, they would be unable to maintain a reasonable standard of health and development, or their health and development might actually be impaired, these being two of the criteria for defining a child as being 'in need'. The Acts/Order also recognise chronic illness as a subset of disability, disability itself also being included among the criteria. It therefore follows that they should benefit from children's service plans, whereby the Acts/Order require the statutory services – health, education and social work – to collaborate in planning effective services for children. The Acts/Order also support children's inclusion in all planning and decision-making related to their lives. While education has not yet fully accommodated these requirements, there are indications of some shifts in policies and practices.

All children in the UK have, indirectly, an entitlement to school education, since education authorities are required to provide 'adequate and efficient' school education and parents have a duty to send children of compulsory school age to school. Some children may be opted out of school by their parents, only with the consent of the education authority, to be educated out of school, and a few carefully designated groups of children may be excused school attendance. Among the latter are children too ill to attend school.

The United Nations *Convention on the Rights of the Child* (1989), partially enacted through the already mentioned Children Acts/Order in the UK, sees education as an absolute right of each and every child. In the case of absent children with medical conditions there is perhaps a special imperative because of their own and their parents' very evident wish for them to be educated. Thus, children unavoidably absent on the grounds of health – who are too vulnerable to infection or too physically fragile or immobilised by surgery or other treatment but who are still well enough to benefit from education – should have education taken or transmitted in some way to them wherever they happen to be, in hospital, hospice, respite care unit or, most commonly, at home.

Education authorities in the UK were legally permitted to provide such a service but it has only recently become a statutory duty in England and Wales under Section 19 of the Education Act 1996, as amended by section 47 of the Education Act 1997. In Northern Ireland the duty has been imposed on education authorities through Articles 86 and 10 of the Education (NI) Orders 1998 and 1996 respectively.

The associated official guidance to education authorities in relation to their statutory duties is contained in *DfEE Circular 12/94* (1994) and *Welsh Office Circular 57/94* (1994). Sometimes even legislation and guidance is insufficient to establish adequate and efficient education. One of the potential weaknesses is that no national standards of quantity or quality of out-of-school education are specified in law or guidance. While it could reasonably be argued that it would be hard to establish what the standards should be, given the enormous diversity of pupils and their circumstances, the absence of standards leaves pupils, to some extent, at the mercy of education authorities' unilateral decisions. This was recently tested in court when the mother of a pupil absent long-term because of ME took their education authority to court for having cut the pupil's home teaching time. The education authority lost both High Court and House of Lords appeals, and was directed to restore the teaching to its original level to meet its obligation to provide 'suitable education', defined as 'efficient education suitable to [the child's] age, ability and aptitude and to any special educational needs he may have'. The authority was also advised that this duty had to be effected regardless of any other resource plans or restrictions.

Further guidance relates more specifically to in-school medical care and its interface with education, recommending among other things that some pupils should have health care plans. This is contained in DfEE Circular 14/96 (1996b) and Welsh Office Circular 34/97 (1997b). Good practice guidance was issued by DfEE (1996a) and the Welsh Office (1997a). Guidance on collaboration between health and education services also appears in the Codes of Practice (DfEE 1994, paragraphs 2.41–52, 3.106–112 and DENI 1998, paragraphs 2.31–36, 3.50–53).

Guidance on medication and medical treatment in school is also contained in DfEE Circular 14/96 (1996b) and Welsh Office Circular 34/97 (1997b). It is made plain that, while there is no statutory or contractual duty on school staff to be involved in this, there is a hopeful expectation that staff, as part of their duty of care towards pupils, would volunteer to undertake reasonable duties in this respect after proper training by qualified medical or nursing personnel and in the security of legal indemnification by their employers.

The current Northern Ireland guidance dates from the 1970s and is due to be replaced. In Scotland the gap in statutory provision of out-of-school education remains although most education authorities do make some voluntary provision. A recent consultation documentation (SOEID 1998) highlighted the statutory anomaly while indicating that, in principle at least, educational entitlement was the right of every child. The ministerial response promised guidance to education authorities and schools in relation to children with medical conditions/health needs. This guidance, along with or including guidance on medication and medical treatment in school, probably similar to that already issued in England and Wales, is expected late in 1999. The report of the Riddell Committee in Scotland, established to examine educational provision for children with severe low incidence disabilities, is expected to include recommendations relating to children with significant medical conditions and to needed legislative change. The report's publication is also expected in the latter half of 1999.

Individualised Educational Plans/Programmes

All four countries emphasise the importance of individualised IEPs for children with special educational needs. Advice appears in the Codes of Practice (DfEE 1994, paragraphs 2.66–67, 2.93, 2.108–113 and DENI 1998, paragraphs 2.56–57, 2.63–67). In Scotland, advice on IEPs and their contents appears in the *Manual of Good Practice in Special Educational Needs* (SOEID 1999, section 2B2).

IEPs are practical working documents which can be used to steer and support the education of children with medical conditions. They can be used to plan and monitor progress and to provide a bridge over absence and changes in location when children are hospitalised and at home working with hospital and home-visiting teachers or on their own. They can help identify children's under-performance although attending school. IEPs should be based on ongoing assessment of ordinary and special educational needs, including those associated with medical needs, and should be simple and concise enough to:

- adapt strategies and adjust targets as changes occur;
- record gaps in learning;
- plan for overtaking these gaps as far as reasonably possible;
- allow clear monitoring of progress by all concerned.

IEPs should, above all, be working documents to which teachers, parents and children themselves may contribute and arrive together at a feasible way forward. Regular review dates should be set, but for children with medical needs it will be particularly important to review the siuation in response to changes in the child's condition or placement.

Educational placement

Parents of children with medical conditions, as all other parents in the UK, may make a placement request for their child to attend a school of their choice. This also applies to parents of children with Records/Statements of Need, even though, subsequent to discussion with parents and other professionals and visits to or discussions with schools, a school will be named on the Record/Statement. Parents of children with recorded or statemented needs have additional placement request rights, to ask for their child to attend a school in another authority or a maintained/grant-aided or private sector special school. While many education authorities try to place children according to parental request, there is a number of reasons for which they may legally refuse a request. These relate to availability of place, suitability of the chosen placement to provide appropriate education for the child, effect of the placement on other pupils, and efficient use of the authority's resources. This last may mean that the authority might not wish to alter premises or employ additional staff in a mainstream school, particularly if they have special school or unit vacancies or budgetary restrictions.

Many such reasons have in the past been given by education authorities in refusing placement requests or in recommending that children with medical conditions attend a school other than their local or chosen school. Lack of on-site medical and paramedical support, lack of access for children who are wheelchair users or have limited mobility, and lack of appropriately experienced or qualified staff have all been evidenced. This is particularly hard for children and parents committed to local mainstream education, especially if it means separation from friends and siblings (see Kelly, Chapter 14). It is doubly hard if this takes place not at the beginning of a school career but part-way through, when it may be suggested that a child should change schools as a medical condition is diagnosed or deteriorates, or if a child who has coped happily and made friends in primary school is directed to a different secondary school from his or her primary school friends.

While appeals against placement recommendations/decisions of the education authority are possible through the Special Educational Needs Tribunal in England, Wales and Northern Ireland – as they are in relation to some aspects of a Statement – parents of children with medical conditions already have many other concerns and responsibilities and may have neither the time nor the energy for what is a stressful process. In Scotland the first line of appeal is to the education authority's own Appeal Committe which may, in turn, refer matters relating to the Record of Needs to the minister responsible for school education in the new Scottish parliament. However, in the case of disagreement over the school named in the Record or the refusal of a placement request, parents in Scotland may appeal to the Sheriff, whose decision is final.

The arguments for and against special schools, integration and inclusion in mainstream provision for children with special educational needs have been well-rehearsed elsewhere (Clark *et al.* 1995), as have the debates around inclusion (Sebba and Sachdev 1997). While the editor of this book is broadly pro-inclusion, no such view has been imposed on other contributors, least of all on young people themselves or parents (see Lyke in Chapter 2 and O'Sullivan in Chapter 5). Trends towards greater locational and functional integration and inclusion have been noted but support for the idea seems stronger than the reality, despite widely publicised national and local authority policies of inclusion. In percentile terms, relatively few children with special educational needs (including some with medical conditions) attend special schools – from less than 1 and up to 2 per cent of the child population, depending on local education authority policies and provision. However, this still means that significant numbers of children continue to attend largely segregated special schools. Many others attend special units with varying amounts of time spent being educated alongside their mainstreamed peers.

The number of children with chronic medical conditions which significantly affect their everyday functioning, and therefore presumably their education, is estimated by the British Paediatric Association (BPA 1995) at just under ten per cent of the child population. This does not include non-chronic conditions so is an underestimate of the total population affected. *The vast majority of affected children are therefore in mainstream schools.* Those most likely to be in special provision are those whose particular conditions result in their having more severe cognitive or physical/mobility impairments or both and who live in authorities that either have special provision of their own or that place children in the special provision of other authorities. Some parents and/or young people make a positive and informed choice for special provision.

There is a clear trend on the part of parents and education authorities to seek educational placement near home and, as far as possible, within the local community. Parents and children who opt for, or are placed within, mainstream provision also want to be assured of access to any necessary specialist services and resources. Parents and children in special school or unit provision want to ensure social contact with the wider peer group, especially where they live, and access to as normal a life as possible. This has led to some blurring of the boundaries between special and mainstream provision, even between day and boarding provision, and a more flexible approach to placement, with children spending most or part of their time in one kind of provision with some time in another or accessing the support of another.

Examples of such sharing include a special residential boarding school for children with acute asthma and eczema, which now offers short courses both to enable children who normally attend day school elsewhere to manage their conditions more independently and effectively and to enable children who have fallen behind in school work through absence to catch up through intensive individual and small-group tutoring. Another special school for children with physical impairments and medical conditions has arranged for some of its abler pupils to attend the local comprehensive for some certificate courses and also shares its paramedical facilities and services with mainstream school pupils. The same school also provides an outreach advisory service for mainstream schools and is part of a 'cluster' arrangement for shared mainstream and specialist staff development. While shared placements can be seen as an advance on completely segregated provision, the effect on children's peer friendships needs to be evaluated.

The concerns of parents of children with medical conditions, of children themselves and most professionals who advise them in selecting or allocating a school placement are:

- being near home, if possible with siblings and with local children;
- availability of an appropriate and effective educational programme;
- availability of medical and paramedical care, preferably on-site;
- willingness and ability of school staff to address health and care needs;
- physical safety, including freedom from all kinds of bullying;
- likelihood of formation of peer companionship/friendships and of being happy.

While the first two and last two items on the list above are common to those concerned with *all* children, the latter may have a particular urgency for children with medical conditions and other 'differences' who are vulnerable in these respects (see Chapter 8). Happiness and friendship, not just companionship, are very much on the minds of parents of children with medical conditions. Some children experience increasing impairment, pain, fear and some degree of loneliness as a result of their conditions, and a small but significant number have a shortened life expectancy. In these circumstances parents hope for more than a good academic education from the school their child attends; they would like it to be a distraction from, and even some kind of compensation for, some of the less pleasant aspects of their lives (Closs and Burnett 1995).

Most children with significant aspects of difference, or even those without external signs, have experienced peer and even adult rejection in some form. They do not want to face it on a daily basis in school. While bullying and rejection also take place in special schools, some families, rightly or wrongly, believe that children with pronounced differences may be more fully part of their school community in a special school and that the need for experience and friendship within the wider local community can be met through the family's own circle of friends and neighbours. They may have visited mainstream schools where children with special educational needs seem to have few friends, or where an adult auxiliary helper seems to be the sole companion of a child with special needs.

While teachers tend to greatly over-estimate the likelihood of requests for help or medical emergencies in the classroom (Eiser and Town 1987), the availability of medical and paramedical services in school and for some help from school staff for children with more significant health care needs – listed as the middle two points above – is not negotiable; they must be provided. This often requires extensive negotiation, both with health services and the school, especially where intrusive treatments or 'unaesthetic' conditions are concerned.

Just as Sally Tomlinson (1982) famously described every mainstream school's most and least favoured potential pupil with special educational needs (a bright little girl in a wheelchair and a dull disruptive boy) nearly 20 years ago, so a competitor for the dull and disruptive child has now emerged. He or she may be doubly incontinent, may require catheterisation of urine, may need rectal suppositories or injections. It is encouraging and reassuring that, generally, the initially highly-resistant head teacher or staff do respond to discussions with families and child health personnel (see Chapter 7), and find a volunteer teacher and/or auxiliary staff to undertake training in the more straightforward procedures. These staff generally become very competent and factually accepting of an additional role which is essential to the child's well-being in school. Thus, preliminary negotiations are necessary but can be interpreted by parents, often rightly in the first instance, as a sign that schools do not welcome their child.

Children with more readily managed conditions may not need medical services in school and, if they have a regime, it may be adapted to take place largely at home or be discreetly self-managed at school, given appropriate facilities and privacy. However, if more children with more complex and severe medical conditions are to attend their local schools, then the child health services in the community will require to adapt and probably also to expand (see Chapter 7). A further requirement is that education staff will need to raise their awareness of the needs of these children and, in time, acquire the skills, knowledge, understanding and positive attitudes which will enable all their pupils to have equity of opportunity. Finally, although some improvements can be made within resources, the needs of children with medical conditions are sufficiently substantial and unpredictable that some additional resourcing for flexibility may be necessary.

Research has indicated that mainstream schools can educate pupils with complex and serious medical conditions successfully. While parents' right to choose special provision is generally defended and while some periods of school absence in hospital, at home or elsewhere may be necessary because of the condition and its treatment, there is a real need to move further along the road to inclusion. An adaptation of Booth's (1998) definition of inclusion is offered as a target for mainstream schools:

Inclusive education is the process of increasing the participation of all pupils in the curricula, cultures and communities of neighbourhood mainstream schools which value diversity, in such ways that they learn effectively in a safe and happy environment.

More schools aspiring to such inclusion might help ensure that, when parents and children with medical conditions make placement choices, these are choices between positive alternatives, not a forced choice because some schools cannot or will not be, or are not resourced to be, sufficiently efficient, imaginative and humane to welcome them.

CHAPTER 2

'I didn't ask to have this': first-person accounts of young people

Kathryn Hegarty, Tanya Lyke, Richard Docherty and Sinead Douglas

Kathryn

I was diagnosed with asthma at the age of two so I don't remember what life was like without it. Fortunately, throughout my younger years the illness never affected me significantly and I was able to do everything other children my age did.

I was lucky to have a supportive family, we had always been very close, but things changed when my asthma got worse. My older brother, Andrew, was very protective, although he had quite a tough time as he was always told to look after me. My Mum and Dad were often shouted at when I was feeling fed up or if I was begging them to discharge me from hospital.

It was when I hit puberty that things started to go wrong. I woke up one morning feeling a bit breathless and I found that my inhaler wasn't helping. My Mum took me to hospital where I was put on a nebuliser. It was the same medication as my inhaler but it was delivered through a breathing mask. I soon felt better and was sent home, although it started to become a regular occurrence. I was put on a very high dose of steroids. The list of possible side effects included weight gain, high blood pressure and brittle bones.

My family moved back to Edinburgh when I was fourteen, which involved attending a new school. Most children find it difficult settling in, but the fact that I was carted off in an ambulance when I had an acute attack at school less than a week after starting made things even more difficult for me.

Over the following months my asthma got progressively worse, which involved my having short but frequent stays in the hospital. My school had a facility called 'The Base' for pupils who needed to work out of their usual class for a variety of reasons. This meant that on days I was not feeling well I could go there and work would be brought down from my classes so that I could work quietly at my own pace. I could also use this facility if the lifts were out of use since it was difficult for me to use the stairs around the school as I would become so breathless.

I certainly wouldn't have been at school half as much without 'The Base'. I became very friendly with one of the teachers who worked there. She provided not only educational support, but emotional support as well. I would often go in feeling fed up and frustrated. She would sit down and listen while I poured my heart out and told her how awful my life was.

Some days, even walking to the bus stop was too much for me, so the school provided a taxi to take me between home and school. It meant that if I was unwell while I was at school, I could telephone the taxi to pick me up early, or if I hadn't been well during the night I could go in to school later. It gave me a lot of freedom but I didn't abuse it. The school knew that I wanted to be there so I didn't have to feel guilty if I was late or even if I didn't go in at all.

A couple of years ago I had a severe attack. I had been at my friend's house when it started so I went home. I used my nebuliser and when it didn't work my Dad called for an ambulance. We waited 40 minutes for it to arrive, by which time my lips were turning blue and my behaviour had become completely irrational through lack of oxygen. I passed out in the ambulance and woke up two days later on a ventilator in intensive care. I was discharged after two weeks. For months afterwards I panicked if I was left alone in the house and I certainly wouldn't go out anywhere on my own. The whole experience had terrified me. Up until then I had always known that as soon as I got to hospital and was given the usual medication I would be fine. Suddenly I realised that if I had had to wait any longer for that ambulance, it might have been a different story.

There were a few occasions where I came across a lack of understanding at school, not only from other pupils but also from some of the teaching staff. A lot of people believe that all asthma can be controlled with one or two inhalers, and don't for a minute think that it can be life-threatening. On one occasion I was questioned by a teacher as to why I was using the lift to go to the third floor. I explained that I was asthmatic and was laughed at and told that even I should have enough puff to walk up three flights of stairs.

After missing 80 per cent of third year I decided to repeat. It was not an easy decision to make and I faced a lot of criticism from other pupils who assumed that the reason was that I was 'thick'. Once I was accused by a classmate of using my asthma as an excuse to have as much time off school as possible. It was so frustrating. I actually wanted to be there, especially as I had big plans to become a doctor.

Unfortunately, my illness did not improve and I went through a period of being rushed in to hospital at least twice a month. I would be admitted for a few days and then sent home, where I would recover for a few days before going back to school. The process would then repeat. I got to know all the doctors and nurses very well and soon I was on first name terms with them all.

I didn't have any form of social life. I didn't live like a teenage girl should. I hated having to think twice before I did anything. I couldn't go and stay at friends' houses if they had pets; I couldn't get up and dance at parties in case I had an asthma attack. If I did make any plans to go out with friends I often had to cancel them at the last minute because my asthma was so unpredictable.

I struggled through my fourth year of school and missed a lot of the course work. When it came to exam time I had special arrangements. I had a room to myself with an invigilator and if I needed to stop and rest I was allowed to do so. I was accused by people of being given an advantage through this special treatment. I wanted more than anything to pass my exams and thankfully I did. Unfortunately, because I had missed the course work, I didn't get an overall mark although I did get a mark for the exams and, considering the work I had missed, I think I did well to pass every one of them.

I was ill throughout my fifth year too, and after much agonising, I decided not to sit my examinations. I felt like a complete failure. My lifelong plans of becoming a doctor flew out the window. I started my sixth year doing the same subjects as the year before. I had decided on a new career, nursing. I realised that if I didn't get my Highers it wasn't the end of the world. I made new plans. I was going to go to further education college to do a Higher Education Access course and then on to university. I left school half way through sixth year. I decided to take a year out to get myself well before going to college. I felt it would give me a better chance; I could concentrate on regaining my health without the worry of school and exams.

I had started taking a new medication at the end of my fifth year at school. I didn't hold out much hope as so many things had failed in the past. After two months I started to feel better. Nine months later I am living a normal life. I managed to reduce my steroids, which meant that I lost two stone in weight. I have been on holiday. I was able to get my first part-time job and I can go out to parties without ending up in hospital. Looking back now, it is difficult to believe how awful things were. I am a different person now, I have a completely different life.

I think the fact that I have such a supportive family has kept me going. I am also extremely grateful to my school. If it hadn't been for 'The Base' I would hardly have been there at all. I could have given up a long time ago, but I didn't. I am a fighter because I have had to be. I will always have asthma. It is part of my life but, hopefully, I am over the worst of it. From now on things can only get better.

Tanya

'I didn't ask to have this' and 'Did I ask to be born?' were recurrent utterances from me from early childhood until now at age 23, sometimes going on 73. I addressed such comments and questions at myself or at my family, and not infrequently at teachers.

I started my school career when I was placed, aged four, in a local special school for children with physical and medical needs. A team of professionals, including an educational psychologist and my hospital consultant paediatrician, decided this in conjunction with my mother. In the late 1970s, 'inclusive education' and 'integration' were not common practice and there didn't seem to be a workable alternative.

I had been diagnosed when a toddler as having a particularly aggressive type of juvenile arthritis, already advanced from affecting a couple of joints to affecting most joints including all the major ones and to rapidly deteriorating vision in one eye and generally poor health. Old photographs show me as a rather pathetic, frail kid, as though a gust of wind would blow me away. No wonder really that my mother and the professionals could not see how I would cope in a robust group of up to 30 five-year-olds in an ordinary primary school. Added to my general frailty were all my medication and treatment needs, painkillers and anti-inflamatory drugs, physiotherapy, hydrotherapy, splinting and lots of additional rest – too tall an order then for the local primary school.

There were gains and losses at special school. Some of the positives were small classes and individual tuition to catch up on work I missed when absent, on-site paramedical therapy and medical specialists who visited school, so saving time, energy and having to be off school. There was more specialist equipment available too, some of my own, some for the use of anyone who needed it at any time. The school was fully accessible. I suppose the other thing was that there was less feeling of isolation or difference in relation to being ill or disabled: that was the norm.

On the negative side, special schools then didn't really encourage assertiveness and pride about being disabled, there really was a prevailing medical model of 'caring' that could result in childlike dependency. In mainstream schools there is an understanding that kids will experiment with so-called bad habits such as smoking and sex, but staff were horribly shocked and dismayed when I was found smoking. The Brook Clinic advisers came to see us individually when we were in fifth year secondary – but that was considered quite daring and progressive then. It is ironic that when I was in special school so many of us would have benefited from more liberal and 'normal' approaches with opportunities for mainstreaming, but now, when so many of the children who attend special school seem to have far more complex and profound disabilities, they can't take advantage of the progress fully.

Teachers in special school have lots of experience and knowledge but my view is that empathy was thinner on the ground. Some teachers were great, committed to enabling us to achieve academically and to understanding us as people – but some could not empathise. Either they weren't that kind of person to start with, or they had grown a bit jaded through being too long in the job.

Staff doubted our capacity to function in a wider world. Maybe some staff, like us, would find it hard 'outside', yet I remain convinced that I could have coped in mainstream if it had been possible to have the access, medical support, specialist equipment and learning support to catch up if I had been absent. Staff sometimes behaved as though all our difficulties related to our conditions but most of us would say that we experienced other stresses, like in my case, the death of my fiancé and several friends and having divorced parents, which left scars deeper than any illness or disability. Some of these emotional matters were not addressed as fully as our physical needs. Schools, whether mainstream or special, need to take an all-round view of children and really listen to them.

The death of a pupil was sadly relatively common in our school but the school's response to death, until near the end of my time there, was to sweep it under the carpet; school friends just disappeared. I think staff wanted to save us from additional suffering, hoping that if little was said then we'd get over it more quickly. They didn't realise that people with disabilities and illnesses have learned to cope with pain better than others. We were glad when things began to be more open, when deaths were properly announced, services held, funerals attended and we could express our grief more 'normally'.

Peer friendships and friction help everyone to grow up but many young disabled or ill people have had to spend too much time with adults – parents, medics, carers, and nurses and with other disabled or ill children – and too little time with the general mass of youngsters. I know I have some trouble relating to some of my peers because some aspects of my life were not like theirs. However, there I was in my special school from age 3 to 18; I made good friends among fellow pupils, teachers, care and paramedical staff. As I grew older, though, there were fewer and fewer pupils who shared my interests and aspirations, so I did spend a lot of time with the staff I liked.

From early in secondary school I hoped, like any able student, to go on to university. I was built up in a way as an academic star in the school, I was going to fly high, relatively speaking, and I was happy about that. I had a lot of good Standard Grades (Scottish fourth year exams) and I was ready to take my Highers and go on to university. I had intensive individual support from my teachers and should have done well.

However, it was at this time that I finally had to acknowledge that my arthritic condition was not going to 'burn out', that a miracle drug did not exist, that my condition had become a serious systemic illness that would get in the way of some

– all? – of my aspirations. I was too ill to sit any of my Highers and, although there were plans that I might catch up, maybe by attending mainstream school for another year of study for Highers, my health really didn't ever fully pick up again. It seemed that after all my high hopes, life was black and purposeless. I became very seriously depressed. Life really did not seem to be worth living. Was the school partly to blame for investing so much in my academic future and encouraging me to do the same? Who knows?

That was five years ago. To summarise what has happened I should look at my illness, what I have achieved, and I suppose, some of the disappointments, especially in relation to education – or maybe I should just call it personal development. In the last five years my condition has deteriorated markedly and become even more aggressive and systemic. I am constantly on a range of drugs related to flare-ups, infections and pain. There are side effects and every flare leaves me a bit more disabled and dependent – though I hate the word – on drugs and help. I spend a lot of time in hospital, sometimes very seriously ill. For example, in the last year I have spent almost half the time in hospital. I try not to get down but it really is hard.

Because my condition fluctuates I never have peace to think clearly about my future or to see through the things I've begun. I began several college courses, some distance learning and so on. Have I become someone who cannot or will not see things through? Is it me, is it the incessant drugs, or is it that maybe I am not convinced that anything so far is worth the huge effort it takes to overcome all the barriers?

I live at home with some degree of independence, but that is still hard for someone who wants to be into LIFE; My mum and carers are essential, though. I have a small circle of really good friends and many more acquaintances, and two great dogs. I drive my adapted car rather competently – a big source of freedom – and now have a part-time job as a news-sheet editor for fellow young people who have arthritis. It is hard to keep to the kind of deadlines the work imposes, but I need the interest and it is nice to have some money that I have really earned myself. I suppose I also want my life to have some significance.

Richard

(His account is a shortened transcript of his views given in a recorded interview with the editor)

I am 15 and my brother is three years older. We're both really keen on sport, in my case particularly rugby and hockey. I am a schoolboy international in both. I'm just coming up to Standard Grades and, if they go well, I'll carry on to Highers and then to college or university, to do Sports Management. In between school and college I'd like to go to Australia with my Dad to watch my brother in the Olympics because he is in the Olympics hockey squad. Then I'd like to stay on to work and travel, but it will take some planning – not the travel arrangements, but the medical arrangements. You see, I am a diabetic.

About five years ago I lost a lot of weight quite quickly and was drinking pints and pints of water and going to the toilet often. I was tired too, falling asleep after school, but I didn't feel seriously ill. My Mum was worried though, and took me to the doctor, who did some tests. Immediately, she said she thought I had diabetes and sent us directly to the hospital. I was kept in for a week. I had to keep on asking the nurse, 'What's wrong with me?' because I had never actually heard of diabetes. There had been nobody in the family with it so we had a lot to learn, like injecting myself with insulin and testing my blood sugar levels.

At first I'd to learn to use a syringe and draw up the right amount of insulin then inject it into a fatty bit of myself, usually my arms, legs or stomach. That didn't really bother me, especially now they have things called Novapens which are really quick. It's basically like a pen but when you pull the lid off it has a needle on the end and the insulin in it, and you click it round to the number of units you need, put it in, and that's it over. Now I inject once in the morning, about half an hour before breakfast, and again before my evening meal.

Really, diabetes is about planning and being sensible. At first there seemed to be lots about not eating chocolate or sugary drinks and so on, quite harsh rules, but now it's more about if you do eat or drink something like that you have to take it in small quantities and balance it with more sensible food. My parents were given some books at the hospital about diabetes, which I read a bit too. They were quite scary, things like 'You can lose an arm or a leg' and 'Your eyesight can be damaged'. There was a time when I felt there wasn't much point in carrying on.

One of the things you have to do, apart from going to your clinics and knowing doctors' numbers and so on, is always to tell the people you are with that you are a diabetic, so that if you start going into a hypo, behaving stupidly or not feeling good or even going into a coma, when your blood sugar level is too low, they will know what is happening and give you something sugary to eat or drink to make you better. Telling other people means *everyone* you do things with, school friends and teachers, team mates, coaches and so on. That's why travelling and doing things on your own can be a problem.

When I went back to primary school after hospital, my parents and I sat down with the teacher and we explained everything. Later the teacher took me aside and said, 'I've got no problems at all, just try to keep yourself under control – manage yourself'. The teacher was great, the whole school was too. A couple of close friends came round to the house and my Mum and I explained everything to them. They were fine about it.

When I first went to secondary my records said that I was diabetic, but the school didn't inform every teacher. There were teachers, when I asked, 'Can I go out? I'm taking a hypo', who replied, 'What's a hypo?'. It was really annoying and worrying, so I went down to the headmaster and the nurse and said, 'Look, I want everybody told that I'm diabetic. I don't want to collapse in the corridor and get taken off to hospital because some people don't know.' It would have been embarrassing going round myself to each individual and saying 'Look here . . .'. I'd rather the school told them because I've got other worries. I've got my exams coming up, I've got to learn, that's what I'm at school for, and there's sport too. My diabetes shouldn't get in the way of all that, if I do my bit and they do theirs.

On the whole they were very good. They said I could go to the canteen any time I felt a hypo coming on and just take something to eat or drink, they would pay for it. The school nurse keeps juice handy. Most of my primary school friends are at my secondary school now and the new friends I've made there don't mind at all. I mean, they worry about me if they see me drinking juice or having a chocolate bar and they check out with me whether I should be doing it. They care, really, and that feels good.

The sports staff have been really cool about it. Once I was left out of a team and I asked if it was because of my diabetes. I had a hypo playing rugby one day when I'd forgotten to eat enough breakfast. But the coach said it was because of an injury I had, not the diabetes, and I believed him. I try to do my bit, not just at the time but by planning ahead. If I'm playing rugby, or hockey, I've to get a bag together the night before like every other sportsman does, but also another bag which has my food, injections, packed lunch, energy tablets, drinks, Mars bar, so I've got a lot of extra things to do. It's not just taking an injection and eating at certain times, especially if sport is involved.

Doing everything right can be hard. I have to go to the hospital every three months for a check-up and they know from the tests they do if I have been managing it properly or if my sugar levels have been too high since I was last there. I know my average insulin dose but I am meant to test my sugar levels once or twice a day and adjust my diet or insulin accordingly, but I don't always test regularly so sometimes my levels have been too high. When I get a bad reading at the hospital, it puts me down. Sometimes it makes me think, 'Come on now, Richard, pull your socks up'. Blood testing is getting quicker; it used to take nearly a minute, but now there is a new thing which does it in 12 seconds, but it does really still hurt my fingertips, not just when I first prick them but for days afterwards. I'm not a guy for sitting down and concentrating – I'm active. I haven't really got time to do regular blood tests, but I know I have to, if that's the only thing I do. It is really important. If I don't, I could become really ill because I could be going around with my sugar levels sky-high and then one day . . . I could get a cut in my leg, get some infection in it and 'Bye-bye, leg'. There is this little part in my brain that says, 'Oh, I don't know, I can't be bothered'. I suppose it is laziness to some extent.

I had a really bad hypo recently. I was at a party, had a couple of drinks, got up the next morning, went to get my breakfast, collapsed in the kitchen and got taken off to hospital, where they put me on a drip to keep my sugar levels under control, so I wouldn't go into another fit. It was pretty stupid really. If you have to drink, you have to eat. Don't go out on an empty stomach, don't go home without having a bag of chips or something. Always have something to eat to last you through the time you are sleeping because alcohol puts your sugar levels high at first, but then it brings it down, which makes you go into a hypo.

I have learned lots from having diabetes. I am glad my school cares about what needs to be done and treats me pretty well normally, giving me chances like everyone else. I think that is how it should be, if someone has an illness or a disability. But I know that, however much my family and my school care, in the end my life and managing my diabetes is up to me.

Sinead

I have just completed my first year at university, living away from home, and feel fortunate to have achieved this and lived such a full life, particularly in my circumstances. I am learning to drive and currently spend my spare time socialising with a great group of friends. Compared to my peers I don't really look different and I have much the same lifestyle. I have an older brother who is in the army. He may not say a lot but I think he cares about me!

At the age of nine months I was diagnosed as having cystic fibrosis (CF). Without regular physiotherapy, courses of antibiotics and an enzyme controlled diet, CF – a life-threatening condition – can be fatal. CF affects different people in different ways but all have some problems in living with the condition which affects breathing and digestion. In my case, due to the relatively late diagnosis, there were some initial difficulties. However, with correct treatment, medical attention and the support of my parents, my condition was brought under control.

I grew up with CF and therefore have not known life otherwise. I have to remember that, while I can live my life fully, I must always pay attention to treatment and never neglect my health – easier said than done! I owe my parents a lot for keeping me well and caring for me until I was mature enough to do so myself. Parents never stop caring and worrying even when their children feel self-sufficient, but I am glad mine are there when I need them. Looking back now over the years that my parents have looked after us – my brother does not have CF, fortunately – I am thankful that they were strong enough to cope with my condition on top of all the normal family crises. Although I do try to carry out my own treatment and therapy, I know that if I need extra help I can rely on them so I can do almost anything – within limits!

Enrolling in my local mainstream primary school was not a problem. My parents had looked into the various issues that might arise during the school day and discussed them with the school staff. They were all confident that if anything happened, it could be dealt with. Initially, the teachers were probably more anxious than my parents. This was understandable; for them it was a first experience of a child with CF, and perhaps they would have worried about any child with a serious medical condition coming into school. As things turned out, they need not have worried. The teachers helped me with tablet-taking until I was capable of remembering them myself, but that was probably the extent of their involvement for some years. Neither my parents nor I wanted me to be treated any differently at school; full participation in everything was our aim.

During the later primary years I participated in several residential stays for outdoor sports including orienteering, rock climbing, and archery. I was fortunate to have experienced such trips then, as my condition now can often prevent me going away from home due to the complications of arranging treatment in a new and perhaps unsuitable environment. My parents and I showed the teachers who were going how to give me my daily physio and how to prepare the antibiotics for vapour inhalation through my nebuliser. It was great that they were keen to learn and to help me maintain the normal treatment regime.

I remember my primary school not just for the classroom learning but also for all the other opportunities it gave me. During my last year at primary school my head teacher nominated me for a 'Child of Achievement Award'. It was all very exciting, going to the prestigious awards ceremony in London, meeting some celebrities and having television cameras covering the event – it felt like quite an honour.

The move to secondary school allowed me to make more new friends and go through the usual 'question time' with them. It was obvious that questions were going to be asked when I took my tablets before eating in the canteen in front of many strange faces, even though I have mastered a quick swallowing technique with the tablets. I have nothing to hide and don't mind answering questions from people who openly ask about my condition with genuine interest. I have, however, received some not-so-pleasant remarks, which I tend to ignore. This situation is very rare, but unfortunately some people don't know how to react and do so tactlessly. I often find people's comments quite amusing. I suppose I take the knowledge of my condition for granted, so perhaps being good-humoured and open helps disarm their embarrassment or over-directness.

The first friends I made at school remain my best friends today, and we can tell each other anything, which is what friends are for. We share the same interests in work, clothes, shopping and travel. Among them are a few very special friends who have been very good to me and supportive when I needed it most. I have said it so often before, but without my friends I honestly don't know where I would be. I know that my parents have always been there for me and always will be, but friends could so easily come and go if they chose. I think it is easy to have lots of friends if you are outgoing and socialising all the time – something I love doing when I am well enough. There are many times now, though, when I do not have the energy to go out, but that does not stop me wanting to be with friends. They have always been there, cheering me up and continuing to include me, finding less tiring things to do together.

It has only really been recently that my health has started seriously to affect my routine in life, which really frustrates me. I know that, gradually, things will have to change and my health will have to be more of a priority. I also know that my friends and family will support me throughout. That's important for me as it takes my mind off the very serious issues which are constantly at the back of my mind. My condition, unfortunately, becomes harder to manage as I get older, due to the deterioration of my lungs. This means that almost everything I attempt to do is harder.

I gained the necessary Highers for university in my fifth year, so sixth year should have been more relaxed with fewer subjects, but it had many highs and lows. We started with a big school show – an exhausting experience! I enjoyed being involved and decided to take drama as one of my Higher level subjects. This was hard as it was assessed on a continuous basis and relied on group work which meant I shouldn't be absent. That year, in which I was also Head Girl, was exciting, fulfilling and very tiring. Staying healthy was difficult because the extra responsibilities and duties brought some hassles and stress and sometimes, even though I appreciated the opportunities it brought, it almost felt too much. I wanted to prove to myself and to show others that, despite my condition, I could achieve what I set out to do.

This was also the year that my social life blossomed. Much to my parents' regret I discovered pubs and night clubs and still managed school Monday to Friday. Of course everyone goes through a stage of 'burning the candle at both ends' but my parents feared that my health would suffer as well as my school work. I think I proved to them that their fears were groundless – not that anything would stop them worrying!

I am pleased that I didn't need to have special exceptions made for me at school, that I passed my exams like everyone else, with a mixture of my own work and good teachers behind us, encouraging us all the way. I could have taken advantage of my situation, taken an easier way out and abused the teachers' trust, but I didn't, even though it was tempting sometimes.

I have many people to thank for my good experience of the education system. I know that school is not for everyone, but it certainly opened many doors for me and provided me with knowledge, life experience and, most important, friends. My parents and I will be eternally grateful for the support and encouragement we received from the schools I attended, which enabled me to be successful despite my condition.

Since writing this account, Sinead has received a double lung transplant and has begun a very different and exciting phase in her life.

CHAPTER 3

The psychological impact of chronic illness on children's development

Christine Eiser

Introduction

The chronic illness of a child has considerable implications for the whole family (Eiser 1994), but the specific issues depend on the developmental level of the child. Whether the illness is affecting a toddler or an adolescent makes a big difference. Attempts to describe these developmental consequences have been made, either with respect to physical illness generally (Perrin and Gerrity 1981) or in relation to specific conditions, such as diabetes (Anderson 1990). The argument is that chronic illness interferes with the attainment of normal tasks. These authors have drawn on the theoretical perspectives of Erikson (1959) and Piaget (1952) who described the characteristic tasks to be acquired at specified times in development. Attainment of these tasks is thought to be necessary for healthy growth and development. For the healthy child, maturation and experience interact to enable the child to achieve a particular set of tasks and proceed to the next stage of development. For the child with a chronic illness, restricted social experiences, hospitalisations and family emotions surrounding an uncertain prognosis may interfere with the attainment of normative goals. The specific ways in which illness may compromise normal development are summarised in the following schema.

Impact according to developmental stages

Infants

According to Erikson (1959), it is important for the young child to acquire a sense of trust in adults. Small children may be adversely affected by periods of separation from their parents. Although many hospitals offer accommodation for parents, it is inevitable that children experience some separations, either because parents must spend some time at home with their other children, or because hospital policies do not encourage parents to be present during medical procedures. At a time when children should be developing a basic trust in adults, they experience multiple physical assaults, through injections and other painful procedures. Parents may feel helpless because it is not possible to explain what is happening to the child, nor to prepare them in advance for painful procedures. The achievements of this period are considerable: infants learn to walk, talk and control bodily processes. In that children with a physical illness are likely to lack energy, their opportunities to master many of the basic physical skills may be limited.

Preschool children

Preschool children are especially vulnerable where they experience multiple separations from family. They need to gain independence and autonomy and acquire fine-motor skills and muscle control. They are physically very active, affectionate and keen to imitate others and learn appropriate gender roles and social expectations. Chronic illness is likely to challenge the attainment of all these skills.

School-aged children

Children may feel different from others, because they are sick or tired, and because they are less able to keep up with peers and normal activities (Spirito *et al.* 1989). Children can feel lonely or isolated and have difficulties with peer relationships (Noll *et al.* 1991) and this in turn can have negative consequences for integration in school. Sadly, children 'must be prepared to handle teasing, questions, and comments from peers, in addition to allaying their own concerns about feeling different and unattractive' (La Greca 1990). Such findings suggest that the child's return to school needs to be supported by a teaching programme for healthy peers to allay their own fears and encourage understanding. Although hospital policy is generally to encourage children to return to school as soon as possible after diagnosis, many experience some difficulties. Absences (Charlton *et al.* 1991) and in extreme cases, school phobia, have been reported (Lansky *et al.* 1975). School absence also has implications for cognitive development and academic progress. Children can become aware of ways in which their illness sets them apart from others. Teachers' lack of knowledge and their own fears about the disease can further compromise the child's successful integration in school, as teachers' response to their own uncertainty is to make allowances and communicate lowered expectations (see Chapter 11).

Young people

The key developmental tasks of adolescence and young adulthood are attainment of independence from the nuclear family, development of a supportive peer group, and adoption of appropriate work and career choices. Any serious illness can very much compromise the individual's ability to achieve these goals. Adolescents may be forced into a position of dependence on parents while also being less able to participate in a normal social life. At a time when most adolescents are experiencing some independence, those with a physical illness may have to rely on their parents to help them with home treatments, or take them to hospital appointments. Extended periods away from school may force young people to rely on parents more than friends for social support and companionship. Treatment can be specially disruptive for education during adolescence, and many are forced to interrupt their studies or delay taking major examinations.

Adolescents, often more than younger children, are concerned about their physical appearance. The problem is specially common for children being treated for cancer who invariably lose their hair following chemotherapy. Loss of hair has frequently been cited as a major cause of concern in young people (van Veldhuizen and Last 1991, Varni and Setoguchi 1991). Even after completion of therapy, there can be permanent changes in appearance. At the extreme, patients with a bone tumour may have been treated by an amputation which poses a major challenge to the attainment of a normal body image.

Consequences of illness for the child's development

The above overview suggests that the difficulties experienced by families in looking after a sick child depend on the child's age. They are not easier at any age, but they are different. The need for visits to the hospital means that children tend to have more absences than other children and this in itself can make it difficult for the child to keep up with the academic work, as well as making it harder to make and keep friends. Added to this is the fact that some treatments compromise the child's learning, concentration and memory.

Learning and cognitive development

This has most frequently been considered for children who are thought to be at risk because of specific medications (asthma, leukaemia) or because the disease itself is known to affect the central nervous system (CNS). This applies to conditions such as brain tumours or epilepsy. In other cases, it is believed that social factors, such as school attendance or family attitudes, are the key determinants of academic success. In truth, it is rarely possible to distinguish between these different variables.

There is some support for the idea that children who are diagnosed with a disease when younger are more likely to experience learning difficulties than those diagnosed when they are older. There is evidence for this concerning children with cancer (Eiser 1991) or diabetes (Holmes *et al.* 1995). In diabetes, learning difficulties have been reported for children who experience severe fluctuations in metabolic control. Explanations have centred on theories of development of the CNS, the hypothesis being that more damage is sustained by the less mature brain.

Social development

Peers have a major influence on the social and emotional functioning of children. Peer experiences help children to develop interpersonal skills necessary to function outside the home environment. There is also evidence that early peer experiences relate to later social competence (Hartup 1983). The establishment of peer relationships is thought to be a major attainment during the period from 30 months to 7 years and related to this, lack of friends is a common source of distress for school-aged children (Hartup 1983). The development of peer relationships is of interest not only for the immediate implications, but also because early experiences have been linked with later peer relationships and adult adjustment (Parker and Asher 1987). An early pattern of sensitive-isolated behaviour is a risk factor for subsequent difficulties and lack of social acceptance by peers, negative self-perceptions, excessive anxiety, depression and dropping out of school (Hymel *et al.* 1990).

One of the more popular ways to assess childrens' social functioning is through the use of the Revised Class Play assessment (Masten *et al.* 1985). In this activity, teachers are asked to imagine they are the director of a school play. The job of the director is to cast members of the class into appropriate roles. Factor analyses suggest three dimensions underlying choices of children for specific roles:

- sociability-leadership (someone who has good ideas; someone everyone listens to);
- aggressive-disruptive;
- sensitive-isolated (someone who can't get things going; someone who can't get others to listen, and someone who plays alone).

Using this technique, Noll *et al.* (1990) obtained teachers' ratings of 24 children with cancer (8–18 years) compared with healthy controls. In addition to the conventional roles, nine additional roles relevant to understanding the adjustment of children with cancer were included. Three of these related directly to the illness (someone who misses a lot of school); two were concerned with the possible impact of cancer on appearance (someone who is very good looking); two were concerned with academic competence (someone who has trouble with work); and two with athletic competence (someone who is very good at sports). Children are given scores for each role according to the number of times they are nominated for that role. Ratings were made by the child's class teacher for younger children and by the English teacher for those in middle or high school.

According to their teachers, children with cancer differ from peers in key areas of social functioning, and show restricted leadership and social skills. However, in a related study the children did not rate those with cancer as different from other members of the class (Noll *et al.* 1991). These findings suggest that it is important to collect information from children as well as adults, and raise questions about why teachers may be more negative in their ratings of the child's functioning compared with classmates.

The relationship between parent and child functioning

Typically, the relationship between coping and adjustment of different family members has not been considered. In part, this is as much a limitation of our methodological and statistical techniques as a failure to acknowledge the interactive nature of family functioning. The way in which parents explain treatments to the child, and their own approach to dealing with the child's fear and pain during procedures, is associated with the child's ability to cope with painful procedures (Blount *et al.* 1989).

Differences between diseases

Diseases differ on a number of dimensions, such as whether or not they are potentially life-threatening, their impact on the child's mobility, the visibility of the disease, the stability of the disease and the degree of self-care that the child or family is required to do. It is evident that the experience of chronic disease can vary widely from one condition to another. We can never be prescriptive and assume that what applies to one condition can readily be assumed to apply to another, neither can we be sure about which limitations are most upsetting for the child.

Life-threatening nature of the disease

Some chronic diseases are life-threatening. Prior to the discovery of radiotherapy and anti-cancer drugs, life-expectancy for a child with leukaemia was just a few weeks. With modern treatment, 60–70 per cent of children can expect at least five years disease-free survival (Stiller 1994). Other conditions, for example muscular dystrophy, remain life-threatening and no current therapy exists. In these cases, medical treatment is limited to control of painful episodes and minimising as far as possible the degree to which the disease compromises the child's quality of life. Most children with non-acute asthma or controllable diabetes have a normal life expectancy and relatively little intrusion of the disease into their everyday life as children.

Mobility

Again, there are some chronic diseases which have very little impact on the mobility demands of daily life. Others, such as spina bifida or muscular dystrophy can severely compromise mobility. Even for conditions that are not normally associated with mobility impairment, there may be periods of acute illness when the ability to participate fully in school and school activities is very limited.

Visibility

Often, chronically sick children look different from others. They may be very small or poorly developed physically. Sometimes particular treatments are associated with changes in body size and shape. The use of radiotherapy and chemotherapy is associated with hair loss in children with cancer. Children with liver disease show characteristic bloatedness and excessive growth of hair as a result of their medication. In all these cases, there is a constant reminder that the child is ill, and this may affect the way in which other people behave. In many other diseases, there are no obviously visible effects. To outsiders, the child looks perfectly normal. For children, this can create much confusion. They look well and can often feel well, yet there are constant reminders about their potential health problem, in the need for daily treatment and regular out-patient check-ups.

Stability

Chronic diseases differ in terms of their stability. A child with poorly controlled diabetes could experience a 'hypo' (low blood sugar) without warning; a child with asthma may similarly experience an asthma attack. With children and cancer, there is always the possibility of relapse or recurrence of the disease, and for many people this remains a real fear, long after the time when there might be considered any real possibility from a medical point of view.

Self-care

By definition, a chronic disease is not curable. One of the goals of modern medicine is therefore to enable the child to live as normal a life as possible. In some cases, this is best achieved when the child and family assume considerable responsibility for much of the prescribed treatment. The degree of vigilance that is necessary to ensure health can be onerous, and is a constant reminder that the child is not 'normal'. Increasingly, parents may be asked to be responsible for a greater part of the child's treatment. This is partly because it is recognised that it is better for the child to be at home rather than in hospital, and many procedures that were once only undertaken in hospital can now be satisfactorily managed outside. Many parents welcome the opportunity to do more for their child, but others may find the responsibility too heavy or worrying.

Quality of life for children

Our understanding of what it is like to grow up with a chronic or life-threatening illness is extremely limited, not least because we have relied on information from parents about how they think their child is affected. As parents, we may often over-estimate the extent to which we think we understand our children's feelings. It is important to recognise that there are contexts in which children do not want their parents to know about what they do, or whom they are with. It is natural that parents themselves are distressed by the child's illness and, for some, this distress can colour their perceptions of the child's strengths and weaknesses. Especially where parents are seriously depressed, there is evidence that they report more behaviour problems in their child (Hobfoll 1991). Although it is difficult to interpret this finding, there are implications that the more parents are depressed or experiencing poor mental health themselves, the more they will report that their child experiences difficulties. Ideally, then, if we wish to know how a child feels about an illness, we should ask the child. However, there have been concerns raised about the reliability of data elicited from children. Certainly, in the past it was assumed that children were unable to give reliable reports about the localisation and extent of pain. As with much work involving children, more recent work suggests that they are more accurate and reliable reporters than was previously suggested. Methods which are acceptable for adults may be inappropriate for children and result in biased information.

Undoubtedly, there are developmental changes in the ways in which children of different ages understand health and illness. Children differ from adults in their understanding of the cause, treatment and implications of illness, their recall of illness events and interpretations, and their perceptions of the risk involved in different situations. They may be concerned about events which do not upset adults, and vice versa. The notion that children proceed through a fairly invariant sequence of beliefs with rather naïve implications for communication and explanations of illness (Perrin and Gerrity 1981) has many attractions. Even this view, however, is increasingly challenged (Hergenrather and Rabinowitz 1991). Although we recognise that treatments can be painful, we have tended to make judgements about the extent of pain or distress based on the reports of adults, especially mothers. Mothers experience stress themselves (Hobfoll 1991) and, as a consequence, their accounts of the impact of the disease may be influenced by their own emotional state.

For all these reasons, it has become important to develop ways to communicate directly with children, in order really to understand their experiences in living with a long-term illness. Particularly for adolescents, some paper and pencil questionnaires have been developed to assess directly children's quality of life.

Coping

Children with any illness experience a wide range of stressors, including those associated with medical interventions and those associated with everyday home and school stressors which affect all children (Chesler and Barbarin 1987). These include:

- understanding the diagnosis, prognosis and treatment
- adapting to treatment and side-effects
- relating to medical staff
- relating to family and peers
- dealing with two worlds, illness and health; 'being special' and 'being ordinary'.

Two common ways of coping have been described by Lazarus and Folkman (1984). These include problem-focused coping strategies directed at changing the environment or personal behaviour; and emotion-focused coping, defined as efforts to regulate emotional states that are caused by, or related to, the stressful event.

Bull and Drotar (1991) studied 39 children, between 7 and 17 years old, with cancer in remission, including 15 who had leukaemia. The children identified many more non-cancer-related stressors than cancer-related, the ratio being 161 to 27. Of the non-cancer-related stressors, 24 per cent related to school, 24 per cent to family and 19 per cent to peers and social situations. In relation to the smaller number of cancer-related stressors, 30 per cent related to impairment or disability and 22 per cent to treatment-related issues.

So how did the children cope with these stressors? Bull and Drotar (1991) were able to identify different coping strategies depending on whether the stressor was cancer-related or not. For cancer-related stressors, adolescents were more likely than children to report emotion, compared with problem-focused coping. (This is to be expected since cancer-related stressors, such as hair loss, cannot be changed, and can only be dealt with by focusing on the emotional issues.) This study suggests that children are able to identify cancer-related and treatment-related stressors and distinguish them from everyday stressors; that they adopt different approaches to managing cancer-related and non-cancer-related stress, and that adolescents may have developed more successful patterns of coping than children.

It can be difficult for the child to return to school following illness and long absences, and therefore some hospitals now employ specialist nurses or social workers to liaise with the school and prepare the staff and pupils for the child's return. Often this involves a class discussion about the sick child's experiences, led by the specialist nurse. A more formal programme has been described (Katz *et al.* 1988). The programme involves:

- preliminary intervention, assessing the child's school behaviour and parental involvement with an aim to arrange appropriate learning support through the diagnostic period;
- conferences with school personnel to help them plan for the child's return;
- classroom presentations, in the child's presence, to provide peers with age-appropriate information;
- follow-up contact after the child's return to provide any further help.

Follow-up evaluations of this programme resulted in positive reports from teachers, parents and children, although it is not clear that there were long-term implications for achievement and social functioning.

Other programmes have been directed more specifically at helping the child with cancer acquire the social skills to cope with school life. It is inevitable that the child with cancer may have to answer questions about what has happened to their hair, why they go to hospital so often, why they do not have to participate in physical education or games. Varni *et al.* (1993) developed a social skills training programme to provide the child with the necessary skills to deal with these questions. The programme consisted of three modules, each of one hour's duration. First, children are taught to identify problems, consider their cause, and explore alternative ways of resolution. Second, they are taught how to express their thoughts and concerns to others. Third, they are shown how to cope with teasing. Children also took part in two follow-up sessions, three and six months after returning to school. When parents were asked their views nine months after their children returned to school, they reported fewer behaviour problems and greater school competence for children who went through the training compared with those who received standard return-to-school instruction.

Ideally, other programmes should be directed at healthy children in order to minimise teasing, but we may still need to prepare children for what might go wrong when they return to school.

Long-term psychological effects

It is, in fact, only recently that we have been able to ask about the long-term consequences of chronic disease. This is the result of the enormous strides made in the care of sick children. The question of how growing up with a chronic condition affects adult development and quality of life is increasingly important. From a society point of view, it is necessary to know how far children will be able to make a full contribution to the workforce, or will need special provision and community care. For parents, it is important that they have a realistic appraisal of the child's longer-term opportunities and potential for future education and employment.

Most of the work in this area has concerned survivors of childhood cancer. Survivors generally do well and have few problems. Some reports suggest they do better than might be expected. Evans and Radford (1995) reported that 55 per cent achieved grades A–C in GCSE examinations (compared with 62 per cent of siblings and 30 per cent in terms of national average). For those who continue to experience physical difficulties, perhaps as a result of their treatment, or because of continuing disease-related problems, the outlook can be less rosy. This may also be so for young people with other unresolved or chronic conditions.

It should also be recognised that prejudices in society generally can compromise long-term opportunities. Some opportunities, especially in the armed forces, fire service and catering, are not open to certain groups, including young adults with a past history of serious health problems.

How schools can optimise the child's psychological development

- Make appropriate provision so that necessary treatments can be delivered at school (see Chapter 7). Children with cystic fibrosis may need physiotherapy during the school day and this may mean that attendance is poor. Providing facilities and personnel so that this can be integrated in the child's normal day is important. Similarly, provision should be made for children to have easy access to their own medication.
- Recognise the need for learning-support (see Chapter 8). Children who had academic difficulties before the onset of illness are likely to experience greater needs for intervention afterwards. Recognition of academic problems needs to be timely and not delayed on a vague assumption that it will right itself.
- Enlist the help of other children (see Chapter 8). Classmates can provide useful practical assistance in helping the child with physical disability make easy transitions between classrooms. They also need to understand why changes in physical appearance occur, or why the child has difficulty learning. Practices to deal with teasing and name-calling need to be in place.

- Designate a special teacher to liaise with the School Health Service and be informed about children with chronic conditions.

In these ways, schools are not only in a unique position to contribute to the development of the child with a chronic condition, but also to ensure their fuller inclusion in their communities and quality of life.

Conclusions

There have been significant improvements in the medical care of chronically sick children, enabling many to lead very full and active lives. In some cases, medical care has, in its turn, created obstacles for the child and family. For this reason, it is important that the psychological consequences of improved technology are recognised.

Recognition of the potential consequences of disease and treatment for the child's psychological functioning has resulted in an increased research interest. This is to be welcomed, as it clarifies the ways in which disease imposes restrictions and care-taking burdens on the family. We must, however, recognise the limitations of research. Too often, we are forced to rely on findings from American research, without reference to differences between cultures in the organisation and delivery of health care, or parents' expectations and attitudes toward childcare. Too often, also, we have relied on the reports of mothers or teachers, rather than listened to the voice of the child.

Acknowledgements

The author would like to thank the Cancer Research Campaign, London, for their continued funding and support. (CRC research award code CP1019/0101).

CHAPTER 4

Researching the education of children with medical conditions: reflections on two projects

Angela Bolton, Alison Closs and Claire Norris

Introduction

This chapter will consider educational research about children with medical conditions, reflecting on its relative dearth, the risks – especially to parents and children but also to educational professionals – in such research, and means of ensuring that their voices are heard. Two separate but parallel research studies provide the basis for the reflection. Overall findings from these studies are summarised here, and many of the individual findings and recommendations arising from the projects appear in Chapters 1 and 8.

The studies had many similarities but were different in several respects. Angela Bolton's research in England and Wales, *Losing the Thread: Pupils' and Parents' Voices about Education for Sick Children* (Bolton 1997), undertaken for the NAESC (see Tait, Chapter 6) over one year, examined parents' and children's views about education for sick children, accessing 100 families by in-depth interview or questionnaire. Most of the children were absent from school at the time, being educated in hospital schools, by home and hospital teaching services in wards or at home, in half-way units, or in hospital without education. This study did not include the views of education staff but NAESC had surveyed local authorities and hospital and home teaching services a year before (NAESC 1996) about the education of children out of school for health-related reasons.

Alison Closs and Claire Norris's two-year research in Scotland (Closs and Norris 1997), part-funded by the Scottish Office Education and Industry Department (SOEID), surveyed all local authorities, interviewed all key authority personnel in one urban and one rural authority, interviewed staff – head teachers, class, subject and guidance and learning support teachers, auxiliary helpers and school doctors –

in four mainstream schools, and interviewed parents and children from 16 families. All the children were enrolled in mainstream schools although many were intermittently absent in hospital or at home. Some were long-term absent.

Thus, the common element was the evidence of parents and children and it is on this that we now concentrate most. However, we will also refer to teacher views from the Scottish research. Just as the current emphasis in policy and research on 'the voice of the child' can seem threatening to the role and voice of parents, so the voices of both parents and children can muffle that of teachers. Yet these three key parties have to hear each other and work together if education is to be effective.

Why so little educational research?

Most studies of children who have chronic or serious conditions (see Eiser, Chapter 3) are medically, psychologically or sociologically orientated; few focus on educational dimensions. Yet education is the largest common ground for the child population and it inevitably helps shape the adult, whatever the form of education or state of children's well-being. The proportion of children with significant health needs is estimated at 10–15 per cent of the child population (Eiser 1993). The British Paediatric Association suggests that just under ten per cent of the under-15 population have an illness which chronically reduces their functional capacity (BPA 1995) and thus, presumably, their education. Why so little study of their education?

Does the health of children, however intrinsically important, not impact on education personnel except through absence or brief visits to the school doctor or nurse? Is it assumed that health and illness belong 'elsewhere' and are the business only of family and medical personnel? Significantly, even in the heyday of categorisation, little provision for 'delicate' children was made in England, Wales and Northern Ireland, and the category did not exist at all in Scotland. Children with health needs were subsumed within mainstream provision, generally without additional support, or, if more severe conditions seemed to cross over into the 'territory' of disability and/or cognitive impairments, they attended special schools and units.

With increasing integration and, in recent years, inclusive approaches to the full diversity of children in local mainstream schools, more research has been carried out into the means of increasing inclusion by improving generic systems and increasing understanding of what it actually takes to include children with specific disabilities successfully. The lack of educational research attention to children with health needs, along with the lack of joint coordinated pressure from understandably otherwise occupied parents and from voluntary organisations, until NAESC came into being in 1993, may account for the very tardy legislation and guidance which would enable their education.

Reasons for the lack of salient educational research may include:

- the ignorance about health-related issues among teachers (Eiser and Town 1987) and educational psychologists (Closs and Norris 1997), two key professions involved in educational research;
- the lack of extensive crossover between educational research and medical and social policy research which has highlighted parental criticism of education services for children with extensive physical care needs (Beresford 1994);
- researcher hesitancy, at a time when medical or child deficit models of special education have been discredited in favour of social models of disability, to become involved in a field where in-child factors and medical treatment are unavoidable issues.

We, too, were very conscious in both projects of the risks of pathologising children and their families. The case for considering children with medical conditions within the social model of disability has been made in Chapter 1 of this book. Children and their families are systemically disadvantaged by societal systems and attitudes when trying to achieve normal human aspirations, including accessing effective education. This was made very evident to NAESC through its membership, and to the Scottish research team through the families and young people with whom they were involved in setting the agendas of research (Closs and Burnett 1995, Closs 1998). We were anxious to include them in the planning of the studies and to ensure that their views had prominence in our reports.

Researching parents', children's and education personnel's views: practical and ethical perspectives

Our concerns can best be expressed in four questions:

- What did children and parents think were priority issues for investigation?
- How should we contact families?
- What methods are best to access parents' and children's views?
- How could we best access teachers' views?

Families' priorities for investigation

The establishment of NAESC and their funding of the research project in England and Wales was in response to the increasing dissatisfaction of some parents and educational activists about the education of sick children, particularly those out of school on the grounds of health, but also those who did not seem to be doing well educationally even when attending school. Discontinuity, under-achievement, uncertain progression and parents' awareness of children's own concerns, which were as much social as educational, comprised a basis of concern which generated the need for greater understanding of the underlying issues. The 1993 legislation in England and Wales had made educational provision for children out of school statutory but without safeguarding standards of quantity or quality of education. NAESC was aware that too little was known of the real educational experiences of sick children and what it actually took to make their education continuous, appropriate and effective. NAESC's director and steering committee, which included parents, therefore determined to chart this policy and knowledge void by means of research.

In Scotland there had been a more consensual realisation among professionals in hospital and home tuition services, some parents responding from their own rather isolated protests against unsatisfactory provision, researchers and lecturers responsible for teacher education, and the SOEID Special Educational Provision Inspectorate, that there was a lack of clarity about the availability, adequacy and efficiency of education of children with serious medical conditions. This was particularly so in mainstream provision, where it was not known whether their school education was indeed 'adequate and efficient' as required by law. Moreover, in Scotland education authorities might make educational provision out of school but this was not a mandatory requirement: some children who could benefit from education might not receive it at all.

A Scottish conference was therefore held in 1994 to explore issues and identify priorities for future development and research. As in NAESC's two studies, the Scottish research was basically charged with investigating policies and practices in education authorities and schools, with finding out the reality of children's and parents' educational experiences and identifying ways forward.

The studies both intended to give prominence to parents' and children's voices, although the Scottish study also sought the views of key education personnel, including mainstream class and subject teachers and hospital and home tutors who worked directly with children with medical conditions.

We rejected the concept of a hierarchy of conditions (see Chapter 1) and included children with conditions of sufficient severity to cause, or be associated with, significant absence and/or difficulties in learning or in accessing the full curriculum. We recognised the major part that educational systems and attitudes played in such difficulties. Children included in the research had main conditions as varied as asthma, psoriasis, recurrent glandular fever, kidney conditions, cancers, severe migraine, cystic fibrosis, sickle cell anaemia, heart conditions, Hurler's syndrome, Duchenne's muscular dystrophy, chronic fatigue syndrome (ME) and juvenile arthritis. This list is illustrative, not exhaustive.

Both studies aimed to produce recommendations arising from their findings to enable the education of all children with medical conditions who were well enough to benefit in or out of school.

Contacting families

Both projects used systems of 'gatekeepers' or 'blind postboxes' to contact families. The parents and children in the NAESC project were recruited in two stages; first, through hospital schools and other teaching services involved in education out of school, which produced 46 parents, most of whom were interviewed at home. Forty of their children aged 7–19 subsequently took part. Secondly, the researchers contacted other medical condition groups through the organisation Contact-A-Family (see Chapter 15), extending the parent sample to 100, with the additional 54 parents completing questionnaires.

The research was based in three broad geographic regions. Most of those selected on the basis of their child's condition agreed to participate because of the endorsement of the project by trusted, familiar teachers who passed parents a letter detailing and explaining the research, with a covering letter supporting the aims of the project. Parents completed a reply slip directly to the researcher.

In the Scottish project, the first five families were contacted through officials of five different parent associations across Scotland, identified through Contact-a-Family. The remaining families were contacted through the child health services of the two demographically contrasting education authorities which were profiled, entailing examination of the research plans by the medical ethics committee of one of the NHS Trusts concerned. Education contacts were not used, since parents would be interviewed about educational provision and might feel inhibited if recruited through this route. Health service contacts gave the researchers access to families not attached to condition-linked associations.

Variety in geography, medical conditions, parental socio-economic and educational status were sought to make the case studies illuminating and salient to as many potential readers of the report as possible. Thus, there were families from remote and rural areas and city dwellers, affluent and economically struggling, graduate and early school-leaver parents, and 17 different main conditions. The small sample precluded generalisation from findings and we recognised that the 'typical family' was a myth.

As in the NAESC project, gatekeepers in the Scottish study passed to families the project information sheet detailing its purposes, the likely time involvement of participants, the intended research products and participants' share in these, and the absolute right to refuse to take part (simply by not answering the invitation) or to withdraw at any time. They were asked if their child/children would be willing to participate but again it was made plain that this must be voluntary and that the child/children could withdraw or be withdrawn at any time. Families had free choice of place and time of meeting but, with the exception of children in hospital, home was preferred. Sixteen families participated, producing 18 profiles of children's educational experiences – two families included two of their children. All 16 mothers were interviewed and six fathers along with their wives/partners.

Fourteen children were 'volunteered' by their parents to participate in Scotland but three seemed less than willing at the time and mutual face-saving ways out were negotiated by researcher and children. In another family a younger sibling affected by the same condition as the older child had not been volunteered by his parents but insisted on participating and gave a lively data-rich account. Thus 12 child interviews or conversations were finally recorded.

The NAESC researcher did not start several interviews where consent was unclear, and cut short others where participation was apparently becoming difficult for the child. The child's spoken or implicit withdrawal of consent overrode parental consent. While we generally found that most children were willing participants, we all found working with very young children challenging. In efforts to work with three five-year-olds, Angela Bolton found herself talking about Barbie with one and coming away with a lovely rainbow drawing, reading stories with a second, and receiving a very firm refusal from an assertive third. Our shared resolve to ensure a positive experience and show appreciation to all interviewees was extended equally to these three youngsters! Working out when we are treading too carefully, denying children the right to speak directly about their lives, or not carefully enough, is not something that can be predicted by age, ability or state of health, certainly not by a researcher and probably not even by parents or children themselves.

Accessing parents' and children's views

Both studies used qualitative methodology, with loosely-structured interview schedules and open questions to encourage expression of what parents and children found interesting and important to them. We also wanted the voices of parents and children to be heard clearly throughout the research reports so used extensive quotations, and illustrations in the case of the children in the NAESC study.

We accepted that parents and their children might not always hold the same views but believe that both perspectives had value. In both studies it was children who gave the most direct and compelling accounts of fear of bullying and worry about missing work and falling behind. But parents were also extremely sensitive to their children's feelings. They were concerned about their children's educational progress but even more concerned about their happiness and inclusion, emphasising peer relations and friendships. It was parents who expressed the most anger when schools gave little or no social support to a long-absent or frequently-ill child. Children cannot always recall earlier events and parents are able to fill gaps, to give a retrospective view or add vital details about medical or educational histories. Overall, parents confirmed and extended their children's accounts; the voices were different but, in general, complementary.

All three researchers were conscious through their training – in one case as a counsellor with additional bereavement training – and their previous research experience of the dangers in doing research on sensitive topics (Lee 1993). We recognised that the most serious concerns surrounded the possibilities of 'conscripting' and 'using' research participants in ways which left them, at best, dissatisfied with the ways in which their evidence had been gathered and used, or worse, feeling in some way exploited, abused, misinterpreted or worse off than before.

Parents
Having ensured by the means already described that the adult research participants were indeed volunteers who had given informed consent, we were still left with several outstanding concerns. Among these were how to interview the parents we thought might be most vulnerable – those whose children had advanced life-threatening conditions – in ways that allowed them to recount fully what they wished yet that minimised distress to them, and offered us coherent data.

In one of the Scottish pilot interviews, a parent talked us through her child's life, the time sequence plainly helping her recall events of significance. However, as it progressed she became tired and began to show signs of distress as her account reached the time when her child's condition began to deteriorate. The mother refused the researcher's suggestion that she might stop and perhaps continue another time, and insisted on completing the interview. She then refused the offer of a meal and drove herself home some distance. We had arranged that she give us frank feedback and were not surprised when she told us how both the length and progressive sequence of the interview had turned what she had hoped might be a cathartic and positive experience into a deeply depressing and draining one. We were very grateful that she generously helped us plan a more successful approach whereby subsequent interviews began with eliciting a description of the child and his or her education currently, and then took parents back to their child's earlier educational experiences. The imposition of a reasonable time limit, with occasional reminders of the time left, reduced fatigue and kept the dialogue on track without apparent loss of narrative quality.

Throughout the research we all learned how to 'lighten' interviews without diluting the importance and seriousness of what parents were saying. We learned to cope with laughter and tears, parents' and our own, and to realise that both could be entirely appropriate. We also learned about the resilience and resourcefulness of families, their capacity for fun and normality and their ability to talk calmly and lucidly, despite deep sadness and anxiety, about the most traumatic and distressing events and circumstances. We perhaps forgot sometimes that, as one mother put it, 'This is new to you, but I've had all my children's lifetime to think about it and just get on with living'.

Children and young people
Despite the efforts described above, researching sensitive subjects with people who feel their views and problems have been ignored or not understood and addressed can mean that, for some, the interview experience may be positive, even cathartic and therapeutic; for others it may be negative, stressful, and painful. While difficult and guilt-inducing, this is a calculated 'risk versus benefit' dilemma in exploring the bigger picture with adults and trying to influence change. As researchers, we take the responsibility for such decisions.

But this is not enough with children and young people. Raising difficult issues with children has even greater ethical and practical implications (Alderson 1995). Continuously checking that children really were informed and voluntary participants was one part of addressing this, but we still had to use child-friendly ethical approaches to access their views.

Mayall (1996) stresses sitting down with children at their level, stepping into their world, letting them talk in pairs or groups if that is more comfortable, to minimise the 'adult as expert' role. This was the approach used in the Scottish study where it was rare for the researcher and child to be sat facing each other with only their conversation between them. More often opinions were sought, rather than direct questions asked, through and round other activities, using a computer, playing a board game or looking at a book on the floor, even watching a television programme together. Some older children were happy to converse, however simply. In the case of two young brothers, interviewed supposedly in sequence but often in a loud and not always harmonious duet, the pace and quantity of contribution was almost too fast and rich to absorb at the time and to unscramble from the recording subsequently.

Over the past decade, researchers have borrowed and adapted visual research techniques from the therapeutic tradition of work with children, particularly in health education (Wetton and McWhirter 1998). Visual methods used with children include drawings, relationship maps, and photographs. Non-visual methods include diaries and child-friendly questionnaires, where the response scale, instead of ranging from 'strongly agree' to 'strongly disagree', goes from a very smiley to a very un-smiley face. Elicitation techniques (Hazel 1996) give children or young people a story, picture, cartoon or scenario and ask them to explain what might happen, what is going on, what it reminds them of or how they feel about it. In other words the material is used as a trigger.

One approach developed by Williams *et al.* (1989) is 'draw and write', which can be used in a variety of ways. Children may simply be asked to draw and write everything they know about a particular topic such as what makes you healthy and unhealthy (Pridmore and Bendelow 1995). Alternatively, they may be given an elicitation scenario and asked to draw and write what might happen. Drawing helps to overcome limited literacy barriers so that younger children can participate – it is a familiar and usually unthreatening activity. Older children may be self-conscious but can be reassured that artistic merit is unimportant or can be encouraged to draw cartoons or use matchstick figures to remove this pressure. Children can be allowed to project their views onto a third person – a less threatening way to think about sensitive issues.

In the NAESC project, the 'draw and write' exercises were used with children aged 7–12 and with slightly older children who were less forthcoming orally. In these instances, they were asked to, 'draw someone who's ill like you' or, 'in hospital like you', allowing medical circumstances and equipment to be represented. Then they were asked to respond to an elicitation question or scenario about what the person might be thinking about missing school, doing lessons in hospital, and returning to school. Most of the children who were offered this approach became absorbed in the drawing and colouring and completed the exercises. Two or three of the more confident under-13s and the older children questioned the 'other person' projection, asking, 'Is this about what *I* think?', perhaps needing to talk more directly about their experiences and not through a distancing medium. On the advice of Sue Occlestone, who has used the technique extensively in health education research, children were told they could represent their figure saying one thing but thinking another, to allow mixed feelings, or public and private views to emerge. In one case a positive response to hospital lessons in a speech bubble was accompanied by a thought bubble containing, '*Great*, I'm in hospital and now I have to do *maths*'.

Parents generally confirmed children's views in their interviews, talking about their children's damaged friendships, the lost thread of education and the children's fear of changes at school during their absence – lost seats and different teachers. In a few cases where children wanted to show their drawings to their parents, parents realised some elements of what concerned their child for the first time or the extent of their child's worries.

Accessing teachers' views

In the last 15–20 years teachers have become accustomed to, and depressed by, the prevailing climate of teacher-focused blame and of constant change. They are understandably wary of inspectors, government reports and development initiatives, the media, research reports and researchers, lest what they say be taken down and used as evidence against them. Those working with children with support needs in mainstream and special provision alike have not been exempt from this oppressive atmosphere. That so many school and educational service staff were so willing to cooperate with us – being interviewed at length in the Scottish study and in the earlier NAESC project, and enabling parent contact in the NAESC Losing the Thread Project – says much for their interest in children with medical conditions. In approaching schools and services we had made it plain that, while we would be looking for gaps in provision and difficulties, we would also be identifying good practice and highlighting issues which they considered important.

In the Scottish project, where school staff were interviewed at some length, we were also able to assure teachers that parents and children who had already been interviewed had made great efforts to be fair, to criticise what they felt were barriers to the children's educational and social inclusion but also to praise efforts on their behalf made by staff and to recognise the difficulties teachers faced.

Teachers were interviewed using the same open approach as used with parents, valuing not just direct answers to questions but also their ideas and feelings – sometimes of anxiety, fear, and sadness and sometimes of satisfaction and happiness at children's achievements, problems overcome, and good partnerships established with parents and other professionals.

Data analysis

Both projects produced huge amounts of data, interview notes and transcripts of recordings and the 'draw and write' illustrations, truly an embarrassment of riches. Interview data analysis was based on reading and re-reading interviews, old-fashioned cutting and pasting, and progressive searching for, and refining of, themes and patterns (Ritchie and Spencer 1995).

It was evident that parents, teachers and children did not merely want to tell their stories but wished to influence policy and practice and to inform educational managers. While the aim of our research was to enable education, many of the messages we received had a strongly holistic underpinning that children needed to be seen not just as pupils or as unwell or disabled children, but primarily as children with all the entitlements of other children. Teachers felt ill-prepared for coping with what they thought might be some of the healthcare aspects of having a child with medication or medical treatment needs in class. They worried too about teaching children with life-threatening conditions. Nonetheless, some who had actually worked with one or more children with such needs had found it less traumatic and much more interesting, rewarding and feasible than they had first imagined. Educational and social inclusion were seen as equally important and inextricably intertwined. Home life and school life could not in any child's case be divorced, and least of all in the lives of children with medical conditions.

The children's 'draw and write' data in the NAESC study were examined for key messages which grouped into five main themes. These were: negative anticipations about returning to school, positive feelings about returning to school, the impact of absence on friendships, whether or not they would be bullied, and being behind with work. Most were able to express these concerns clearly, for example, drawing a child 'like them' thinking 'Who's the bully now?' on return to school, 'Who am I going to hang around with?', and 'I'd better find a new friend to play with'. Sadly, more of them expressed worries than confidence about return to school. This finding ties in with some of the Scottish interview data with children where they referred to having 'sore tummies', 'cramps' or 'feeling sick' at the thought of returning, with some thoughtful children explaining how they sometimes had these very unpleasant feelings even when, in some ways, they wanted to go back. Even younger children in both projects were also able to express ideas about what would help other children, much of it centring on additional help with work and on friendship.

Conclusion

To summarise, the parents', children's and teachers' accounts of, and comments on, their experiences helped establish what did and did not work in organising and delivering education. Overall, both research projects shifted the scope of attention much more towards mainstream schools and education authorities, valuing additional specialist services and provision highly but seeing them as essentially supportive partners with mainstream provision rather than an alternative education. They drew attention to issues around interpersonal relationships and inter-professional working, and communication. Catching up on school work or, whenever possible, not falling behind, through more support for learning introduced more promptly and by filling gaps in the curriculum, were identified as important ways forward. Inclusion in the special educational needs systems and processes to codify, coordinate and prioritise planning and provision for children with health needs was a high priority. Blaming of teachers was rare; efforts made to include the diversity of children in classes were recognised, but more awareness-raising and training for education professionals around relevant issues were thought essential.

The research points to the value of talking with children, parents and teachers, and, above all, of them finding the ongoing time and space to talk to each other.

CHAPTER 5

Parents' expectations and experiences of their children's education

Sandra Mason, Amanda and Tony O'Sullivan, and Mairi Ann Cullen

Andrew's mother Sandra Mason talks about him

Our son Andrew was born on 5 March 1983, a healthy 5lb 10oz. He continued to be a healthy, happy child until he was six years old. He suddenly became ill in October 1989.

One morning he was rushed into hospital and diagnosed as having a kidney disorder called nephrotic syndrome. Andrew was in hospital for 14 days in isolation. He blew up like a balloon with fluid retention, his immune system was 'down', he was seriously ill. We did not know then what his life or future was – his education did not even enter our heads. Andrew was very ill when he came home from hospital and continued to be in and out of hospital for quite a few years. Initially, he was not back in school until February 1990. By that time we knew a lot more about his illness and we knew that his future was going to be very unsettled, so subsequently his education was almost certainly going to suffer.

As the months went on we got through one day at a time, trying to come to terms with our new way of life, trying to be strong for Andrew, each other and our extended families, which was almost impossible. At that point we did not put much emphasis on his education; his health was more important and dominated most of our time and all of our energy. When Andrew felt well enough the education authority gave us a home tutor, a super person and simply a godsend to me. She has a lovely nature and quickly became a friend. She and Andrew gelled together and built up a close relationship. She understood Andrew and knew when he was too tired to concentrate – she would just call it a day.

Somewhere along the line, somebody asked us if Andrew had a 'Record of Needs'. We had never heard of this. Andrew was in Primary 5 by this time and our life was completely taken up by hospital appointments and with our home-visiting teacher coming in to work with Andrew. Sometimes he was able to go to school. We were always told he was doing well and had caught up with the classwork he had missed.

Andrew's health had not improved and kept fluctuating. His education was becoming more and more dominant in our minds, so we decided to find out what a Record of Needs was and how it might benefit him. I approached the educational psychologist and had a meeting with him; he explained what the Record was, how it was a legal document which set out a child's needs and what the education authority would do to meet them. The psychologist agreed to do an assessment on Andrew. When this was done we were told a Record of Needs was not necessary. We accepted this decision for approximately a year. We began to think about Andrew moving up to High School which was a daunting thought. We wanted guaranteed support there so we approached the Psychological Services again about a Record of Needs. They agreed to do a further assessment. This was done and we were asked to attend an informal meeting to discuss Andrew's assessment. This time it was agreed that Andrew needed a Record of Needs. The support options that were put to us were: a mainstream school with a special unit, a school for children with special needs, or a supervisory assistant to help Andrew in a mainstream school.

We felt Andrew did not need to go to a special school, as he was 'just ill', although he needed a lot of support, both in and out of school. It was explained to us when, and where, the official meeting about the Record would be held and who would attend: the educational psychologist, the home tutor, the head teacher, the paediatric consultant, the senior educational psychologist, myself and my husband. We were told what the agenda would be and that all the 'professionals' would be putting in a report on Andrew. Fine – but what about *our* report? Well, the parents don't usually put in a report, was the reply. Later we discovered this was misinformation and that the Record has a special section for parents to complete if they wish and also that parents and young people should be encouraged to have their say in all decisions.

Over the years we had become completely different people, much more cynical, harder, more aware and ready to take on the world to make sure that our son got what we felt was his right – to be educated, the same as every other child. We put together a report and handed it out at the recording meeting. Prior to the meeting we were provided with the rest of the reports which we read until we had almost memorised them word for word.

The day of the meeting arrived and we went in feeling very apprehensive, but ready to put up a good fight to get what we wanted. We thought Andrew needed a special needs auxiliary for when he came back to school after treatment and also that he should be formally recognised as having top priority for a home tutor. The meeting went very well with everybody sharing their own ideas of what would be 'best for Andrew'. Fortunately, both my husband and I were very strong people by then and we did not accept anything with which we did not agree. At times I felt quite angry and upset that all these people were discussing what was best for our son. Basically, I just did not want to be in this room and most of all I did not want to be in this situation at all. I wanted my happy, healthy son back, but that was not to be, so all we could do was to get on with what was in front of us.

The satisfactory conclusion of the meeting was that Andrew would have a Record of Needs opened and he would have an assistant in class, and be top priority during any absence for the home tutor. We would also be kept informed on Andrew's school progress at regular intervals.

Andrew's health continued to be very unsettled and he was losing a lot of schooling. He always had home tuition as soon as he was able. I used to go up to the school to collect and hand back work for Andrew. When he was well and back to school for a week or so, I would go up to see his teacher to check his progress. I was always told that, considering he had been off for so many weeks, he had caught up well with the rest of the class, and was doing very well. Naturally, we were very pleased to be told this as his health was still an enormous worry to us. We felt relatively relaxed that his education was 'something to worry about less' or so we thought. His Record of Needs was really a good thing to have.

It was now time for Andrew to go up to secondary school. A review meeting was called before Andrew left primary school. The meeting was very informal, and relaxed. It was explained to us how learning support works at secondary level, which we thought was good, also that Andrew would have a supervisory assistant – whom we knew and liked, a real bonus – in most subjects. The assistant was also a really nice person, so we felt confident about Andrew going to secondary school.

The day arrived for Andrew to start his new school. All went well for a couple of months until he came home and said he was being bullied. A group of boys had pushed him and called him names – 'dwarf', 'fatty,' and many more. Because of his illness he was small for his age and also he was puffed up through fluid retention. I went straight to the head teacher and explained the situation and how serious it could be if Andrew got punched or kicked in the stomach. The head teacher was excellent in the way he dealt with the matter. Because Andrew had not been in the school long enough to know a lot of people, he did not know the bullies' names, so the head teacher got out all the class photographs and Andrew pointed out who the bullies were. The head teacher wondered if it would be a good idea if pupils should be made aware of Andrew's condition, but I thought it might make matters worse as children can be very cruel. The head teacher assured us the matter would be dealt with and it would not happen again. I was very impressed with the head teacher's way of dealing with bullying – and felt reassured that this would be the end of the matter – and so it was.

Andrew seemed to be doing well enough at school and it was time for our first parents' night. We went up feeling quite confident about going in and speaking to all his teachers. The maths teacher was last on the list to see. We gradually worked our way through them all; each one said Andrew was a pleasure to teach, always tried his best and was doing well. 'It was a shame about his health', was the common feeling among the teachers. We finally reached the maths teacher and we were really shocked when we got her report. She also said Andrew was doing well but because he had missed so much maths at primary school, there were some things he had never done which were now affecting his overall work. We were led to believe in primary school that he was always quick to catch up with the class, but what Andrew did not recognise was that there were some crucial bits of maths that the teacher had not filled in. We got this sorted out by asking for an urgent further meeting with the learning support department. It was agreed that Andrew should have a reduced timetable. It was suggested that he drop languages and have extra periods of maths and English to fill in any remaining gaps. This has worked very well for him and that was what we needed – a flexible response to his particular situation.

Andrew is now in third year and specialist subject home tutors have been appointed to come to the house when he is absent. He also has, exceptionally, the use of a room to himself in school where he can do technical drawing and art work if he is absent because of low immunity. This means he can still have all his subjects, but in safety from infection. The school and the education authority have been very helpful and supportive in ensuring that Andrew gets the education that is his right.

Andrew is now in fourth year and is doing extremely well. He sits his Standard Grade examinations this year and his teachers are confident he will get good grades in all his eight subjects*.

To summarise what it has been like for us in the last nine years, I can only say it has been hell. We started out as a very 'normal' family, ordinary people with our children going to school every day and not knowing very much about the education system, but now we have learned so much about 'the system' that we could almost apply for the Director of Education's job if he were to retire! Now, as organiser of a local voluntary special needs group, I use some of what I have learned to benefit other parents and children about how education can be made to suit children, with a bit of give and take on both sides, even when children have big health and attendance problems.

---

*Andrew got a very severe attack of chicken pox not long before his exams and valuable time was lost trying to find home-visiting teachers who would brave the possibility of getting shingles. Fingers are crossed for the exam results!

Amanda and Tony O'Sullivan, parents of Amy, talk about her

Amy, age 8, is our first child and Gemma, age 6, our second. Concerns about Amy became more focused when Amanda was pregnant with Gemma, although we had lived with some of the features of Amy's condition well before this. Amy has an extremely rare genetic condition known as Dubowitz syndrome. This was tentatively diagnosed – no definitive diagnostic test is available – by a specialist children's hospital when Amy was 3. We have a one-in-four chance of carrying a child with this condition. Gemma was nine months old when the diagnosis was made, and luckily shows no features of the syndrome. We decided to have no more children.

The characteristics of the syndrome, which matched well with Amy, were: small physical stature, global developmental delay, distinctive facial features, eczema and a propensity to have fits. We became aware of there being a problem gradually. Each characteristic of Amy's condition emerged at a different point in Amy's growth and initially they seemed unconnected.

Amy was a very unsettled colicky baby. She had difficulty feeding due to oesophageal reflux which corrected itself after a year. Her eczema first appeared when she was six months old, with her first tooth, as a small patch on her chin. Eczema is a dry skin condition where the skin is inflamed, itchy and sore. Very quickly it spread over her whole body. Next came the breath-holding, a form of tantrum in which Amy, in over-reacting to certain situations, ceased breathing until she became unconscious. Quite often a small fit would follow a breath-hold, but she never had a fit without breath-holding and, after tests, epilepsy was ruled out. Next came evidence of learning difficulties. Amy developed into a placid child, and was, and still is, very affectionate. She constantly sought adult company, and looked to be entertained. While this could be very tiring, there was no reason initially to believe anything was amiss. Increasingly, however, her contemporaries began to outstrip her in inquisitiveness, dexterity, personal awareness, speech and the quality of play. At her age-3 assessment, Amy was referred to a community paediatrician who confirmed developmental delay. Finally, her size and facial features put the medical profession on the track of the correct overall diagnosis.

Amy has immense positive qualities that have been important for both the way we have come to terms as a family with her condition, and for shaping the nature of her education. She is a tremendously happy child, and very loving. While naturally shy, she has a great sense of humour. She delights in being helpful and in being praised.

Our first reaction to the confirmation of learning difficulties was naturally one of grief. To cope with it Tony set out to 'do something' – to get Amy into an appropriately resourced nursery as quickly as possible, knowing that early intervention is important for the development of children with learning difficulties. This proved easier said than done as the only local nursery equipped to deal with children with special needs had 22 applications for seven places. This was our introduction to the chronic lack of resourcing for children with additional needs and caused us and other parents great heartache. Amy eventually got in because the parents of another child turned down a place.

Around this time we began to realise the really nasty nature of Amy's condition. Being developmentally-delayed she could not understand why she was in seemingly constant pain or itchy, and looked to us to do something about it. Seeing her so distracted and upset, and being incapable of doing anything to solve the problem, was very difficult for us to cope with and the source of much distress. Our inability to help our own child as she scratched and implored us for relief was frustrating and horribly painful. It is easier now she is mentally older and more self-aware, but still unpleasant.

The nursery was overall a very positive experience for Amy and beneficial to her subsequent development but it threw up unexpected management and educational problems. The warm cosiness of the nursery, suitable for most children, was overheated for Amy. The heat would trigger severe itching and scratching bouts. In addition, dust in the nursery atmosphere or from soft toys, furnishings and dressing up clothes, and contact with numerous common substances found in nurseries such as chalk, paint, sand, soap and water – all very drying to the skin – and certain foodstuffs could trigger powerful reactions. While the staff were sympathetic, there was little they could do about the heating – the needs of the many outweighing the needs of Amy – and protection from contact with substances meant Amy could not join in many of the common activities through which social and other skills develop. If she did, she had to suffer the consequences of her skin reaction to them.

Amy experiences urticaria – nettle-rash – if she eats lentils or split peas, beans and pulses, or if she touches raw egg and sometimes citrus juices, tomatoes and fish. Because of this, the nursery had to be careful when baking – many times Amy came home with her hands red raw – or with arts and crafts, as often lentils and pulses were used to make collages. At lunchtime staff had to be careful what Amy ate. Once Amy ate some lentil soup and suddenly became so itchy and hot, covered in urticaria, that a staff member had to take her outside to cool down. Luckily it was snowing at the time!

About this time we were referred to the paediatric allergy clinic and then to the dermatology outpatients' department where we were given a new skin-care regime and shown how to bandage Amy. This was extremely useful; at last we could do something to limit the damage eczema was doing to her skin. However, effective as it was in protecting her skin from scratching and harmful substances, the bandages added to the over-heating problem and so did little to relieve the itching.

During Amy's time at nursery her breath-holding peaked. She might have up to eight attacks in one day, such was her frustration. A deep sleep would often follow a breath-hold, and the nursery staff allowed her to sleep it off in a play bed in the 'house corner' which meant Amy was missing out on nursery activities. When we realised this and discussed it with the teachers, we asked them not to allow her to sleep, as Amy was using this to opt out of things she did not want to do. Slowly, Amy became more settled at nursery and able to participate more fully. The breath-holding reduced so that by the time she started school they were quite infrequent. Amy no longer breath-holds now.

Prior to Amy's transfer to her current school at age 5, the education authority opened a Record of Needs for her, at our instigation. This explicitly recognised Amy's eczema as having locational, curricular, school facility and physical access implications. We observed in the parental section of the Record:

> Amy remains an unconfident and introspective child by nature. Her eczema continues to contribute to this. About 40 to 50 per cent of her day is spent in scratching at any and every part of her body, during which time it is exceedingly difficult to attract her attention. Amy's medication is geared totally to the control of her eczema.

We further noted:

> Amy's eczema is both atopic and contact in nature. Her skin responds adversely to heat, dust and a number of food products including lentils and, to a lesser extent, eggs, fish and citrus fruit. These factors will need to be taken into account.

For its part the education authority noted in the Record that:

> Amy requires to be placed in an educational setting where the educational environment does not exacerbate her skin condition thus providing her with equality of educational opportunities.

We had started looking for Amy's school very early. Little information on options and possibilities comes parents' way routinely. By chance we heard of a Scottish Office list of special schools detailing size, location, level of learning difficulty provided for and so on. We requested a copy of this nine months before Amy was due to start school and selected eight 'possibles'. We visited all the schools, comparing each with an agreed list of criteria her school must meet. We had decided to send Amy to a special school for a number of reasons relating predominantly to her developmental delay. These were: firstly, that any extra resources spent on Amy's education were likely to have a positive effect; secondly, that Amy's shyness would be exploited and misunderstood in the rough and tumble of a mainstream school, and she would withdraw into herself as a consequence. We felt Amanda's extensive social contact out of school hours with friends with small children would provide ample opportunity for Amy to socialise normally. We have never regretted that decision.

Although Amy's developmental delay drove our choice of school type, general and specific conditions within the school, attitudes to eczema and competence to deal with it medically and educationally all figured in our final choice. One nursery head teacher had looked dubiously at Amy and said, ' I think we can deal with her if she doesn't shed skin everywhere'. Less obviously crass, but more subtly damaging, most schools and teachers see eczema as a medical condition solely, without understanding that it has implications for how education must be arranged and delivered. At one school, staff references to their pupils lacked respect. Others proved unsuitable because of the levels of learning difficulty for which they catered.

Our final choice was between two schools of obvious high quality in terms of teacher ability and professional commitment. One was in our local authority area, the other not. We chose the latter because the physical conditions were more suitable. The school was cooler, bigger, airier and not hemmed in with busy roads throwing up fumes. We made it clear to the education authority that we had invested considerable time and forethought into what we wanted, that we had good reasons for our choice and no intention of being dissuaded. After a minor scuffle, our request was granted. We expect Amy to stay there at least until she is 16.

Her attendance at this school has been a wholly positive experience. With a chronological age of nearly nine, she has an assessed mental age of around three but her social and self-care skills have blossomed. She adores school, hates to be away over the holidays, and frets if she is unwell in case she won't be able to attend. This is due to a curriculum and learning approaches sympathetic to Amy's general strengths and weaknesses. The school's positive approach to the care of Amy's skin and their willingness to learn what to do, putting aside several hours to be taught by us how to deal with scratching and itching bouts by applying an emollient, by using distraction, but most importantly by keeping her cool, have been crucial. We are lucky that they have a qualified nurse to apply Amy's creams when required, to change bandages when worn and to administer antibiotics if Amy's eczema becomes infected. We have had to reiterate that it is useless to tell Amy to stop scratching or indeed to try to restrain her physically, by holding her hands. We have taught Amy to respond to such attempts with, 'I can't help it, I am very itchy'. It is always best to say something positive such as, 'Rub it instead', or to find a cooling approach: removing some clothes, opening a window, using a fan, running the itchy bit under water or pressing a cold wet cloth against it.

Amy's skin affects her behaviour. She can become 'non-responsive', blanking out everyone and everything except the itch. Amy has also developed some ritualised behaviour, banging her head with her hand and touching things repeatedly. We are not certain why she does this but it is usually when she is tired and itchy and it makes concentration very difficult. One of Amy's teachers once said to us very perceptively, 'It is always best for Amy to be in maximum response mode before introducing a task and it is also important to know when to stop teaching her something'.

Occasionally, the school makes mistakes, forgetting once that Amy reacts particularly badly to lentils. Consequently, she suffered a severe reaction. Once, a pupil in Amy's class had a nasty cold sore and because of the school's and our own over-reaction, and fear about the condition eczema herpiticum – a very serious condition caught from the herpes virus – Amy, not the infectious child, had to stay off school. We have tried to understand when the school makes mistakes – we make inadvertent mistakes ourselves. It would be inappropriate to over-react, given the school's obvious commitment to working closely with us on Amy's behalf. The school staff are focused, as we are, on meeting the needs of Amy pragmatically, helping her development, learning willingly as we go. We believe that it is this honesty and integrity that makes the difference in responding to all Amy's educational needs.

Mairi Ann Cullen, mother of Patrick, talks about him

At the time of writing, my son, Patrick, is 12. He was born with a genetic predisposition to suffer anaphylactic reactions to a variety of common foodstuffs.

Anaphylaxis is the name given to the most severe type of allergic reaction. If untreated, an anaphylactic reaction can involve the whole body and is life-threatening.

One major impact of Patrick's medical condition was that it greatly curtailed his opportunities for social interaction. Sadly, we never found a playgroup or nursery which had staff willing to accept Patrick and to take on board the implications of his condition. For a term, I attended every playgroup session with him but, as I was the only mother doing this, I came to resent the fact that Patrick had been denied a place on the same terms as other children his age. In addition, my presence made the playgroup leader, used to working on her own or with 'one-off' volunteers, uncomfortable. At the end of the term, I withdrew Patrick.

The local playgroup was our first experience of organised educational provision. The reaction of the playleader made us feel that we had no right to expect other adults to take responsibility for our child in the way they took responsibility for the rest of the community's children. We were made to feel that we had to cope alone. This impression was strongly reinforced at the very first discussion about starting school.

At Patrick's age-3 medical check-up, our GP told us that it would not be possible to send Patrick to the local school. No-one will take him on, we were told, it's far too risky. If anything happened they wouldn't be able to get him to hospital in time, we were told. Such is the power of professionals that we accepted these bald statements. Reflecting on this now, I can look back and understand that at the time we lacked the information to make a rational judgement. When the doctor told us that something was so, we accepted it.

As a result, we felt we had no choice but to teach Patrick at home. From the time Patrick was 3 until the age of 6, no medical or family health professional we encountered ever suggested to us that school was a possibility. The problem was not only ensuring the safety of our son, it was also to do with the legal issue of liability – if adrenaline was administered by a teacher in school and problems occurred, the fear was that we might prosecute the teacher and/or the education authority.

Over the years, the effect of the lack of access to mainstream school on us as a family was cumulative. One of us always had to be with Patrick. Our solution was that both worked part-time but our careers and finances suffered as a result. Psychologically, the situation was very stressful. We had the full responsibility of maintaining Patrick's health and safety and the full responsibility of educating him. Because he had not started school and so had never been registered, we had no contact with the education authority. Our social life was non-existent – our fear of leaving Patrick with a baby-sitter was reinforced by the perception of his problem as so great that even the schools could not accommodate it.

Reflecting on the experience of those years now, it seems to me that the key issue is the importance of health and education professionals talking to each other. Why was it that not one of the many GPs, health visitors, dietitians, nurses and consultants we encountered made, or helped us to make, any direct link to an educational professional to discuss Patrick's educational needs?

In the end, it was through a chance encounter that we learned that there was one independent school in the local area that might take on Patrick and his medical problem. The school had a policy of ensuring that all staff were trained in first aid. The whole staff were consulted and agreed to having Patrick in their school. Patrick started school just before his seventh birthday. Since then, we have moved twice and he has attended two other schools. Looking back, some key experiences stick in our minds.

Schools accepting a pupil with known anaphylactic tendencies must work with medical professionals to ensure that a sufficient number of staff has been properly trained to give the necessary medication. Medical expertise is also vital in drawing up an emergency plan of action. We refused the offer of a place for Patrick in one school because the head teacher would not accept that medical professionals had to be involved. His attitude was that there was no need to make a fuss; Patrick would be 'safe enough'. We knew such an attitude meant that we couldn't trust him with the life of our son.

In another school, however, we were fortunate to encounter an example of best practice in this respect. Before Patrick began attending his second school – a state primary school – an individual action plan for the management of a severe allergic reaction was drawn up. This was a requirement of the education authority, and the procedures were in place to link up education and health professionals. The process involved the school staff, the school nurse, ourselves, our GP, the GP surgery nearest to the school, the hospital consultant who dealt with Patrick's case, the local education authority's health and safety officer and the community paediatrician.

Finding a new school for Patrick after moving house was a fraught experience but we were deeply impressed by one head teacher's approach. His attitude was that the medical problem was only one small part of Patrick. While it was vital to learn about anaphylaxis and about how best to ensure Patrick's safety, he felt that the most important thing was to welcome Patrick to the school and to begin to find out about all the other aspects of Patrick's character and interests. This sums up exactly how Patrick, and I am sure anyone with a medical problem or other 'difference', wants to be treated – acknowledge the situation and its implications but then concentrate on the person, not the difference.

We have always considered it vital that all adults in the school know about Patrick's allergies and what to do in an emergency. In his current school, this was done in a particularly effective way. The head teacher invited me along to the in-service session immediately before term started and allowed me to talk to all the staff and to answer their questions face to face. From my point of view, this allowed me to be certain that all the staff knew about Patrick's allergies. I also felt that the school was willing to use my knowledge and experience of coping with anaphylaxis. From the school's point of view, it allowed the teachers to take the opportunity to ask how Patrick's condition would affect him in class. I, in turn, was able to reassure the staff that, despite the severity of his allergies, no serious problem had occurred in school previously and, with information and care, was not likely to happen in their school either. Other schools might like to think about how they could learn from the knowledge and experience of the parents of pupils with chronic medical conditions.

Classmates also need to be informed about anaphylaxis. In one school this was done at assembly with no prior discussion with us or with Patrick. In another school, a better way was found. The head teacher and class teacher asked Patrick who should be told. He replied that he thought all his classmates and their brothers and sisters should know about it but not the whole school. Before Patrick joined the class, the teacher informed the class of the situation, playing very much on expectations that they would react responsibly and in a caring manner. Their empathy was called on – imagine life with no coke or sweets or pets! We have found that if adults create a responsible, caring environment, children mirror that in their behaviour to their peers.

Patrick's allergies make him very vulnerable. His peers know of his allergies and, 99.9 per cent of the time, have been supportive. But for his sanity and ours, it is vital that teachers take seriously the slightest hint of intimidation. For example, one young boy became jealous that Patrick had a special place reserved for him during packed lunch time in the classroom. This boy wanted to sit in Patrick's seat and so he threatened Patrick with an egg. The classteacher took action immediately and no further problems arose. She could understand that, for Patrick, being threatened with an egg was just as frightening as being threatened with a loaded gun.

Teachers are busy professionals with a million things to think about – sometimes it is easier to exclude the pupil who is different rather than changing the activity to include that pupil. For example, his class was studying techniques of dyeing in art and the teacher wanted to use an activity that she had used many times before involving a simple, flour-based glue. Fortunately, Patrick immediately realised that this was dangerous for him and told the teacher. The teacher suggested that when this activity happened, he could leave the room. Discussing this at home, we decided to phone the school and suggest to the teacher that an inclusive alternative would be to use candle wax in place of flour-based glue. The teacher was willing to listen to our view and to take up our suggestion. We felt valued and Patrick felt good about having spotted, and averted, a potential danger to his life.

An anaphylactic reaction is extremely frightening for those watching but much more so for the person experiencing it. It helps when teachers and school medical professionals show their awareness of the emotional and psychological effects of this. For example, anaphylaxis has meant that Patrick has had a different pattern of schooling from many of his peers – as a consequence of not beginning school until he was 7, he learned how to be a self-directed learner. This has caused some problems in school when the teacher did not understand the source of the behaviour. Patrick also learned from having anaphylaxis that not everyone can be trusted to be responsible. His awareness of his own vulnerability has led to a certain maturity and that has caused some problems with peers. He has been upset when teachers have called him 'a loner' but some teachers have helped him by easing his social relations with peers and by discussing his fears with him.

Key messages for educational professionals

(Written with the help of Patrick Cullen, age 12)

- Please take the time to find out from the parents or guardians of the young person as much as possible about the condition and about the implications for everyday life.

- Please take the condition and its effects seriously. This means taking the action necessary to make school safe and pleasant for the young person. This requires vigilance that the condition and its implications are not forgotten.
- Please take time to find out how it makes the young person feel.
- Please treat the young person as a valued and interesting human being who will contribute to the life of your school.
- Please try not to blame the young person for being different.
- Please try to find ways of including the young person in all activities.
- You may find that the young person responds to your care by working extremely hard.

CHAPTER 6

The role and achievements of voluntary organisations supporting education

Kirsteen Tait (PRESENT/NAESC) and Helen Hart (Ataxia Telangiectasia (A-T) Society)

PRESENT/NAESC – A national 'umbrella' organisation

Why NAESC was established

Why did we start the NAESC? Another new voluntary sector organisation, yet another organisation dealing with children, and yet another education charity! Was it really necessary – especially when there are already too many competing causes for funds?

The answer is simple. NAESC was set up because something of great importance was not being provided, and would not be provided, without an organisation to fight for it. A campaigning body was needed in order to focus on the education of sick children as a target in its own right.

In the summer of 1993 a group of sick children, concerned professionals including the hospital and home-visiting teachers working with the children, and officials from the newly established association, went to 10 Downing Street to petition the Government about the inadequacy of out-of-school education for sick children. The petition described how such services renew children's hold on life, normality and future potential and how they were not sufficiently available to all children who needed them.

It was ironic that the impetus for NAESC came from the 1993 Education Act for England and Wales.

> Each local education authority shall make arrangements for the provision of suitable full-time or part-time education at school or otherwise than at school for those children of compulsory school age who, by reason of illness,

exclusion from school or otherwise, may not for any period receive suitable education unless such arrangements are made for them.

Education Act 1993, section 298 (1)

Thus, for the first time it became a statutory duty on local education authorities (hereafter referred to as LEAs) in England and Wales to provide 'suitable education' for children absent from school on the grounds of health, that is, hospital teaching and home tuition. The new duty, paradoxically, threatened the very thing it apparently set out to secure. It placed sick children together with excluded and truant children whose needs are emphatically no less important than those of sick children but are different and already have a much higher political profile. The statutory obligation was to be implemented without additional funding and without national standards, and we correctly predicted that, without NAESC, sick children would be at the end of the queue for scarce funds.

Truants and school excludees make headlines – they are the focus of both opprobrium and compassionate support, but there is a unanimous clamour from politicians, professionals and lay people who all insist that these children must have education to support them now, to reintegrate them into school and society and to ensure their future.

There was no such demand on behalf of sick children. Children with all manner of conditions (see Chapter 1) missing weeks or months of school, revolving between hospital, home and school, often facing long and disagreeable treatment and altered and uncertain futures, needed *their* entitlement to high quality education to be ensured.

The absence of these children's educational needs from the national and local policy agenda is explained by a lack of understanding of children's health and the role of education in their lives, what hospital teaching, home tuition and better liaison with schools could achieve for them and what would happen if it were not available. Putting that right was the starting point for NAESC.

Hospital teachers' associations had signposted the way. They campaigned heroically despite their other demanding commitments. NAESC was needed, however, to flag up sick children's interests with national and local politicians and officials, to campaign on behalf of their overburdened parents and teachers, and also to forge powerful links with health service staff who recognised the importance of ongoing education for children. Paradoxically, it was the education world which, with notable exceptions, seemed blind to sick children's educational rights and needs.

Establishing the information base

Control of information is the power base of many voluntary sector organisations. For NAESC there were three distinct stages – establishing reliable facts and figures about the problem, documenting the inadequacies of provision, and publishing evidence of the losses they cause in the words of those affected. Once recorded, this information had to be relentlessly broadcast countrywide, since relevant people and organisations were engaged in other matters or would rather not hear. The cause was not 'trendy,' nor very attractive to funders. I would like to pay special tribute to the large and small trusts who provided start-up funds and supported the initial research. Without them, change for the better is impossible in many fields.

Putting the subject on the map was relatively straightforward. In 1995 NAESC published the first national *Directory of Current Provision* (NAESC 1995), listing the hospital and home tuition services of each LEA in England and Wales and, more recently, in Scotland and Northern Ireland (NAESC 1997a and 1998). The Directory embodies these distinct education services – its physical weight alone symbolises the importance of the subject. The information assembled in it could not be ignored. LEAs were asked for numbers of teachers both in the hospitals in their areas and providing home tuition, the amount of teaching and home tuition offered, and the criteria for eligibility for them. In 1994 some education authorities did not know which officer was responsible, or even whether they employed teachers for sick children. Some, we suspected, had to formulate their criteria for child eligibility in order to complete the returns.

The level of information detail required was deliberate. The returns raised the profile of education of sick children, the listing of a responsible officer meant that someone was accountable and could be contacted by parents, by officers in other LEAs, by hospitals outside the LEA to which children had been admitted for specialist treatment, and by local mainstream teachers. It was the first step in establishing the channels of communication with LEA officers and heads of service on which NAESC depends, to update and refine its understanding of current issues. Its links with hospital teachers, home tutors and other interested parties are built on hundreds of visits to services, and also through a quarterly NAESC information newsletter introduced in 1994 and expanded and streamlined since to become *Present Newsletter* (NAESC/PRESENT quarterly).

No-one knew the numbers of sick children, which hospitals they were in, what their illnesses or medical conditions were and their pattern of absences from school, nor what was being provided and what educational needs were being neglected. This state of ignorance included the Department for Education and Employment (DfEE) which kept some statistics but only for designated hospital schools and for limited purposes. As Scottish research would subsequently show (Closs and Norris 1997, also see Chapter 4), and informal inquiries in Northern Ireland, the situation was similar elsewhere in the UK. Winning a research grant from the DfEE to find answers to these questions was a landmark in NAESC's development.

The single most significant finding from this research (NAESC 1996) was that there were at least 10,000 school-age children each year in England and Wales in hospital or out of school long enough to need education elsewhere if they were not to fall behind and have problems reintegrating into their own schools. This statistic proved that children with medical needs were not a tiny inconsequential group but a pupil population the size of an average LEA, although scattered across all of them.

It showed that about two-thirds of education for sick children was provided not by registered hospital schools but in an immensely varied range of LEA hospital and home-teaching services, in small hospital teaching units with two to three teachers, or by lone isolated hospital or ward-based teachers cut off from their profession, or as an afterthought or 'add-on' to an out-of-school service dealing primarily with truants and excludees. These were not recognised as schools, whatever their size, so did not receive Government Circulars as of right and could remain ignorant of developments and policies. Many, for example, knew little about Statementing processes. They had no independent governing bodies and therefore had no protection from the annual round of LEA cost-cutting, often had pitifully small budgets and little or no funds for professional training.

The research showed incontrovertibly that, in spite of valiant teacher efforts, hospital teaching and home tuition were being provided inequitably and to very different standards, and in some places not at all. It was no longer possible to ignore the fact that some children were being deprived of their rights to education, many service teachers were cut off from professional support and development and two-thirds of the entire national range of provision was outside any form of independent quality assurance and development. The education of children accessing these services was vulnerable, even though these children were advantaged relative to the many we knew were still not receiving education at all.

The third and possibly most important investigation, required to create the information basis for change for the better, was the Pupils' and Parents' Voice Project (Bolton 1997, also see Chapter 4) which recorded the views of sick children and their parents in their own words on the value of education and the effects of missing out on it. It revealed vividly and poignantly that sick children almost invariably want education, want and need more of it than they are getting, and dread returning to school if they have missed it. Children and parents highlighted problems by describing in telling simplicity what was generally missing and the ill-effects on confidence and achievement.

NAESC's focus had been very much on out-of-school services, but this research turned the spotlight on the inadequacy of mainstream schools to help sick children maintain social and educational contact with their schools and to reintegrate successfully on their return, something noted also by Larcombe (1995). Because of lack of understanding and information, being overworked and overburdened with new regulations and duties, many teachers were not only failing to help sick children academically and socially, but were unwittingly actively adding to problems which could increase loss of confidence, fear of school, isolation and bullying, and attendance problems.

From action research to action

The research and information collection established the preconditions of change for the better, but they were not enough to make it happen. Extensive recommendations were addressed to the DfEE in their commissioned research report. Some required additional funds or legislative changes which, realistically, made them longer-term objectives, as were improvements in guidance to LEAs and better recognition of sick children's needs within the *Special Needs Code of Practice* for England and Wales (DfEE 1994) and its Scottish and Northern Irish equivalents.

Quantifiable out-of-school education minimum standards emerged quite clearly from the research and from professional and parent opinion. Although these are not yet officially adopted there is widespread agreement about them. NAESC therefore, after the legislative changes in 1993 and their re-enactment in 1996, contested cuts which would endanger these minimum standards and promoted improvements. Every LEA proposal was countered with constructive proposals, by discussions with officials, through joint meetings between health and education, through membership of local advisory groups and management bodies. A three-year outreach project, funded by BBC Children in Need, formalised the standards-setting work.

Meetings in an LEA might halt damaging cuts but still not create adequate provision. NAESC's membership of committees overseeing new services was useful but too labour-intensive for a relatively small organisation. Conferences and good practice publications were more widely effective. The publicity arising from a House of Lords ruling against an LEA, for using funding constraints to justify providing so little home tuition for a GCSE-age child that it made nonsense of the statutory duty, was another boost. It takes a long time to achieve a change in political will, but some LEAs have improved provision without additional funds and others will heed the implicit warning of this case.

The Pupils' and Parents' Voices project, which led to a published report (Bolton 1997), helped to set the agenda for several new action projects. The first provides guidance for mainstream teachers on supporting sick children's education and social confidence and on helping them settle back into school smoothly after absence. It also fed into a 16+ entitlement project. The statutory duty applies to children aged 5–16. Many LEAs fulfil their minimum duty and cut off hospital teaching and home tuition on young people's sixteenth birthdays, even if they are sitting external examinations and returning to school. This denies youngsters education at a time crucial to their whole future. The 16+ project should help remind LEAs of their moral obligations to children and of the sheer waste, not just to the individual but also nationally, of stopping education at this arbitrary point.

Conclusion

The needs of sick children will not be secured without a voluntary organisation dedicated to them but, paradoxically, what is achieved for them can generate opportunities for others who face educational disruption and discontinuity. Making up for lost time should be an entitlement for all within the concept of lifelong learning, now being espoused nationally.

Five years on, the cause is firmly on the political agenda – at national and local level. Keeping it there and moving on now require different tactics. In 1997 we launched an award scheme to recognise the extraordinary efforts of sick children and young people to keep their education going in spite of severe and life-threatening illnesses, painful and arduous treatment, and absence from school. The awards deliberately celebrate also the value of education and the skills and professionalism of school and service teachers. The next step is to pass on the message that there needs to be better understanding and sharing of skills between school-based and special service teachers – true collaboration to support children who need both.

During the founding five years NAESC has set out an agenda, identified and publicised the needs of the children and their teachers and drafted national quality standards. It is not enough to call LEAs to account about standards. NAESC has to help develop effective and cost-effective methods of achieving them. Much remains to be done. I am confident that NAESC will continue to pursue its cause through innovative work with my successor as Director.

The Ataxia Telangiectasia Society: a small condition-specific voluntary organisation

The second part of this chapter is an account of the development and changes that one small voluntary condition-specific organisation has gone through in the last ten years in response to wider changes which have taken place in the field of education, care, medical practice and organisation, for individuals and for families affected by physical disability. The Ataxia Telangiectasia Society is a small charity working throughout the UK, supporting families which have a member with ataxia telangiectasia. It could be a description of the experiences of any similar group over this period of time.

The condition – history and pathology

A-T is a very rare neurodegenerative condition which affects three in a million people. There are fewer than two hundred people with the condition in the UK. It is a complex, multi-function syndrome which was identified in 1956 by Dr Elena Boder in America. At that time the main features of the condition (the ataxia – a loss of balance and coordination – and the telangiectasia – web-like prominent blood vessels most commonly found in the whites of the eyes) had been described, but understanding of the effects of the condition was limited. The disorder was known to show itself in children between the ages of 1 and 5 and the prognosis was bleak, with children rarely living through their teens.

Gradually, as genetic research information and knowledge have grown, it has become possible to gain a greater understanding of the many facets of the condition and the impact of A-T on the lives of the children and their families. It is now known that there are early and later onset variants of the condition, that there is a variation in the rate of deterioration and that the condition is caused by a defect in DNA processing and an inability to repair damage to the DNA. A-T affects motor control – neurological findings show selective nervous damage of the cerebellum, brain stem, basal ganglia and spinal cord. Speech may be slurred and eye movements can become restricted as the condition progresses. Seventy per cent of children with A-T have poor immune systems and suffer from recurring chest infections. All carry a greater risk of developing cancers – leukaemia and lymphoma in particular – and most need to use a wheelchair by their teens. The gene, which was located in 1995, is an important and complex one and may hold the key to understanding other medical conditions. Research in the UK is continuing, and advances have led to better management of the condition. People with A-T are now living into their thirties and forties.

The A-T Society

The A-T Society, like many small charities, started as a self-help and support group for parents who had an affected child or children. From an initial meeting of nine families in Birmingham in 1989, the Society was formed with three main aims:

- to raise money for research
- to raise awareness of the condition among the medical profession
- to act as a contact point for families.

To do this effectively, the management committee drew up a five-year plan identifying the main areas of activity as sponsoring and supporting a specialist clinic, promoting research, providing information and providing family support.

At the end of the first five-year period the Society had succeeded in raising awareness about A-T among the medical and paramedical professions, had drawn on its expertise to publish a range of leaflets, and was then in a position to respond to requests from professionals who were working with the families. Providing social workers and teachers with information about the condition was a priority.

Political initiatives at national and local levels over this period brought about shifts in policy affecting support services for people with disabilities. In practice, this meant moving from residential and segregated services to community-based services. Moving from the 'medical' model to the 'client-centred' model of services meant adopting a multidisciplinary approach involving many professionals working with individuals and families. This move has directly affected how children with A-T receive their education.

Ten years ago, children with A-T began their education in special schools and many completed it in residential schools. Today most children with A-T start in mainstream primary and some continue into mainstream secondary. Others move into special schools in their teens, depending on the availability of suitable local provision. The introduction of parental choice in requesting school placement has affected the work of the Society and shown a growing need for relevant, up-to-date and accurate information. It is needed both to assist and support families and to inform the professionals, teachers and others with whom they must work when making decisions about education and exercising choice.

Living with A-T

In order to help families and professionals alike, it is important to understand and have some insight into the effects of living with this condition day-to-day.

Living with a rare degenerative condition means that the family dynamic is constantly under pressure and parents can feel isolated and unsupported. With A-T there is the problem of variable health day-to-day as well as ongoing deterioration. Trying to balance the differing needs of the various family members can be difficult, especially in times of crisis.

Meeting the needs of children with life-limiting or life-threatening conditions and those of their families calls for cooperation, awareness and understanding. Both parents and professionals must have awareness and knowledge of the condition and be prepared to cooperate in managing the effects of the condition continuously. Professionals must be able to exercise understanding and flexibility in their approach to the family. Cooperation and communication among the professionals involved with those who have complex educational needs is also vital. Parents of children with these special and specific needs have their own particular requirements for support. However, dealing with a range of different organisations and, worse, with constantly changing representatives of these organisations, brings its own stress. Wherever possible the statutory and voluntary bodies should work to provide their support in tandem.

Voluntary organisations come in all shapes and sizes. Large voluntary organisations may be able to provide specialist schooling, work or leisure projects and respite care services; smaller organisations tend to concentrate on information services and advice on health issues, benefit rights, disability access and education provision. Very small organisations, such as the A-T Society, have very specific contributions to make in providing focused advice, information and support for families and the professionals with whom they work – medical, social work and educational.

A-T and education

One of the most important tasks which the Society has undertaken has been to help those educating affected children to understand the condition. In practice, this has meant giving class teachers information about the effects of A-T which are relevant to the classroom situation. These include matters which affect the day-to-day health of the child, his or her ability to move about the school, his or her social interaction with the rest of the class, and a range of practical issues relating to learning and communicating.

The first leaflet for teachers, published in 1993, was based on the observations and experiences of the teaching staff of a residential school for physically disabled children which at that time taught the highest number of children with A-T. This gave valuable insights into how the condition affected intellectual, emotional and behavioural development. This was the first time that the educational needs and abilities of children with A-T had been described. By 1997, most parents were opting to enrol their children in local mainstream schools where possible. This meant that the Society needed to give background information to a wider circle of teachers and schools about the condition and its implications – for the child, teaching and support staff, other children in the class and the wider school community. In presenting this information the Society had to recognise the constraints and demands of teaching and learning in a school in 1997 and take these into account.

The teacher of a child with A-T needs information which will directly help in supporting the child's progress. This information has to put the condition into a manageable context and identify the kinds of skill which are needed to deal with the effects of A-T. All of this now appears in a leaflet, illustrated with photographs of young people with A-T. The leaflet, *Ataxia Telangiectasia: A Guide for Teachers*, was published with support from charitable funds and is available from the Society's headquarters (see References). The Society also publishes a regular newsletter which gives an insight into the effects of the condition.

Physical implications of A-T

A-T affects children and young people physically in a number of ways that can have important consequences in an educational setting. These include:

- high levels of fatigue;
- immune system problems, which may mean frequent coughs and colds;
- deteriorating ability to coordinate movements, which affects manual dexterity and mobility;
- speech which is slow and may be slurred;
- tiredness, which may make breath control difficult for speech;
- eye problems affecting focusing and tracking ability.

Daily responses

Although A-T is a progressive condition, the rate of deterioration is specific to each individual. Some need wheelchair assistance in primary school, others do not. Some children have better immune systems, others have frequent infections which can result in many or prolonged absences from school. Parents need to be kept informed of any infectious diseases among fellow pupils and schools also need to liaise with them about coordinating schoolwork so that children do not miss out as a result of absences. Fatigue is experienced every day due to the physical effort of moving about, walking and talking.

Education

Many children with A-T will have had their individual needs assessed before beginning primary school or will be in the midst of that process. If a child does not have a Statement/Record of Needs, this may be something to discuss with home, school and education authority. A support assistant may, in some cases, help the class teacher and pupil with everyday routines and classroom activities.

Children with A-T show the normal range of ability – one young man is presently undertaking postgraduate studies and teaching duties at a university. No specific learning disabilities have been definitively associated with A-T. However, recent research appears to show that some children with A-T may have a form of dyslexia and for some there may be a slowing down of thinking speed as the condition progresses.

A supportive environment and understanding from the teacher and classmates is very helpful for a child's self-confidence and esteem. Although unable to keep up with peers, a child should be encouraged to try new things. They may feel more self- conscious or clumsy when doing practical tasks, and a supportive friend or partner to work with can help. Tremors or involuntary movements of the arms, body and legs can be present and this can be upsetting. Understanding on the part of the teacher and others can minimise distress.

Growing up with A-T

Adolescence is a difficult time for all young people, and for someone with a disability it can be even more difficult. Physical appearance becomes increasingly important, so anyone with a disability such as A-T may have a poor self-image and low self-esteem. They may face teasing or bullying by others or find it hard to make or keep friends. School life can become stressful and frustrating. Some may cope with this by becoming overly independent and reject the help they need, others may withdraw socially.

People with A-T have been described by teachers as quiet, easy-going individuals who value their own space and privacy. This can mean, however, that they can become isolated unless teachers are aware of this possibility and help to draw them into the class/year group. Whole-school support from teachers and fellow students is vital if a person with A-T is to make the most of his or her school experience and fulfil his or her potential. Schools can assist by implementing policies which promote a positive ethos and tackle bullying and discrimination.

Conclusion

The A-T Society has tried to respond to requests from professionals by providing relevant and helpful information. Feedback from these professionals has been a valuable resource when preparing and updating the range of leaflets that the Society publishes. This information may seem general rather than detailed but there are two reasons for this:

- The Society has limited funds so that leaflets often have to meet several needs. For example, it is not possible to produce separate leaflets for different parts of the UK although in each there may be significant differences in educational arrangements and structures. This is a problem shared by many small voluntary organisations.
- Although A-T is rare and has a number of clearly recognisable features, the number of variations in the combinations of effects which the condition can have is surprisingly large. Thus few people with A-T have exactly the same needs. This is a significant feature of A-T.

There are continuing concerns for parents of children with A-T about education in the next millennium and a number of questions are raised by current education policies and practices, for example:

- It is difficult to know yet what effect, if any, league tables of pupil and school performance and attendance will have on the decision-making process as regard school placement offers to children with conditions such as A-T. For example, how far, if at all, will individual schools be able to negotiate with

LEAs over the levels of achievement they must meet and over the use of standardised tests (like curricular attainment tests) in the interests of a child with A-T or other conditions?

• Similarly, how much flexibility will examining and qualification awarding bodies have in assessing students with special and specific needs? This is already an issue where qualifications are based on very specific standards or are vocational in nature, but with increasing public scrutiny of standards, will these bodies feel driven towards an increasingly conservative position on special arrangements?

• Will the increased use of Information and Communication Technology (ICT) in education, including the Government's plans for a National Grid for Learning, make learning easier for children with A-T, or will the fact that sophisticated resources are available to all put additional strain and pressure on them to keep up?

• Similarly, as ICT becomes more sophisticated, will it continue to become less expensive or will expectations grow in a way which will counter this trend and make it hard for some families to access the necessary hardware and software? This could put considerable strain on local authority budgets. Will these authorities find themselves able to provide only basic packages and look to voluntary organisations to provide top-ups as is increasingly the case in other areas?

In other words, the role of the voluntary sector, even in essential services such as education, seems set to change and grow over the coming years, and factors which will shape this growth are going to offer major challenges to small bodies such as the A-T Society.

CHAPTER 7

Health services: supporting children, families and schools

Patricia Jackson

Introduction

Full inclusion in educational settings creates very significant challenges for those who work towards it. Parental expectations that schools can adapt to meet their children's needs is both an encouragement and a pressure. The treatment of children's medical conditions in a community setting has advanced and increased greatly. Parental involvement, after appropriate training, has also increased in many practical procedures in order to maintain their child at home, and technological advances have simplified many procedures and associated training packages produced so that they can be safely undertaken by parents and carers.

The unique position of teachers as 'parent figures' within the school setting needs to be formally recognised through training and in discussions with parents on meeting medical needs in school. Sometimes parents assume teacher willingness to tackle specific tasks, but this needs to be sensitively negotiated to avoid excess pressures on teachers. Parents and doctors have an inbuilt trust of teachers and know they can sort out problems, but this must not lead to more worry or new responsibilities than can realistically be addressed.

There must be a negotiated balance between school, health service and parental responsibilities and a realisation that teachers' key role is as educators of all their pupils. However, children with medical needs, as others, spend a significant part of their day at school and fitting in all the required treatments can mean that some of them must be accommodated within the school day. They are often necessary to ensure children's comfort and ability to participate. A good example would be children with cystic fibrosis who need regular medication at meal and snack times and who may also require intermittent bursts of chest physiotherapy to clear their lungs and keep them active.

However, these things take time and someone to do them. Careful thought needs to be put into the 'who, how and when', so that they do not detract from the central task of delivering education. The aim is to enable all children to participate in their school community in as natural a way as possible. How do we achieve this?

In this chapter I will explore:

• current health service structures and processes to support inclusion at school
• the prevalence in the community of different childhood disorders
• ideas to improve the way the system works.

In some areas processes described will not exactly match local practices.

The School Health Service

In most areas of the UK advice on children's health in school comes from the Community Child Health Service. This service was built up post-war, with the emphasis on monitoring children's nutritional state and on the prevention and spread of infectious diseases. It focused on the health of the majority, with relatively little input as regards children with special needs. It was accepted that chronically or seriously ill children would either not attend school or, with the increase in special provision between the 1950s and 1970s, go to a special school. The aims of the school health service have been progressively redefined, especially in the last 15 years. There is, and should be, emphasis on the prevention and early identification of disease but, with the advent of inclusion as an educational aim, a major role for school health teams is supporting children with special needs in their school environment.

The training and responsibilities within the school health team continue to improve and adjust to perform this role adequately. School doctors require to have postgraduate training in Paediatrics and, at a senior level, subspecialty training in Community Paediatrics. Likewise, school nurses will have undergone specific post-qualification training to best equip them for this special role. Trained health assistants support the school nurse in appropriate tasks, with her guidance and supervision. Future service provision (DoH 1996) is modelled on a consultant-led team at district level, with a named school doctor, school nurse and health assistant responsible as a team to support 'cluster' of nursery, primary, and secondary schools in their area. Visits are planned depending on the needs of the school population. In addition to the core team, trained nursing staff may also be provided when a child – in mainstream or special provision – requires nursing skills for their day-to-day functioning. In special schools the school nurse may perform both roles.

Boundaries between members of the school team merge, with sharing of skills and tasks, to achieve the central aim. Consultant community paediatricians offer accessible specialist advice within the school health team. Specialist community paediatric nurses offer particular expertise, for example in management of epilepsy, diabetes, cystic fibrosis, oncological diseases, palliative care. Coterminosity with social work and education boundaries greatly facilitates locality planning but presents challenges when, as is the case in many areas, there are geographical overlaps. From a health perspective it is vital to have good links with general practice and hospital colleagues, to work towards a 'seamless service' to children and their families (see Figure 7.1).

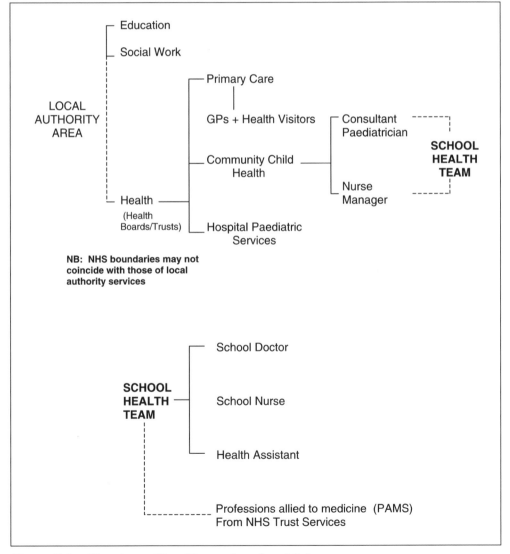

Figure 7.1   Structure of health services for children

The central aims of the School Health Service (Hall 1996) continue to be :

- health promotion
- health-related screening programmes, e.g. vision/hearing
- health advice for individual children and their families
- support and training to school staff in relation to children with special needs.

Which children have medical needs?

Children with physical or sensory impairments, learning difficulties and social, emotional and behavioural difficulties are recognised as having special educational needs. They may sometimes have medical needs arising from these impairments, or they may, as with any other child, experience unrelated illness or medical needs. Some children may have multiple and complex special educational needs and medical needs.

The focus of this chapter is on children with chronic and/or serious physical health difficulties, with or without additional special needs. Dealing with their needs should be just an extension of the service available to all children but focused to support their particular needs.

There are many diseases/disorders which cause a child to have significant needs for health care or monitoring. In order to look at whether health-related support and staff preparation for each child's school placement has to be approached on a

Table 7.1

Some chronic/complex diseases/conditions	Incidence (expressed as percentage of child population)
*Epilepsy	0.4
*Cerebral palsy	0.3
Severe disabling forms of cerebral palsy	0.01
*Oncological disorders e.g. leukaemia	0.17 (60% cure rate)
Neurodegenerative disorders	0.00033
Muscular dystrophy	0.03 (males)
*Cystic fibrosis	0.2 (decreasing)
*Diabetes	1.33
*Asthma	12.5
Spina bifida	0.03 (decreasing)
*Down's Syndrome	0.17
Congenital heart disease	0.02/0.03 (symptomatic)
Autism	0.04/0.05
*Anaphylactic problems	percentage unknown
(Adapted from Bone and Meltzer 1989)	

'one-off' basis, or whether some basic training for all schools would be useful, we need to look first at the prevalence of some conditions (see Table 7.1).

If schools are unlikely to see many/any children with a condition in a generation, then it is not an effective use of time to run regular training sessions on that condition – better to wait until the enrolment of an affected child is expected, although preparation should never wait until he or she is actually there. In planning to raise the awareness and coping potential of schools it is more helpful to think initially in terms of general problems/needs which are common enough to affect all schools at all times regardless of cause of illness. General themes for care and treatment emerge for children with chronic and/or serious conditions which may also appear frequently as short-term needs in other children.

This suggests a need for some basic general training for school staff (see Chapter 15), on a regular basis, as well as some specific preparation for working with children with more commonly occurring conditions, such as those asterisked on Table 7.1, perhaps adding eczema and other skin conditions which may be particularly lowering to children's self-esteem, and migraine. Infectious diseases are also important, particularly the special implications for children on immuno-suppressant therapy during treatment for cancers. They are more vulnerable to infection and may experience life-threatening reactions.

While advocating that school staff have some understanding of specific conditions as well as competency in meeting more general medical needs, they must keep the individual child, his or her rights, interests, responses, abilities, coping skills and views to the fore in planning educational and social goals for children. While children's medical conditions must be taken into account, school staff, medical personnel and parents must not lose any of these individual aspects of children in their understandable concerns about medical needs.

Who else can help?

Problem-solving requires knowledge of how others can contribute to that process. As well as the school health team, therapists, or professions allied to medicine – PAMs as they are now known – will be major contributors. School staff should be aware of their roles, in order to use their skills and advice appropriately.

Occupational therapists (OTs)

OTs advise on suitable aids and practical training to enable children's independence, for example, in feeding, toileting and dressing. Specialist paediatric OTs also advise on aspects of children's sensory function, e.g. visuo-perceptual skills and body awareness. They may also have expertise in splinting to enable better hand function, or in seating systems. Some have special skills in working with emotionally disturbed children.

Physiotherapists (PTs)

PTs advise on mobility aims for children. They develop positioning and movement programmes for each child to encourage mobility and maintain range of body movement. Their aim is to facilitate optimal independent movement for children. For those with limited or no independent mobility they advise on mobility aids or positioning equipment, such as standing frames and walking aids. They also design specific programmes related, for example, to a child's post-operative needs, or to underlying disease such as cystic fibrosis or arthritis.

Speech and Language Therapists (SLTs)

They advise on all essentials in the development of speech, language and communication. Many also have knowledge about feeding skills in children with disabilities and alternative communication systems, including augmentative communication aids.

Many of the therapists work together, particularly with children with more complex needs, in order to achieve their objectives. Collaboration with parents, school staff and the children themselves is essential.

Issues for all schools

Physical/mobility needs

One of the greatest practical barriers is poor or non-existent school access for pupils who use wheelchairs or other mobility aids. Children should be able to go to their local school. It is tragic for a child well settled into a school community to have to leave because the school cannot cope with wheelchair users. This is sadly sometimes still the case for children with muscular dystrophy, or cerebral palsy, who often 'go off their feet' just as the move to secondary school is being planned. For want of access, they lose friends and vital peer support at a vulnerable time. At any time, the need for wheelchair access in schools may be required for children who have broken limbs, or following surgery, in addition to those with longer-term chronic conditions. Legislation ensures that new buildings have good access, but achieving this in some existing schools is expensive and sometimes impracticable.

Local planning must take such barriers into account and honesty is required with parents at an early stage about what is, and is not, possible. Advice can come from OTs and PTs involved with children's care. The prognosis and timescale for continuing independent mobility and the need for a wheelchair can be estimated – albeit not with absolute certainty – by the community paediatrician to allow forward planning. All districts should have a rolling programme of planned adaptations to all schools. All new schools should be fully wheelchair-accessible, with appropriate adapted bathroom areas, for toileting, changing and washing.

Knowledge should be shared on special seating, standing frames and equipment essential for the optimal inclusion of children with physical disabilities in the school programme. Classroom planning needs to take into account the additional space required. Classroom staff need to have appropriate training in the aims and practice of basic physiotherapy programmes:

- positioning, and passive movement programmes, to maintain good body posture and assist in the prevention of contractures;
- active physiotherapy treatment programmes, e.g. chest physiotherapy for children with cystic fibrosis or limb movements for children with cerebral palsy;
- moving and handling skills, essential for the protection and safety of children and of staff assisting them, e.g. for transfers and toileting. Back injuries can be a major problem if staff are not trained in these skills.

Sensory impairments
Staff working with children with sensory impairments should have enough understanding of sensory pathways to respond appropriately to how particular impairments impact on function and learning. Differences between types of visual and hearing defects, whether it is a peripheral, eye or ear, or central brain-based problem, and information on what can or cannot be corrected or improved, are all important in planning appropriate classroom experiences, although individual aspects, as mentioned before, must be taken into account.

Support for children with sensory impairments is usually given by specialist teachers, often peripatetic, who work with class and subject teachers and link closely with health colleagues. This cooperation, along with advances in technology, has resulted in real strides towards inclusion.

Communication difficulties
Teachers should be well informed about their local speech and language therapy team's approach to assessment and treatment of children with communication difficulties. The identification of difficulties – receptive, expressive, articulatory, and/or communicative interaction – should be followed by ensuring a shared understanding of their nature by all involved with the child.

The success of any communication support programme will depend on the ability to use that programme in the educational setting. Close links, and an agreed mode of collaborative working, must be made between these agencies. In nursery school and primary settings it may also be helpful for education staff to have a baseline awareness of the use of signing such as Makaton or Signalong as a facilitator of communication. They, like parents, need to be convinced that it does indeed support rather than hinder the development of oral speech. Knowledge of appropriate alternative augmentative communication aids will be required for some children, with education staff and parents cooperating in programming such aids appropriately.

Medication issues and health care procedures

All education authorities and schools should have agreed policies for the administration of medicines in school. There should be clear instructions from the parents and a signed notification of the medication prescribed which the parent wishes to be given to their child and the timing of this. Similarly there should be clear instructions and agreement from parents about health care procedures. School staff will look to the School Health Team for advice and appropriate training on these issues. Joint planning meetings, including children, can help greatly.

Doctors, children and families need to plan a medication/therapy regime that minimises interference with the school day – necessary interruptions will then be better tolerated by all. However, it is the reality for a small group of children with complex special educational and medical needs that their day has to be planned to integrate the regime as part of their programme.

As outlined earlier, huge changes have occurred in both the types of treatments and the expectations that parents and carers will manage them and this can, understandably, cause concern to all involved, at least initially. Not all staff, as not all parents, may feel comfortable with all procedures. The wishes of those who would prefer not to be involved should be respected. However, school staff are sympathetic to the needs of all children in their care and many initially hesitant staff become competent after the necessary training and are willing to provide additional care as needed. They understand that the normalisation of children's lives depends on those naturally in contact with the children being able to assist, and they do their best to make this happen.

Those assisting need to know that they are working within a recognised framework, and are indemnified by their employing authority in the unlikely event of any mishap. A clear statement from central government, as well as the statements already made by many local authorities reassuring staff of legal cover, is essential. This largely exists in England, Wales and Northern Ireland, and guidance is awaited in Scotland.

What about children with chronic/complex medical needs?

Over and above basic training and knowledge that should be built up in any inclusive school environment, these children should have an individual healthcare plan with information specific to them. It is *essential* that this plan is the result of discussions between the parents, child if appropriate, healthcare professionals and the school. Usually, the head teacher or other designated person – the SENCO in England, Wales and Northern Ireland – and the particular child's class teacher will be involved, and often it will also be important to involve classroom or school auxiliaries.

Guidelines to facilitate healthcare planning have already been agreed in England and Wales in a joint Health and Education good practice guide (DfEE/DoH 1996a) and Circular (DfEE/DoH 1996b). There is no doubt that a similar practical guide is much needed and eagerly awaited in Scotland.

The individual healthcare plan (IHP)

What should it include?

1. Child's personal details:

- school attended
- contact telephone numbers, including GP details.

2. Details of child's condition and individual symptoms.
   (It is often helpful to include a pertinent reader-friendly article on the condition. The Contact-a-Family *Directory of Conditions* (CaF no date, biannually updated and accessible on the Internet, see Chapter 15) could be helpful in this respect.)

3. Daily care routines:

- any required medication – routine/emergency
- timing of medication, e.g. pre-exercise becotide ventolin (inhalers)
- programmed procedures, e.g. physiotherapy, gastrostomy feed.

4. Emergencies that may occur:

- action to be taken
- whom to contact

5. Responsible adult in school/on out-of-school activities (should also include the following as relevant to individual children):

- request to school to administer medication and/or carry out particular procedure/s;
- record of staff who have volunteered for training and dates of completion of training;

- individual plan for emergency treatment of seizures by administration of rectal medication (Joint Epilepsy Council proforma);
- ambulance emergency service contact plan (if required).

Case example

Chris Smith
Age 10
Condition

- inherited neurodegenerative condition
- spastic quadriplegia (increased tone in all four limbs)
- seizures poorly controlled on medication
- profound learning disability
- cortically blind.

Symptoms

- great difficulty with feeding, now requires gastrostomy feeds
- tonic/clonic seizures most days. Requires emergency medication at least once weekly.

Daily care routine

- requires careful attention to daily positioning programme to allow chest drainage and prevent contractures (see Physiotherapy programme)
- gastrostomy feed (500 mls) required at 12 noon
- medication (anticonvulsants) given at home. Emergency medication 10 mgs Stesolid may be required for fits lasting more than four minutes (see prescription sheet and epilepsy record sheet).

Emergencies
Responsible adults

- Within school the class teacher (Lee Brown) or the class auxiliary (Sandy Jones) will administer Stesolid anticonvulsant as prescribed.
- If prolonged fit occurs on transport, child to be taken direct to Accident and Emergency Department of Children's Hospital.

Overview

So what structures do we have in place and what do we need to develop further to ensure good health support in the community to these children, their parents and schools?

Basic level information is provided by health, education and voluntary agencies, e.g. *Capability* on cerebral palsy, *Enlighten* on epilepsy and *The Cystic Fibrosis Trust* on cystic fibrosis. Organisations can be contacted directly or via the School Health Team. Other organisations such as *Contact-a-Family* (see Chapter 15) can provide information on rarer medical conditions and there are many support organisations specific to individual conditions, e.g. cri-du-chat syndrome, muscular dystrophy, metabolic disorders and Down's Syndrome.

Most areas of the UK are now working towards the described model of the School Health Team as an integrated nurse/doctor model (RCPH 1997). Every school should have access to this baseline support. Unfortunately, prior to the publication of this guidance some areas had decided that it was not appropriate to deploy qualified nursing staff as school nurses and removed the service. This is a very serious loss in these areas, and should be reversed.

Education colleagues need more information about the different roles of individuals in the health care team, as there is often an expectation that the nurse has only a 'hands-on' role, rather than also being trainer and facilitator. It would be helpful to have a trained first-aider within all schools, as this would give reassurance to families and staff.

Further health service assistance

Anticipating needs/early identification

Most children with chronic conditions will be identified through the medical route, although parents are very often first to express concerns. Notification systems in most areas pick up children with significant medical needs at preschool level through the preschool child health surveillance programme. There will also soon be a national Special Needs database system to allow supportive interventions and monitoring throughout the childhood of these children.

Experience in the Lothians area of Scotland over the past ten years suggests that this is particularly helpful for children with severe chronic disabling conditions. With good cooperation among all statutory agencies – social work, health, and education – as required by the various UK Children Acts, and services' cooperation with families, it is possible to anticipate needs and plan for these children at preschool level through the Preschool Multi-disciplinary Team

(Robards 1994). The system also ensures that there is at least a yearly medical review of children's needs, normally linked into the school review system. Identification of children with conditions significantly affecting their health, with onset at any age, is also achieved. Information about anticipated needs should transfer easily among statutory agencies, so common information storage systems would be extremely helpful.

Sharing information and expertise

Most children's services now run courses organised by their health care staff for education and social work staff. Training packages are available for the following: administration of medication via inhalers/nebulisers, tracheostomy care, gastrostomy care, administration of emergency rectal medication, emergency treatment of anaphylaxis, and urinary catheter care. These training packages should be agreed at a Health Trust or Board level and the education authority should be in agreement that they will indemnify their staff, if appropriately trained, to carry out the agreed procedures.

Information about health care and therapy needs for any school wishing to achieve an inclusive approach is a necessity. The head teacher, however, in planning appropriate use of limited professional development time, is confronted with difficult prioritising decisions. Health-related issues sometimes seem a low priority beside curriculum planning needs. With league tables in mind, it may not seem to be to a school's surface advantage to devote time to non-curricular topics and ultimately to encourage the inclusion of more pupils with special needs into their school community. *The costs of inclusion and associated training should not fall to the school and a school's success in including diverse pupils should be properly recognised as one of the key markers of an effective school.*

Community clinics

Currently, many children are seen in clinics within their special school setting. This avoids long treks up to sometimes numerous out-patient clinics, missing schoolwork, and it facilitates a more comprehensive and helpful review. Clinics are often of a specialist nature, such as Orthopaedic, Ophthalmic and Paediatric Neurology. This is seen by everyone, especially parents, as a useful provision. With greater degrees of inclusion and the development of community schools, careful consideration of how best to provide this type of service on an area basis will be needed so that the increasing numbers of children attending mainstream schools may also benefit.

Using the recording/statementing procedure

Although recording/statementing is not seen to benefit large numbers of children, and the usefulness of health information has been rightly questioned for some children, for children with chronic illness and high health input needs, the system could, in fact, be made to work more usefully (see Chapter 1). The current medical report to the education authority on a child with special educational needs could easily form the basis of the healthcare plan for that child.

In our area we have redesigned the format to give a clearer and more 'user-friendly' form. The information is a product of medical professionals working with families and is shared with parents. With parents' consent the document is available to those working directly with children in school. The restyled form provides information that will advise the class teacher on how children's illness or disability affects their day-to-day ability to learn. Used in conjunction with forms specific to administration of medicine and healthcare management, as detailed previously, this could be the basis of the IHP. Used in an inter-agency recording meeting with parents, it would be a helpful working document.

Sharing basic essential information and ensuring good support and practical training for those involved with children during the school day is obviously the starting point for cooperative care, but there are other issues for which children, parents and school should expect support.

Factors which affect school attendance

The health pattern of children with chronic and/or complex disorders may be marked by spells of good health followed by troughs of ill health and intermittent poor attendance. Others may follow a slowly progressive and unremitting deterioration, often the case for children with neurodegenerative disorders, with timescales of months or years. The decision as to whether it is in children's interest to be at school on a particular day is difficult. If a child has a chronic problem with his or her breathing, when is it so bad that he or she should not go to school?

These dilemmas and the balance of risks versus benefits to children are the day-to-day business of caring for and educating children with severe disability and chronic illness. Most parents with children with life-threatening conditions are well aware of these risks and most are confident of the benefit to their child in attending school. But the school may be anxious about these decisions. It is so easy for parents to be thought of by teachers as either over-protective or uncaring, when, in reality, they are struggling to do the right thing. It is essential that there are regular review meetings with the education staff, health care team and parents to ensure that the pattern of attendance benefits children and that this decision is supported by all.

Case Example

Jackie Evans
Age 10
Condition

- neuro-degenerative disorder
- profound physical disability
- mentally deteriorating – but still alert and able to participate at around a three-year-old developmental level
- feeding problems and often has chest infections due to aspiration.

Prognosis

- child will probably die within the next 1–2 years
- chest infections will be recurrent and increasingly more frequent.

Options
1. Send child home from school if he or she appears to have any chest symptoms.
2. Accommodate child in school and arrange additional positioning programme and physiotherapy to help chest and ensure comfort through the day.

Plan
If option 1 is followed, the child is likely to spend most of his or her her remaining time at home. If option 2 is followed, the child's quality of life will be improved and being stimulated and moved throughout the school day in the company of others will benefit his or her physical and mental health.

However, in order that the school staff feel happy to support option 2 there must be due discussion with, and assurance from, the parents that they feel this is best, and from the health care team that this will not be detrimental to the child's health or long-term prognosis. Given the preferred option, can the school staff support this? What are the implications as far as staff are concerned to accommodate this? If extra time is needed for 1:1 care of this child, will it be available?

The alternative assumption is that a child with a chronic disorder needs time off school. For any child, illness may be used as an excuse not to be at school. As with any other child, absence from school should be examined and accounted for; assumptions should not be made. Children may be depressed as a result of their illness or the side effects of their treatment; they may find it hard to keep up, or they may have been bullied or teased and feel friendless. They need social support and encouragement to attend. Parents may need reassurance that potential risks to their child can be managed in school. These are very sensitive issues and can only be handled with good up-to-date health and education information to enable all to find the best solution. Often, social work colleagues are very appropriately involved.

Sadly, particularly in school communities with children with profound, complex or degenerative disorders, the death of a child may occur (see Chapter 13). The support and expertise of the school health care team should be fully available to, and utilised by, pupils, families and staff in this situation.

Health-supported respite care is an important health provision for families of children with complex conditions. Dovetailed transport arrangements and good communication between schools, respite facilities and families are essential if families are to benefit fully (see Chapter 8).

The way ahead: questions for the future

Some schools' experiences have shown that inclusion can work for even the most profoundly disabled children with high health care needs. The basis of good practice (Russell 1995) appears to be:

- active involvement of parents in planning
- a cooperative joint approach from statutory agencies
- good information and training for staff
- appropriate sharing of skills
- clear acknowledgement of legal cover for education staff involved in medication and medical/paramedical treatment procedures.

Inclusion in the local mainstream school is the wish of many parents for their children, and the approach should be the same whether children are placed in mainstream or specialist schools or units.

Issues that need to be resolved include provision of enough trained support staff in children's chosen setting, agreement on legal cover and training to enable skill-sharing between health and education, and adequate funding for provision of 'hands-on' therapy and nursing support where appropriate. Urgent consideration also needs to be given on how this approach can be continued into the further education system.

The commitment to inter-agency work and care planning with parents and children to facilitate inclusion is strong at practitioner level. Let us hope that through the joint development of children's service plans and central government legislation, the support and resources will be made available to ensure that successful inclusion is a real choice.

CHAPTER 8

Issues for the effectiveness of children's school education

Alison Closs

Introduction

Unlike the general population of children who receive their education in schools, children with medical conditions may receive their education either in schools, at home, in hospital or in a variety of other health, social service or voluntary organisation contexts such as children's hospices and respite settings (although a few children may still receive no education). Education can therefore take place in domestic, care and health settings and, conversely, when children do attend schools of whatever kind, they may require medication and/or medical treatment, as outlined in Chapter 7. There is, therefore, a need for a particularly holistic approach to children's education if it is to be effective and, in mainstream schools, inclusive.

This chapter looks particularly at a range of issues which may challenge schools, whether they are day or residential, mainstream or special. The degree of challenge will vary from school to school and within each school according to school ethos, staff experience, training, cooperation and attitudes, and according to individual pupil needs. The issues are discussed briefly under five headings. Suggested responses – based on existing good practice in schools – are given. (The suggestions given do not cover the administrative ground already addressed within the various guides and circulars already referred to in Chapter 1.) The five headings are:

- family matters
- communication
- educational continuity and support for learning

- peer relationships and social continuity
- children's physical and/or cognitive regression.

Family matters

It is all too easy to problematise or pathologise children with medical needs and their families – to see them primarily in terms of children's impairments, symptoms and conditions and what they cannot do, rather than as children and families with much common ground with others in terms of abilities, interests and aspirations, but with some different strengths and needs. Eiser (1993) acknowledges that family life can never again be fully normal where a child has a serious medical condition, but school staff should recognise that normality is a key aspiration of families, socially and educationally.

Even if children's conditions are relatively mild and respond well to treatment, parents and many children become at least vigilant – medical regimes need to be followed, however tiresome. For families facing very serious conditions, sometimes life-threatening, the impact may be traumatic. Hornby (1995) describes how families of children with pronounced special educational needs may develop a different pattern of relationships. Their 'ecology' adapts, by the close family focusing on the affected child, circles of friends and neighbours becoming partially displaced by medical, social work and other professionals, and community and leisure activities falling away or being replaced by activities linked to the special needs.

All family members may experience emotional, practical, physical and financial stress: anxiety and depression around uncertain or negative prognoses, time spent on medical-related activities rather than on each other, one parent – usually the mother – often unable to work because of child-care roles (Kagan *et al.* 1998), yet expenditure for diet, heating and transport may increase. Children's disturbed sleep patterns inevitably result in tired parents. Siblings may be protective, sensitive and helpful, or jealous, neglected and detached, or all of these at various times (Meyer and Vadasy 1997, see also Chapter 14). Such stresses are greatest on families who are socio-economically disadvantaged or who lack a supportive network of family and friends, but no affected family is exempt. Family choices will be influenced by each family's contexts and values, some of which may not coincide with those of education staff – for instance, a family holiday taken in term time.

Beresford (1994) found that greatest parental stress came not from child care but from what parents considered to be poor service provision and management, with education sometimes the worst offender. Generalised anxiety and feelings of isolation may result, which overspill into school. While most parents want to look after their ill children themselves, hospitalisation may sometimes be inevitable. The recent introduction of Diana Nursing Teams and associated community paediatric nurse training (ACT1999) should ease some of the stress of caring for seriously ill children at home.

Community respite care, whether through share-the-care schemes with alternative families or through health, social work or voluntary organisation units, is very scarce, but invaluable to parents (While *et al.* 1996a and 1996b) when they are sure of the quality of the child's experience there (Russell 1994, Morris 1995). Hospices for children with life-threatening conditions are becoming more numerous and provide respite, general support and terminal care, both in the hospice and sometimes also at home, to optimise the lives of children and their families (see Chapter 15). Despite all they face, most families find some time for fun and positive future plans and should be supported in this.

Some parents, and even children, become knowledgeable about the condition, through their own efforts or by joining condition-specific support organisations. They may become empowered and assertive. Some education staff may deny or reject parental expertise and may resent parental assertiveness. Wolfendale (1992) promotes parents' expertise about their own children and their place in contributing to their children's educational assessments and programme planning. Children, too, should be involved. The understanding and practical skills of families can certainly benefit schools and teachers, just as teacher knowledge and experience can benefit families.

Suggestions for schools

- Show awareness and understanding of the child's and family's aspirations, strengths and constraints, and allow some flexibility around school norms (see Communication, below).
- Plan monitoring procedures with the School Health Team (see Chapter 7) and the family.
- Show respect for, and willingness to learn from, parents' and children's experiences, knowledge and skills, and from relevant reading.
- Put worried or isolated parents in touch with useful organisations. Contact-a-Family (see Chapter 15) is a good generic starting point.
- Medical concerns should be referred back to the school medical service and not tackled by education professionals.
- Schools should support respite care arrangements by liaising with respite carers and by re-routing school transport to and from the respite address.
- Share in families' happiness as well as their worries.

Communication

Behind every apparently 'difficult' or diffident parent lie any or all of the following: real unmet needs in their child's education or other services, not being heard, not being understood and/or not understanding, fear for their child's future, exhaustion, multiple domestic stresses, and unhappy experiences of school and teachers in their own childhood or more recently.

Good communication enables better education and is best established by school staff who understand the basis of interpersonal relationships. The core conditions for Carl Roger's person-centred approaches (Mearns and Thorne 1988, see also Chapter 15) are, along with active listening skills, a sound foundation for working with stressed parents. They are:

- having unconditional positive regard for others
- being genuine
- being empathic.

As teachers, we are sometimes inclined to tell, improve and criticise rather than listen, accept and affirm, even when we know that the sun is stronger than the north wind!

Recent Governments' emphasis on reducing the unauthorised absence of truants is understandable but has perhaps obscured the numerically far larger issue of authorised absence on the grounds of health. It has also put increasing pressure on educational welfare officers (EWOs) to return to their old role of attendance officers and to narrow the wider concept of care and welfare which many of them realise is so important. Children absent because of longer-term medical conditions and their families tend to receive calls from EWOs only when their school suspects that the absence is no longer genuine. For some families a more supportive contact with the EWO could be a valuable link with school. A few education authorities are fortunate or wise enough to have home liaison teachers based in schools located in areas of disadvantage who could also link with absent children.

Suggestions

- Get it right from the beginning! The head teacher, principal teacher of guidance, SENCO or other designated contact person should set aside substantial time – at least an hour – to talk in a relaxed way with parents before a child with a medical condition first comes to the school. Older children and a supportive friend or named person should also attend, if parents wish. The School Medical Officer, or, in more serious cases, the Child Health Consultant, should participate.

- Any nursing or auxiliary staff likely to be involved should have time to talk about more personal aspects of care, informally and privately, with the child, parents, named school contact and medical staff.
- If the child is recognised as having actual or potential special educational needs, this meeting may form part of the wider special educational needs process set out in the *Code of Practice* for England, Wales and Northern Ireland (DfE 1994 and DENI 1998) and in *Circular 4/96* for Scotland (SOEID 1996) (see Chapter 1). A similar meeting is suggested if a child is diagnosed as having a serious medical condition while already at school.
- Staff involved in the meeting should be familiar with the relevant parts of the above documents and with *A Good Practice Guide: Supporting Pupils with Medical Needs* (DfEE/DoH 1996a) or with Scottish guidance to be issued later in 1999.
- The invitation to the parents/carers should make it plain that you are pleased the child is coming to the school, and that you want to listen, to support the child's education, to establish partnership with the parent/s, and to discuss any points they want to raise.
- Encourage parents ahead of the meeting to list things they want to tell or ask you and any worries they have.
- Establish what the parents' and child's understanding of the child's condition is. Medical support with this is useful.
- In an ideal inclusive world, pre-briefing and support for teachers and fellow pupils might not be necessary before a child joins a school or when a condition is diagnosed in an enrolled pupil. However, when a child looks or behaves in ways which might be thought strange or less acceptable, or when needs are substantial, the SENCO or other support-for-learning staff and the school doctor or nurse should explain the situation to ease the child's inclusion. Briefings and written communication content should be negotiated with families and medical staff. There should be acceptance of at least initial uncertainty on the part of teachers and pupils, and also belief in their ultimate coping capacity. This dual message can be very effective. Parents and children with medical conditions themselves, medical and voluntary organisation staff may be involved in staff's and pupils' briefings.
- Parents and children should be told of school measures to meet medical needs in school and also about anti-bullying measures, particularly if the condition or its treatment affects the child's appearance.
- Don't promise immediate solutions to more problematic issues, if any are raised, but do negotiate another meeting *soon* after to discuss the school's response to these. Meantime, work urgently with medical and school colleagues to develop provisional strategies.
- Pupil records and programme plans should be open to parents, both for them to read and for their own contributions.

- Establish a two-way communication system with as free access to the named contact person as possible. The more liaison offered, the less likely are parents to become over-anxious and contact needs may actually reduce over time, unless the situation changes. Review dates should be negotiated well in advance with the option of bringing them forward if need be.
- If a child becomes seriously or terminally ill then parental choice of contact should be offered rather than a person being allocated (see Chapter 13). The chosen contact must be supported by school management.
- School communication with parents should not just be problem-related. Messages about progress, achievement and positive regard help parents feel more secure about their child's well-being.
- Schools should consider with the education welfare service how to deploy EWOs as a supportive – rather than 'policing' – link with families of children with medical conditions.

Educational continuity and support for learning

There is a general belief that educational discontinuity and absence invariably have negative effects on school progress, achievement and qualifications. Clear research evidence, however, is surprisingly limited. Recent research in Scotland (Malcolm *et al.* 1996) established a positive correlation between slightly lowered performance in some Standard Grade examinations and all kinds of absence – authorised and unauthorised – in the general pupil population. However, the statistical link did not actually prove that educational discontinuity/absence itself caused lowered performance. Despite the overall positive correlation, the researchers also found a very wide variation among individuals, with some very high achievement among poor attenders and vice versa. This suggests that other factors, e.g. pupil motivation and ability, parental support, alternative educational inputs and support for learning on return to school, play a part in raising, sustaining or lowering achievements of absent pupils by their availability or otherwise.

Fowler *et al.* (1985) in America examined the absence and achievements of children with chronic illness, taking ability, nature of conditions and socio-economic status into account. They found that the level of absence for children with chronic illness was very much higher than annual average – 16 days in comparison with seven. Despite this, the undoubtedly lower achievements of the sick children appeared to correlate more with low socio-economic status and with specific conditions which may be associated with disadvantaged communities (such as sickle cell anaemia in America's black population) or with possible cognitive impairments (such as epilepsy and spina bifida) than with absence in itself.

This warning flag to educational support providers – that some pupils' education may be more vulnerable than others, both at school and particularly when absent – must not be ignored. Ill health and medical care are not equitably distributed across the general population, as the Acheson Report (1998) indicated. Families at both social and health disadvantage may want to support their children educationally but may be less able to do this themselves or to push for services from education authorities. Where resources are limited, assertive families, competent in their dealings with officialdom, tend to 'win'. However, responsibility for ensuring equity of educational opportunity and support lies with schools and education authorities, without reference to, or blame for, parental characteristics or attitudes.

Recent case-study research with families (see Chapter 4) shows clearly that absent children with medical needs and their parents become extremely worried about education. Gaps in learning, falling behind in school work with the resulting need to catch up, and reduced achievement and qualifications can all cause acute distress (Larcombe 1995). The prospect of return to school can generate psychosomatic symptoms and absence may be extended beyond real – that is, physical – health need. Some previously well-adjusted children, after genuine absence, may seem almost school-phobic. Underlying reasons are very often related to disruption in peer relationships (see next section) and loss of self-esteem, as well as to school work. Returning children are sometimes moved down to a lower class group and find themselves working not only outside their usual group but possibly also with children who, although at the same stage of work, are less able.

All support-for-learning staff have a vital role in educating children with medical conditions. It might be thought that the learning of children who were absent for long periods would be most vulnerable, yet the one-off block of absence may actually be better accommodated, by children themselves and staff, than shorter, recurrent and continuing absences so often experienced by children with chronic disease, or even than the continuous feeling of 'being under par' experienced by some children who continue to attend school.

The traumatic car or burn accident or the onset of leukaemia will bring a burst of sympathetic energy, goodwill and supportive cooperation from most school staff. A really effective school, however, can sustain support throughout the whole of a child's school career if need be, however demanding and variable. It requires enduring empathy, energy, good management and attention to detail. SENCOs and support-for-learning staff are key to this, but they in turn need the support of their school managers and education authorities.

Support staff need to act as facilitators when a child has complex and sustained needs. They may make difficult decisions – with the child, parents and other staff, for instance – about differentiating the curriculum, and about how far the full breadth and balance of the curriculum can be sustained over very extended absences. They may work supportively with a member of staff who is genuinely anxious about having an epileptic child in class or who does not like going near a child who has acute psoriasis. They may be responsible for collating, selecting and packaging the missed work of a child, absent irregularly for over 60 per cent of the time, in order to fulfil the IEP for work at hospital or home. The need for time for staff to support children with medical conditions is certain even if the answers to 'when, how much, and where' questions cannot be predicted.

A support auxiliary may resuscitate a child with a serious heart condition and give rectal suppositories to an epileptic child in a seizure, and also work with teachers to foster both these children's independence and fullest inclusion in the activities of the class. The auxiliary has therefore both protective and emancipatory roles which can cause him or her inner conflict. Much is currently being written about the value of classroom and school auxiliary staff (DfEE 1997, Dew-Hughes *et al.* 1998, Clayton 1993), yet their deployment can be problematic. There is a significant risk that they may inadvertently increase the difference factor in the child and alienate peers. They may also, in a genuine wish to help the affected child, reduce direct access to teachers – some of whom may collude in this. A mini special school, but without any of the benefits of special school, can be created in the midst of a mainstream class and school.

What can be done by schools to support educational progress, inclusion and continuity?

Suggestions for schools

Management of continuity and inclusion

- Whole-school staff development in equal opportunities and disability awareness will enable teachers to accept the equal value and rights of all children, including children with medical conditions.
- Training in healthcare procedures should be given and an IHP set up (see Chapter 7) as necessary. Children should be encouraged to assume responsibility for their own medical regimes as far as possible.
- Schools should continue to feel responsible for absent pupils, and act accordingly, including when out-of-school education services are involved.
- A record of all missed work should be kept by a pre-designated person. Teachers' notes of work covered should be collated to use in planning work in hospital, at home and on return to school.
- If the absent child is well enough, school-set homework should be agreed by the named contact person, out-of-school teachers, child and parents. Reasonable expectations of pupil and school should be negotiated!
- The burden of managing this should not fall to over-pressed mothers nor to

one sympathetic teacher, nor should the procedure be reinvented each time. Strategies for collecting, transmitting, supporting, marking and returning work should already be established school policy and practice. Post, telephone, fax, e-mail, auxiliary helpers and neighbouring pupils may all be deployed.

- School-contact people should liaise closely with out-of-school educational services to ensure that educational programmes delivered are, as far as possible, in line with that followed by pupils in school. Achievement out of school should be tracked so that return can be planned to be as smooth as possible.
- A home/hospital education pack, containing the basic resources to enable pupils to continue with their education, may be prepared in advance for pupils who have a scheduled absence or for whom absence is a frequent occurrence.
- Where keeping up with school work during absence is not feasible for health reasons, children and parents should be reassured that planned specific support for learning will be available on their return to school.
- Young people with significant medical needs must be made aware of opportunities for continuing education beyond school through further and community education, especially since out-of-school education ceases to be a statutory duty on education authorities at age 16 (and is not yet a statutory duty in Scotland at any age). This will be particularly important for young people who have gaps in learning or who have not yet achieved the qualifications of which they are capable (see Tait, Chapter 6).
- For young people, with or without a Record/Statement of Needs, the local specialist careers officer should be involved timeously with the youngster, the family, the school and post-school services in preparing an appropriate transition plan which addresses continuing education and vocational prospects.

Practicalities of support for learning
- School management should allow enough flexibility in staffing to cover the fluctuations in demand of such pupils; full timetabling of support staff is not the mark of an effective support service.
- IEPs are essential for children who may under-perform while at school or have significant absence. IEPs help ensure that expectations are sustained, losses and gaps – and achievements – are noted and learning support/recovery planned. Additional reviews after longer or accumulated absence are important.
- Attention should be given as to whether the criteria to request assessment for Statementing or Recording are present (see Chapter 1).

- Support for learning should be given to pupils within the classes and groups to which they belonged before absence wherever possible.
- Where pupils have lost substantial ground because of being too ill to learn, it may sometimes be better to reduce the breadth of the curriculum to allow learning recovery in core subjects and in subjects particularly enjoyed. Some specially designed curricular packs are available through NAESC (see Chapter 15).

Auxiliary staff support
- Auxiliary staff should facilitate the child's independence and peer interaction while providing care and practical facilitation. Ways of reducing auxiliary presence and individual attention while maintaining safety should be identified, e.g. by using bleepers between teachers/auxiliaries and pupils/auxiliaries.
- Children should be full members of the class and remain the *educational responsibility* of the relevant teachers, with *support* from auxiliary staff as necessary.
- Selection of auxiliary staff should bear in mind children's practical and emotional needs as well as their age and gender.
- School managers and SENCOs/support-for-learning teachers should ensure continuity of auxiliary staffing when appropriate. While changing auxiliary staff working with some children may reduce dependency, children with advanced deteriorating conditions and their families must have security and continuity with their support workers because of the need for very detailed knowledge of children's physical and emotional well-being. Even then, however, more than one helper should be involved with each child, for absence cover and to reduce excessive stress on helpers.
- School managers should consult with and advise parents about any possible changes in amount of auxiliary support time or in support personnel. The consultation should take place well in advance of the changes being effected and reasons should be given clearly. Possible problems or objections on the part of parents or auxiliary personnel should be anticipated and allowed for as far as possible.

Children's peer relationships

For many children, school is more about peer relationships than about academic learning. For children with medical conditions, relationships may be even more significant since absence can disrupt relationships and create loneliness. Bullying is, sadly, a pervasive and persistent reality in most schools in the UK and worldwide. Children with health conditions, especially those with readily discerned 'differences', have been victims of physical, verbal or emotional abuse;

> …in addition to learning how to do complicated long division problems, friends continue to play key roles in what are often our most memorable positive and negative social learning experiences in school' (Deegan 1996, p. 5)

It might be thought that children with significant medical conditions could be at some disadvantage in the friendship and companionships stakes. There is a wealth of research about children's peer relationships including friendship (James 1993), bullying (Smith and Sharp 1994, Eiser 1993), and isolation or rejection (Asher and Coie 1990). There is agreement over some aspects of commonality which make friendship between children more likely: similar interests, similar cultural backgrounds, a common language or mode of communication, a similar degree of attractiveness, and others. Deegan (1996) notes that children in a minority whose differences are not valued by the majority may find themselves socially rejected.

However, there are also factors that enable friendship and are more amenable to change, including teacher-initiated change, than those listed above. They include: shared experience, time to form relationships and establish intimacy, and good social entry skills (behaviour which makes their welcome from other children probable). Many shared experiences in childhood are essentially active and children with health conditions may be disadvantaged in these. Time to form friendships, and to establish the kind of confiding, more intimate friendships favoured in particular by older girls, may be limited for children who need to follow medical treatment regimes, who are absent or have to rest more.

For some children with special needs including medical conditions, attention comes as of right from parents and family members and medical and paramedical professionals, and may be given as an intended kindness by others. Such one-way attention, and experiences of rejection to their own overtures to others, may make children less skilled and less confident in seeking friends. Does having a serious condition induce a level of self-absorption in some children or young people that peers find off-putting and adults hesitate to correct? Does it accelerate some aspects of maturity in children and young people so that they are out of synch with their peers? Young people themselves may question how far the existing relationships they enjoy with peers and with younger medical and paramedical staff or other professionals are real friendships and how far they are just acts of duty or kindness (Closs 1998).

The fact remains, however, that many children with special needs, including those with serious medical conditions, do establish real and close friendships, despite 'differences' and other potential barriers, while others have reached out to make a tentative start. How can schools work with other affected children, their peers and parents/carers to ensure their safety in school and to enable good peer relationships, including friendships?

Suggestions for schools

- Teachers must model for their pupils, valuing all pupils in their classes, and develop a positive ethos, building a sense of community and belonging. Peer potential for supporting pupils who might be at social disadvantage can be fostered by example and positive reinforcement. Circle time can be used effectively with primary *and* secondary pupils if adapted appropriately.
- Physical and social safety must be ensured by effective anti-bullying policies.
- *All* children need opportunities and encouragement to help others and be useful, including children with medical conditions who may all too often be frequent recipients of such attention.
- *All* children need to understand and agree acceptable norms of behaviour and ways of initiating and establishing positive relationships (see Chapter 15 for recommended reading). They can be helped through specific social skills training. Various forms of support or scaffolding (supporting) of behaviour may be particularly helpful when relationships are being sought tentatively by more vulnerable children or where existing relationships seem at risk. It should not be assumed that children with special or medical needs require this more than other children, but neither should they be excused if it seems they might benefit.
- Opportunities should be created for children with medical conditions and other special needs to spend significant time together with healthy peers in a variety of interesting activities which enable those with health needs not to be at a disadvantage, especially activities which make little physical demand on children.
- Social continuity should be prioritised, especially in prolonged absence. Some schools encourage key staff and classmates to visit absent pupils (after consulting with parents) and send cards or reports of special events. The social use of telephone, fax and e-mail can be very effective and the relatively small school outlay can be justified. 'Little, often and continuing' is better than 'lots, rarely and not sustained' – pupil effort in this will almost certainly need staff support. Teachers can model 'remembering' for pupils through natural reference in class to absent peers, by suggesting that younger children select some school diary entries to send to their absent friend, by older children writing a chain letter with a sentence or a few paragraphs each from closer classmates. A relatively small effort from schools can make a huge difference to absent children and enables them to return without dread.

Children's physical and/or cognitive regression

We have already looked in Chapter 1 at how education can be not just a source of satisfaction but also a 'normalising' and continuous positive influence throughout the lives of children with medical conditions. However, some conditions, and some treatment regimes, can bring about changes in the child himself or herself. In this section we look at how loss of physical and/or cognitive abilities in children can be addressed.

The suggestions are again drawn from the policies and practices developed by teachers from special and mainstream schools working positively with parents and children in this situation. For mainstream schools, such an experience may be rare and responses can include: sadness, and fear of the downward slope, of its probable outcome and of its effects on pupils, parents and teachers themselves in terms of loss of self-esteem. There may be panic and rejection: 'This is not our job, we cannot manage, where else can the child go and how soon?' Yet most parents and affected children want to stay with the familiar people and placement. How can staying in their original school, particularly in the mainstream, continue to bring satisfaction to all concerned?

Suggestions for schools

- Seek support (see Chapter 15). This is a sign of professionalism, not of failure. Colleagues in special schools, medical and paramedical colleagues, special needs advisers, voluntary organisations and families themselves, all need more than ever to communicate and work together.
- Timely professional development by a short-term placement or visit to a school facing similar challenges is time well spent.
- Think of education being more like a diversely challenging journey in uncertain conditions rather than a steady uphill climb towards ever higher achievements. Make sure that pupils' IEPs and Statements/Records of Needs reflect this approach.
- Acknowledge losses to yourselves, with colleagues, and with families, and try to share the inevitable sadness with them. Some children, parents or close teachers or helpers may find coping with such losses particularly difficult. Medical colleagues or some education authorities may be able to refer them to suitably qualified counsellors if necessary.
- However, each physical or cognitive loss brings with it a challenge of new learning that renews purpose in teaching and offers a continuing sense of achievement. The previously independently mobile child who has to become a wheelchair user has many new physical skills to acquire. The child with memory and skills losses caused by cognitive deterioration needs help to

remember things in different ways – by oral or pictorial instructions, for instance, or tactile signs rather than written words. Physical and sensory activities that empower and offer enjoyment, such as riding, music and water activities, may become increasingly relevant.

- Human contact and communication continues to be registered positively by children at some level, effectively to the end. For children who have complex communication and cognitive difficulties, 'circles of friendship' (Jupp 1992 and 1994) – organised supportive groups of peers and adults with a positive interest in the youngster concerned – may be developed to ensure companionship and advocacy.

- Remember that previous achievements, although lost now, were real and remain as things and events to be valued.

- Record achievements as they happen – they may be different from those of many peers but they should be genuinely and overtly valued. Records of Achievement should be kept for pupils who are experiencing the loss of previous learning but who are simultaneously adjusting to their new situation.

These children and young people are experiencing in cruelly premature and accelerated form what some of us will experience on our way to old age and death. We have the ability to make it more bearable and to enable children to retain a positive identity. Schools and teachers who have gone on these challenging journeys with children and families grow enormously as caring places and as human beings and teachers.

Conclusion

While the range of issues addressed in this chapter is not exhaustive, it includes some of the most troubling and recurrent. The kind of measures suggested can have positive effects on many other children too. The suggestions are not cost-free. As with all kinds of good educational developments, they take time, thought, imagination, sustained effort and some, but not all, require resources and training. What they create are happier pupils and more effective learning, less stressed families and more satisfied teachers – a very significant return on the investment.

CHAPTER 9

'There were more than I thought': reflections on a medical audit and its implications for a primary school

Joy McFarlane

Background

Just over four years ago I was asked to speak at a conference which was looking at a variety of ways of enabling the education of children with chronic, deteriorating or other significant medical conditions. At the time we had a child in school with muscular dystrophy and I also had experience of two children with cerebral palsy. In my naïveté I wondered how I was going to speak for any length of time about three children, albeit all with varying kinds and degrees of needs within the school. So I decided to consult with our school doctor to ask her advice and professional opinion. She was extremely interested, particularly in the area of children with chronic conditions, and this is where my learning process began.

In a busy primary school of 325 pupils there are so many priorities waiting to be dealt with that on-going health issues tended to be delegated to the school medical team who visit regularly, and, apart from the routine exchange of notes and telephone calls from parents, I am ashamed to admit that the health of my pupils appeared to be a matter for home and the medical establishment. This was to change.

My first discovery was the variety of ailments that were covered under the adjectives 'significant' and 'chronic' and my second dismaying discovery was just how many of my pupils fell into this population. In preparing for my part in the conference, our school doctor agreed to go over the roll with me, indicating instances of chronic conditions. I have to say that it was a salutary experience for both of us. Even she was amazed at the number of children and variety of conditions that were apparent in our school.

Outcomes

This whole exercise began to change my thinking. Until then we had considered really only the needs of the children with the most obvious conditions. There was a ramp in place from an early stage, with a lift and toilet for people with disabilities following later. We were very aware within the school community of a need to ensure inclusion and to avoid 'differences' becoming in any way a negative issue for children whose needs, because of their diagnosed conditions, were clearly recognised within the school. But after conducting our unofficial but careful audit of other chronic conditions, I became very aware of issues such as embarrassment for children with urinary or bowel ailments, discomfort for those with asthma or eczema, frequent periods of absence in cases of children with migraine, asthma and conditions which require regular hospital checks, and possible isolation and stigma for those with more obvious differences. Irvine (1997) refers to schools as potentially caring communities, thoughtful, supportive and flexible in their efforts to look after the well-being of their pupils. We needed to be sure that such aspects of conditions which might seem unpleasant or socially challenging had to be treated in a way that showed practical translation of the school's ethos of valuing each child.

This original audit of health conditions and needs proved to be a pivot for us in trying to bring about this aim, despite all the implications in terms of extra workload that it might mean. The first essential for the school was to have a list of children with functionally significant conditions updated on a regular basis and available for each member of staff, but retaining the necessary confidentiality. This allows each teacher to be aware of the needs of the children within his or her classroom and to respond appropriately at all times and especially if a child shows any degree of distress. It also allows for continuity throughout the school. Previously, children with, for example, a urinary problem relied on their parents to write an explanatory note for each new teacher to ensure permission was given for frequent toilet visits. Now, that information is automatically passed on through the database, and children are secure in the knowledge that their new teachers are aware of their needs.

Because this information is regularly updated, I am now no longer surprised, although I am still saddened by the growing number of children who have such conditions. The school is also, of course, attentive to the needs of children with transient conditions of whatever degree of severity.

Current audit

Out of a roll of 325 the following conditions have been indicated by parents and the medical profession. Some, as can be seen, are more prevalent and one or two are conditions that are now beginning to be commonly named, in a way that did not happen in previous years. A small number of children had several conditions.

Foot deformity	1
Rheumatoid arthritis	1
Diabetes	1
Alopecia	1
Hyperactivity	1
Foetal alcohol syndrome	1
Bowel problems	3
Migraine	4
Heart conditions	5
Hearing impairment	6
Visual impairment	7
Urinary problems	11
Allergies	14
Eczema	15
Asthma	47

Although I have written that I am no longer surprised, because of the procedures we now have in place, the percentage figure of 31 per cent (allowing for children with dual conditions) with a significant medical condition and 14 per cent with asthma still leaves me saying 'There were more than I thought'. The other rather worrying feature is that out of the 47 children with asthma, 37 are the four lower age classes in the school and only ten in the three upper primary classes. It would appear that this particular condition is on the increase with all its particular implications for both children and staff for the organisation of medication. This is backed up by Irvine (1997) who states:

> The frequency of asthma appears to be rising. This may be partly due to better recognition of the condition by doctors, but there is concern that there has been a true rise in frequency due to environment factors such as atmospheric pollution. (p. 48)

He goes on to suggest that the average class will have four or five children with asthma. Of these a proportion may not yet have been diagnosed. This, together with the increase in myalgic encephalitis (ME), which the medical profession is at last acknowledging, means that there may be a significant number of children in school who have broken or erratic attendance causing disrupted progress. ME in children can often be so difficult to diagnose and uncertain in its progress that periods of absence can go on for a considerable length of time, causing the child added distress and thus aggravating the condition still further. Even if medical diagnosis has not taken place, sensitivity is required for children feeling unwell or chronically tired.

The children who currently have medical needs in our school, identified by our most recent audit, fall into four broad categories of care. The two children with a foot deformity and alopecia, together with those who have bowel or urinary conditions, require to be treated essentially with sensitivity, ensuring that they are not teased or put into embarrassing situations.

The two with rheumatoid arthritis and diabetes, together with those with heart conditions, need to be monitored discreetly for any change in their conditions. For those with bowel or urinary ailments and visual or hearing disabilities, action must be taken to allow comfort and positioning in class, to enable both physical and emotional ease. Only for the last category is treatment generally required – those with allergic type responses – eczema, asthma or migraine – but as can be seen from the audit, it is into this category that the greatest number of children fall, 80 out of a total of 118.

Perhaps mention should also be made here of the two children who suffer from hyperactivity and foetal alcohol syndrome, at opposite ends of the activity spectrum. Both have conditions that are chronic, although not deteriorating, and both need sensitive and patient handling, although medication is not part of their requirements. Nevertheless their conditions cause disrupted progress and have implications for their educational achievement, with staff requiring to be supportive and patient in building up their self-esteem. So, although we can broadly categorise the conditions in our medical audit, there are implications for the school in how we go about treating, monitoring, putting actions in place and handling all of this sensitively; in other words, how we organise ourselves to meet the varying health and educational needs of each individual.

In looking at the implications for a primary school with regard to this organisation, it is obvious that there will be times when school is an appropriate place to be, but also times when other factors take priority.

Implications

Clearly, a balance has to be struck between giving children the right to be fully involved in normal school life whenever possible, while not exposing them to potential risks. However, there is also a very fine balance between staff who are anxious to do their very best for their pupils, but are becoming increasingly aware of potential legal liability should things go wrong. The whole question is not helped by the fact that there are no national guidelines yet in Scotland, such as have been introduced in England and Wales, although there are some good practice guides, and each school and local authority is advised to have a policy and procedures for managing medication. As there is no legal duty requiring education staff to administer medication, this is a purely voluntary role and has to be supported by parents and local authorities with the necessary updating of information and training. With these, together with clear communication and effective partnership, it is possible to give children with chronic and other longer-term medical needs the best possible opportunities and the least possible disruption to their education. Children with shorter transient conditions also benefit.

Nevertheless it is also apparent that, despite the best efforts of everyone to ensure involvement in normal school life, there will be times when children with functionally significant medical conditions are unable to attend for varying periods. The implications that come into play at this point are curricular. These absences are broadly covered in three main categories. Firstly, if a child is in hospital for a period of time, his or her education is handed over to a hospital tutor. All kinds of factors determine whether this is successful for the child or otherwise. If there is liaison between the hospital tutor and school staff, with the child well enough, even in short bursts, to access learning, it can be most successful. It is least beneficial when the learning is unrelated to school and happens in an isolated context.

The second category is when a child is absent for a longish period of time and is based at home. In our school, if the parent feels the child is able to focus on some tasks at specific points, he or she will contact school to arrange for work to be sent home. This has varying degrees of success. Class teachers are able to send only revision and consolidation work to be covered at home. Any new concepts or skills have to be taught in context in class and must await the child's return. Then the teacher, having taught the new work, can encourage the child to catch up on what he or she still has to cover or, on occasions, use time given by promoted staff on a regular basis or learning support staff to help the child make up what has been missed.

Time is precious, however, and this system is usually only offered to children who have a lengthy period of absence and also only to those who will be able to benefit without added stress. In some cases it is preferable to let the child progress more slowly in order to consolidate areas that need more practise. In those cases it is often more practical to let the child slip back a group and work at a rate that is more comfortable, although the teacher must safeguard the child's self-esteem in such a situation and still retain expectations that match the child's real ability.

The third category is when a child has frequent, intermittent and unpredictable absences for one or two days at a time. This is the most difficult group of children to manage, in that they return to school, are taught what has been missed, are often just beginning to catch up, and then are absent again. This can be very frustrating for both child and teacher and is often the type of absence where most difficulties arise. Some staff and children are able to manage to develop strategies to help them cope with the curriculum, such as using peer support. If this is used in a positive way, such as through group help and cooperative discussion, it can allow a child to understand and progress, and both partners may benefit. However, negative peer support, such as copying answers without comprehension, can lead to further problems as time goes on. Sadly, many children with this type of absence, despite the best efforts of staff, miss out on vital stages of learning and fall behind, requiring to be taught individually when the concept arises again. Sometimes a short period of learning support, or the specific help offered by a classroom or support for learning or special needs assistant can be used to try to keep a child progressing as steadily as possible, but again, pressures of time, and commitment to large numbers of children with varying learning and behavioural needs, often make this an unrealistic proposition.

The fourth aspect of curricular implications is not to do with absence, but with children who are present in school but are not functioning at the normal level because of the effects of their condition or its medication. Here, each individual class teacher is of paramount importance as he or she knows the child very well in a primary school setting, and is able to gauge whether to ease the pressure at times of relapse, constantly encourage and praise at points where a plateau seems to have been reached, and gently push and demand the higher standard that a healthy period of time might allow. In this situation a class teacher is using experience and skills that he or she would use with the majority of children, taking into account knowledge of background situations. With the chronically ill child, the teacher is perhaps just more constantly alert for indications of children's health and attention as they come and go.

Variety of approaches

Different approaches need to be made to cope with varying conditions, and no two children with the same condition have the same needs. In the past when we have had children with deteriorating conditions it has been very important to put in place an IHP or protocol as advised by the guide (DfEE/DoH 1996a) and circular (DfEE/DoH 1996b) issued in England and Wales, so that the child's day-to-day condition can be monitored and allowances made for days when the child is clearly below par. As previously indicated, the teacher's judgement is of paramount importance in gauging changing capabilities, whether to put in extra support, to push gently or take a step back. When our pupil with muscular dystrophy was with us previously, the teacher became adept at judging when he should be encouraged to write manually, when the computer was more appropriate or indeed when to have his work scribed by another child or adult. A protocol allows for flexibility and is unique to each child.

A protocol or IHP is outlined in Chapter 7 with the various aspects to be covered. There should also be some indication of how far others should have access to knowledge of the child's condition or whether greater confidentiality is appropriate, and to whom information may be communicated.

For some children with chronic but not deteriorating conditions, such a protocol or plan might also be appropriate. Indeed, for a child with epilepsy or an allergy such as peanut anaphylaxis it would be very necessary (see Cullen, Chapter 5). But many other children might not need the formality of a protocol if the parent/guardian were happy with the school's awareness and ability to handle a more straightforward condition appropriately.

However, a parent might still wish the opportunity to discuss the child's needs formally without necessarily setting up a protocol. In our school we sometimes give parents an opportunity to discuss the matter with the school doctor and me on the understanding that any decision can be reviewed at any time if needs or circumstances change. This fulfils a kind of 'middle way' approach, allowing full discussion without formal documentation. It is also open to any of us, parent, school or medical services, to initiate such a meeting if it would be beneficial.

Children with medical conditions need to know that there is treatment available when it is required, that their condition will be treated sensitively but practically. This combination of awareness, sensitivity and practical treatment forms the basis of how we are currently coping with the medical conditions presently apparent in our pupils. For the majority, only awareness and sensitivity of response are required – awareness of when a child might be suffering from another child's teasing or when a condition itself might be 'flaring up' and requiring a different approach, or increased sensitivity, while allowing for a greater than normal degree of flexibility.

This is often the situation with children who have urinary tract infections or bladder control problems. In the early years of school a child is often not able to ask the teacher in time to reach the toilet, and our pupils know that they may go quickly without asking to be excused. Our school helpers are very understanding and sensitive if clothes have to be changed or 'accidents' cleaned up, and if a child is being teased for being 'smelly' this is dealt with quickly and matter-of-factly. These problems tend to lessen with age, but one young girl in the top class suffers great discomfort on a regular basis. Not only does she have to pay frequent visits to the toilet, but she has extensive periods of absence when the pain of her condition does not allow her to concentrate and focus on school tasks. In line with our policy, during these absences we are careful to keep her up to date with the language, mathematics and topic work that the class is studying, so that she can tackle these tasks as and when she gets periods of relief. On other occasions a half-hour lie down on the bed in our medical room is enough to allow the worst to pass and enable her to function again in class. For staff, and sometimes for children and parents too, the difficulty is in recognising how severe the symptoms really are and how long they will last. Will she recover soon and be able to carry on, or should we arrrange for her to go home for a longer period of rest?

For some, practical treatment in school is required, either sporadically or regularly. The majority of these children have migraine or asthma, which need to be dealt with promptly when the occasion arises. John has migraine. He has tablets to take when he feels a headache beginning to come on, and often this is as much as he needs to control the symptoms. On some occasions he also needs to lie down for a period, and rest in a quiet place until he is sure the tablet is taking effect. Usually these preventative measures are sufficient to stop the migraine developing, but if not, a telephone call is made to get him home. We went through a period when he seemed to be needing a tablet almost on a daily basis. Fortunately, it settled down after a short while and required only sporadic treatment.

Amanda, who has asthma, is a much more regular 'patient'. She needs to use her inhaler on a daily basis and is usually looking for me after the lunch hour as her friends are going back to class. She is always quite badly out of breath and sometimes her colour is very pallid. She is able to take the required puff(s) from her inhaler by herself, needing only supervision rather than help. She and perhaps six others need to use their inhalers regularly. Most of the other children come before gymnastic times or if the day is muggy. Sometimes on these days we have such a long queue for medication that my room resembles a doctor's surgery. For a very few there can be emergency procedures which need to be put in place calmly and quickly. This might involve a child with diabetes, but is more likely to be concerned with allergies, especially the growing number of children with 'peanut allergy' or allergic anaphylaxis (see Cullen, Chapter 5). Although currently we have no-one in school with this condition, our neighbouring school has several, and our school doctor has advised us that it is likely that a child with this condition will enrol in our school soon.

This allergic reaction is alarming for everyone – the child, staff and fellow pupils – and it is essential that some staff members are trained in the use of the Epipen syringe for auto-injection. The most worrying aspect of allergic anaphylaxis is how quickly the reaction can occur, how it can in its most severe form become life-threatening, and how it might occur from seemingly unrelated incidents. For instance, a child with peanut allergy might be affected by a cereal box on the junk table, or an allergy to eggs might be aggravated by egg boxes, both of which are common items in a nursery or infant classroom. Some children are so sensitive that merely being in the same room as a minute trace of the allergen can trigger a reaction.

Management and organisation of medication and medical treatment in school

Clearly such a variety of responses to conditions needs to be very carefully managed and organised in a school. Children are encouraged, of course, towards self-management, but the onus is on teaching staff, and more often management staff, to carry out procedures and to ensure that the level of self-management is appropriate for each child.

Children's capacity to manage their own regimes

In our education authority parents are advised that children should take responsibility for their own asthma medication, but we recognise that young children may require help. However, from experience we have found that even older primary children can use inhalers either wrongly or inappropriately. Indeed, on more than one occasion inhalers have been passed round 'for a go'. While not seriously harmful, it is inappropriate behaviour and is strongly discouraged. Nebulisers can also be difficult for children to carry around on a daily basis. Therefore, in consultation with parents, we often advise that the medication is kept centrally in an easily accessed location. This, of course, gives rise to other implications of organisation, safety and administration.

The school's and parents' organisational roles

Parents are encouraged to come into school and dispense medication to their child as generally the most desirable option, but often this is clearly impossible. Also sometimes it is simply not desirable. Our whole aim in school is to help children become as independent as they can be. Where we can, we encourage them to take medication under supervision only, and are on hand to offer help if a child is too young or is finding it difficult. We also try to treat all our children in as matter-of-fact a way as possible, and parents coming in to administer medication may make what should be routine seem too 'special', both adding to children's anxiety and making them seem different from the majority. As always, it is a question of balancing needs – the needs of the child and of the parent – always emphasising the importance of the child's requirements. If I feel that children need this contact and time with their parents I would encourage parents to come in to administer medication. If, on the other hand, I felt that levels of stress were being increased for both parent and children, I would discourage it.

As an alternative they must deliver the medication personally to me or a member of my management team, with accompanied written instructions giving clear details as to the administration and the dosage. This information automatically expires at the end of each school year and must be re-confirmed at the start of each new session, with the parent taking responsibility for expiry dates, and changes of medication.

Safety

It is of course of the utmost importance that parents have confidence in the safety and security aspects of medication being administered in school. Each individual item of medication must therefore be clearly labelled with the child's name and the dosage required. To reassure all parents that medication is securely stored it is kept in locked accommodation which is also readily accessible when required. Any training which is required for specific administration, such as auto-injection, is carried out before I or my representative would embark on such treatment.

Records of medication and medical treatment

As in all areas, the administration of medication or treatment must be meticulously recorded, and the administrative details of this can be quite onerous and time-consuming. Each pupil has an individual record detailing the issue of medication or treatment. It gives the pupil's name, date and time of administration, name of the medicine and dosage and signature of the administrator. All of these records are kept on the premises for a period of five years.

In the absence of a national system in Scotland, our education authority, in common with many others, has devised its own system with the appropriate administrative guidance and documentation (Stirling Council 1998). However, it is somewhat cumbersome and time-consuming, especially in terms of storage of outdated medical data for a period of five years. Perhaps there is no way round this, but a national system which recognised and supported schools in their care of pupils with medical needs would be very much appreciated and welcomed. It would also ensure that all pupils with medical needs were being treated in a similar way and would allow for continuity of management across authorities.

Union perspectives

While Scottish councils are currently advised to formulate their own policies in the light of local needs, all the literature points out that there is no legal duty which requires school staff to administer medication; this is a voluntary role.

The Professional Association of Teachers (PAT) – one of our professional unions – points out that staff who provide support for pupils with special needs require support from parents and from employers (PAT 1996). They need to be assured that the employer will accept responsibility for any alleged negligence by school staff while administering medication in the course of employment. They also, as a matter of necessity, need information and training. Our authority's own health and safety regulations require us to be informed and trained for all tasks we undertake.

Our local branch of the Educational Institute of Scotland – the largest teachers' union in Scotland – is similarly cautious in its advice to staff (EIS – Alloa 1996). It suggests that teachers should not volunteer to administer medication unless it is an emergency with a potentially life-threatening situation. It also suggests that the education authority provides every teacher who does volunteer with a formal statement of indemnification signed by both staff member and a representative from the authority.

Conclusion

In conclusion then, it is important to see that children with everyday and more serious chronic conditions are as carefully managed as children whose conditions are even more serious and more obvious. Every child has a right to the best provision possible, enabling him or her to access education despite challenging circumstances. Sometimes it is easier to meet the requirements of the most needy children simply because it is plain to see and understand their condition. It is the challenge for the school to ensure that each child's condition is managed in the most appropriate, sensitive and caring way. Children and staff have to share their strengths with one another. It is often children who treat a peer with equality, accepting a person for who he or she is regardless of disability or condition, while some staff may be over-sympathetic, feeling that a child has more than enough to face with a serious health condition. They can create an unintentional and unhelpful discrimination. If we can all strive to reach a situation where, regardless of conditions, regardless of impairment or difference, each child is supported with an appropriate mixture of practical care, empathy and realism, then this may enable every individual to get the best from education.

CHAPTER 10

'People took a lot for granted': a secondary school's support for pupils with chronic illness and medical conditions

Ronnie Hassard

Introduction

This chapter describes how the educational system in Northern Ireland – unfamiliar to many UK readers – has only recently fully acknowledged and begun to accommodate more effectively pupils with special educational needs in all its schools. The frameworks within which resources are allocated are explained, and found wanting, in relation to making desired improvements. I describe the mixed intake, traditionally caring and academic grammar school where I am one of three assistant principals, and then, using two case studies and pupil perspectives, look critically at the school's policies and practices in relation to pupils with medical conditions. Finally, I list suggestions in relation to aspects which could be improved.

Northern Ireland educational systems and the locus of grammar schools

Northern Ireland grammar schools have not traditionally prioritised young people with special educational needs; the concept was simply alien to them. An outmoded but persistent stereotype represented selective institutions' sole justification for existence as academic success – high examination pass rates – and the pupils as able and unproblematic. Those with significant special needs would, it was assumed, not reach the academic standard for entry and, if their needs became apparent after enrolment, they would be unable to survive. Sooner rather than later, they would 'drop out' to a more suitable place, i.e. a non-selective school. The very idea of 10–15 per cent of their pupils having special needs would have been laughable.

Grammar school pupils did indeed, and still do, experience high levels of success for which the schools were happy to accept credit. Any difficulties experienced by their pupils would tend to be attributed to individual or familial deficiencies, and any outstanding academic success of pupils in non-selective schools would be dismissed as statistically insignificant and not worthy of professional critical reflection on the system.

A growing awareness of the inadequacies, inaccuracies and unfairness of this perspective, the advent of GCSE structures, the legislative requirements of the Northern Ireland Curriculum and advances in knowledge about how pupils actually learn, eroded old certainties and reshaped the educational topography. Other influential developments were open enrolment, free transport to the school of choice for those living more than three miles away, pupil-driven budgets, as well as the publication of examination results and Department of Education of Northern Ireland (DENI) Inspection Reports. Grammar schools may have come late to special educational needs, and their initial motivation may have been suspect, but they are now genuinely involved.

More recently, the Children (NI) Order (1995), and specifically the *Code of Practice on the Identification and Assessment of Special Educational Needs* (DENI 1998), made adequate and effective support mechanisms part of each pupil's legal entitlement. Our educational psychology services, central to the identification and assessment of all special educational needs and their Statementing, has been embedded in the local education authorities (the Education and Library Boards 'ELBs'). The recent experience of this school has been of under-provision and long waiting lists for the service. It is fair to add that the ELBs have faced their own difficulties. Contraction is the common experience and, while the goodwill of ELB personnel is not in question, obtaining extra provision such as transport, home tuition or specialist facilities, including classroom assistants, can be difficult. Statementing has been particularly convoluted.

For the most part, this state of affairs arises from a shortage of qualified educational psychologists, resulting in a quota system, limiting referrals from schools and allocating the majority of assessments to the preschool and primary sectors. In the post-primary sector the quota is largely based on 'the number of children in the school who obtained a grade 'D' or opted out of the transfer procedure'. ('Transfer procedure' refers to the government-supplied tests on which selection at eleven is based.) The number of 'Ds and Opt-outs' acts as a proxy indicator for determining referral quotas but, since pupils in this school fall into neither category, accessing the beleaguered educational psychology service is bound to be difficult. To the credit of those involved, some capacity is held in reserve, and occasional requests for assistance beyond the limitations of the quota framework generally meet with a positive response.

The Educational Welfare Service, which may also have a positive role in relation to pupils absent on the grounds of health or with social needs, is also located within the ELBs. This school has more direct contact with Educational Welfare Officers (EWOs) than with psychologists and the experience has been positive. The introduction, however, of a bureaucratic referral system may change that perspective.

Overall, however, our school's situation echoes that cited by Closs and Norris (1997), that the quality of provision for pupils with special educational needs, including those with medical conditions, in a given school 'will depend almost entirely on the knowledge and experience of the people in that school' (p. 49).

Our school: its location, systems, ethos and the constraints upon it

From the school's upper floors, the cranes of the Harland and Wolff shipyard, made famous by the 'Titanic', seem relatively close at hand. Beyond the cranes, the angular profile of Cave Hill confirms Louis MacNeice's line about Belfast, city of his birth: 'between the mountains and the gantries'. Elsewhere, the view is of red-brick suburbia or of fields across the nearby Castlereagh Hills. This combination – industrial cityscape, suburban housing and rural landscape – reflects the diversity of the pupil population. Having begun life in 1945 as an inner city grammar school, in territory to the west of the Lagan, in improvised accommodation, serving an economically deprived Protestant ghetto, the school moved to purpose-built premises on the eastern edge of Belfast in the late 1950s. Within the divided society of Northern Ireland and its fragmented educational structures, it was thought of as a grammar school for an exclusively Protestant and mainly urban working-class constituency.

This is the school's 'defining myth'. Although one would argue the validity of such a perception at any time, the records prove the school population was neither socially nor religiously homogeneous – but the myth, in large proportion, engendered the caring ethos. It is widely accepted that pupils succeed here who would probably fail in other grammar schools. In the past, such pupils were marked out by their addresses, their accents and their fathers' occupations, but they were part of a school in which a number of pastoral care and support structures were installed, long before they became current in other grammar schools. Many of those features are still recognised as strengths.

The practice of the caring ethos and some of those 'strengths' may be questioned in the course of this chapter, as they apply to young people with medical conditions, but a few comments should be made:

- This *is* a successful and caring school, with a geographically, socially, religiously and culturally diverse student population.
- Only a minority of the eleven-hundred pupils come from the Belfast City Council area, but the pupil population is a more representative cross-section of society than that of most other grammar schools.
- Any criticisms are offered constructively, from a position of relative strength: a well-founded confidence, but not complacency, that our young people are given the care to which they are entitled by a school committed to practical and continued improvement.

The school, which describes itself as 'interdenominational, coeducational, increasingly multi-national and catering for children from a wide range of social backgrounds', is a 'Controlled School' of the Belfast Education and Library Board (BELB). Local Management of Schools may have loosened that 'control', but this is the least independent category of Northern Ireland's schools. Maintained, Integrated and Voluntary schools benefit from budgets determined by bodies such as the Catholic Council for Maintained Schools (CCMS), the Northern Ireland Council for Integrated Education (NICIE), or the Department of Education for Northern Ireland (DENI), rather than the financially straitened ELBs. An illustration: at a very conservative estimate, ten per cent – about 110 – of our pupils are entitled to free school meals (FSM), a generally accepted proxy indicator of need, and normally a trigger for extra funding. The connection between disadvantage, ill health and special educational need has been too well documented to need further rehearsal here, but BELB operates a funding threshold; under 20 per cent of pupils on FSM and no extra funding is made available. No such barrier has existed elsewhere. Only two schools in the entire Province were excluded from FSM funding in 1997–98, this being one of them. Part of the explanation for this anomaly lies in the nature of the urban population served by the BELB; economic deprivation and social need are more prevalent than in any other ELB and the budgetary pressures of this should not be underestimated. However, no distinction is made between the haves and the have-nots when it comes to school comparison. The crude statistics of the annual School Performance Tables apply the 'Northern Ireland Grammar School Average' to all such schools, although the extra funding, beyond normal provision, varies enormously.

Regardless of funding allocations, there are still questions to be asked about the educational provision and monitoring of progress of pupils whose education is interrupted or impeded by illness, and about the particular measures put in place to support them. But it seems that financial considerations cannot be avoided. There has been little room for manoeuvre within the school's budget, and the funding of pupils presumes they are learning in school, not off-site, or, if they are off-site for anything other than relatively short periods of time, that extra funding, from another source, should be applied. We are in a very competitive situation in the market-place of open enrolment but lack the financial cushions which many of our rival schools enjoy. Statistics in the public domain show the annual cost per pupil is consistently lower than that of any other Northern Ireland grammar school. It is difficult, in the face of such realities, to see how Government is discharging its obligation to ensure fair resourcing of adequate and efficient education for all.

Educational care for individual pupils with medical conditions

The caring ethos and strong academic focus of the school are complementary. Year-on-year improvements in results – in 1998 99.4 per cent of Year 12 pupils obtained five or more GCSE A–C passes – and Inspectors' comments on the quality of care support the claim. We would not be caring for bright pupils if we failed to hold high expectations of them, or if they failed to achieve their academic potential. Efforts are also made to keep staff aware of pupils' circumstances. In relation to their health, for example, details of illness, medical condition, severe allergic reactions, etc. are filed in a secure but accessible location. The Heads of Year, who monitor attendance and progress, ensure all teachers working with these pupils know about these matters.

There are about 6–8 pupils in each year-group with moderate to severe health problems. This estimate excludes mild asthma or eczema for instance and is based on parental comments and a cross-check of the pupils' attendance records and progress reports. The impact of these conditions on the learning of individuals varies considerably and is not easy to assess. Some were born with their condition, and the severity of symptoms may vary; others have contracted the condition much more recently and are still learning to live with what can be devastating effects.

In dealing with pupils' long term illnesses which result in absence, the school informs the ELB Special Needs Department, which then arranges hospital or home tuition, this having become a statutory entitlement in Article 86 of the Education (NI) Order 1998 and, for children with Statements of special educational needs, in Article 10 of the Education (NI) Order 1996. Beyond that, there are no institutional imperatives on either side, for a coordinated approach. The relationship between school and tutor, for example, is undefined. In our school, each Head of Year maintains ongoing contact with the family, largely but not exclusively by telephone, and provides some limited academic support, if appropriate. The home tutor, if one has been allocated, can be provided with texts, areas of focus, assignments, tests, past papers, etc. The school is not automatically informed if a tutor is allocated; some tutors have not initiated contact and, if there is a mechanism for monitoring the effectiveness of the tutors, it has not yet involved this school. There is difficulty in getting tutors with the subject specialism(s) and expertise to work with pupils across the range of subjects and at the necessary level for GCSE or GCE A' Level. The ELB cannot make finance available for teachers in the school to act as home tutors, or even to pay travel expenses if they are prepared to do so in an unpaid capacity. The explanation is that the home tutor system is in place and further expense cannot be sustained.

Overall responsibility for special needs is accepted by senior management in this school. A Senior Teacher has responsibility for pastoral matters and liaises with the Heads of Year. There are monthly meetings involving Heads of Year, the Senior Teacher coordinating pastoral matters, and the Principal. Heads of Year meet regularly with their teams of form teachers. The School Counsellor – who is also the SENCO – undertakes referrals to the psychology service, liaising with the EWO and the ELB Special Needs Department, as well as completing assessment and review procedures. Attendance, recorded twice daily, is entered by optical mark reader, using codified data. Agreed procedures enable prompt response to unexplained or lengthy absence, but there is no specific policy statement or clear strategies relating to the way in which the learning of pupils with chronic illness and other medical conditions might be promoted and monitored away from the classroom.

The school aim for all pupils is to 'stretch and support' them. The Prospectus and the Staff Handbook are emphatic that the academic and pastoral dimensions ought not to be separated. The recent enhancement of disabled access, including ramps, lifts and toilet facilities throughout the buildings helps to explain an increasing number of statemented pupils. Parents are confident that there is a growing pool of experience and expertise within the staff and they have expressed their satisfaction with the provision for, and approaches to, pupils with special needs. However the gap in policy and practical strategies in relation to pupils with medical conditions would indicate that constructive criticism is needed. The recent experiences of two pupils are instructive.

Kerry and Sharon: two young people who experienced health difficulties

Kerry is a young person of very considerable presence and determination. Diabetes Mellitus Type 1 was diagnosed when she was in primary school; very soon after that she was self-administering insulin and adapted well to the regime. Aged 10 she was on four daily injections, but blood sugar levels proved hard to stabilise, and from the beginning of her grammar schooling there were headaches, low concentration levels, occasionally erratic behaviour and frequent fatigue, despite her adherence to the regime under supervision of the school nurse, in keeping with the policy on administering medication. Intermittent hospitalisation, generally 4–10 days, averaging six days, was needed to achieve stability. Examination times, with increased stress levels, were especially difficult. High blood sugar levels brought urinary tract infections and kidney pain, but these responded well to antibiotics. Alongside these atypical symptoms, Kerry had chronic back pain. The unhelpful tendencies to infections and chronic back pain, coupled with intermittent hospitalisation, meant schooling was often disrupted. Having obtained six GCSE passes at A–C grades, Kerry was offered a sixth form place although her results fell short of the overall entry criteria. She did not request special consideration, but it was felt that such consideration was appropriate. She now attends a further education college, her decision prompted by a house move across the city, rather than any dissatisfaction with the school.

Sharon, currently in Upper Sixth, contracted post-viral chronic fatigue Syndrome (ME) at the age of 13, during her second year at the school. Sharon's recollections centre on gross physical fatigue, inability to do anything, and long periods of not wanting to do anything either. As testing eliminated other possible diagnoses, symptoms became increasingly intense and Sharon was out of school for over a year. On return she attended when able, but seldom for a whole day. There were home-based tutors, provided by the ELB but withdrawn once the symptoms abated sufficiently for her to be able to return to school, however irregularly. As Sharon recollects the experience, she says the tutors varied, both in their interest in her and in what she was supposed to be learning.

Sharon speaks calmly about the experience; for most of the time her extreme lassitude and her understandable concerns at the apparent inability to explain or to treat her condition meant she had little motivation towards friendship or interest in her peers, much less any inclination to learning; her energy level was so low that she could not concentrate for any length of time. Her condition had improved by the time she sat her GCSEs and she was able to enter the Sixth Form, as she had always planned, on the strength of her results. Now in the last year of her 'A' Level studies, her immediate aim is to enter higher education. Sharon is a sociable young woman with a well-developed and infectious sense of humour and a thoughtful frankness about her ordeal.

As Kerry reflects on her particular experience, she stresses the school's understanding and emphasises that people went out of their way to accommodate and support her. She is not uncritical of some aspects of that support, however. For instance, she found on several occasions that new teachers or substitute teachers had not been informed. She resented having to explain why she needed to leave the classroom, or why she was late, and feels this sort of thing should not occur. There were a couple of embarrassing moments when she was unfairly reprimanded for failing to understand material that had been explained during her absence. In conversation, Kerry now attributes that embarrassment as much to the teachers as to herself. Pressed on the point, she admits that she found these lapses hurtful and annoying in equal measure and recognises that they served to emphasise her 'difference' from her peers, a feeling already exacerbated by the absences, the visits to the school nurse's room for the injections, and the very existence of the condition in the first place.

It is evident from her conversation that this sense of 'otherness' is something with which she has struggled, and which still frustrates her as she moves into adulthood. There were a couple of her peers, two boys with whom she was on good terms most of the time, who occasionally teased her about her diabetes. She thinks this was not done maliciously, as she believed at the time, but she is equally emphatic that it did not feel like 'friendly banter', to use her own words. Kerry is sure in her own mind that the thoughtlessness and immaturity from which it probably proceeded could have been better counteracted. Her parents, then and now, felt that such teasing was inconsequential, probably inevitable and might even have been well-intentioned. They point to the fact that Kerry had good friends at school. Kerry would say that she was part of a smaller network of acquaintances than most other girls of her age and that her absences and illness inhibited the development of wider patterns of acquaintance and friendship.

With those exceptions, the pastoral structures were seen as helpful. The form teacher/Head of Year combination worked to her consistent advantage and the positive relationships in the school helped her fit back into class after absences. As for support for learning, while Kerry praises the efforts of most of her teachers, in terms of their encouragement and making sure that she had notes and other materials and for taking time to go over problem areas, she does make some interesting comments. The Head of Year coordinated the setting, marking and return of work to Kerry during some of her absences. Kerry is mindful of the effort that went into this, and thankful for the progress that was made possible. However, each of Kerry's intermittent absences was treated as a separate event, rather than one of a series. 'You'd think they could have known that I was going to be absent,' she says, articulating not just a criticism of the lack of an overview or understanding of her diabetes, but also a frustration that it seemed as if no one cared enough to find out about it, or to draw conclusions from the available evidence.

One unexpected point which Kerry volunteered was her exclusion from extra-curricular activities. She had been very active and was interested in hockey and netball, but her back pain in particular ruled this out and gradually she dropped sport entirely. However, when she cast around for another feasible activity, one to match her interests, in which occasional absence might not matter too much, she could not find one. The school does have a varied programme of extra-curricular activities but there is certainly room for expansion; Kerry's own suggestion of a cookery club, for example, deserves further consideration.

The impressions that relationships in the school are constructive, that people-to-people they work well, but that aspects of the pastoral structure, especially monitoring the progress of pupils with long-term and frequent absence, could benefit from careful review, are confirmed by Sharon's comments. While she herself was not troubled by Kerry's sense of 'otherness', she commented that when she returned to class on an intermittent basis a few teachers never commented on her return. The treatment she received was unfailingly courteous, but she feels that there ought to have been a more explicit, even if informal, low-key and individual sign that her return was important and worth celebration. If that had taken place before her peers it needed only to have been a simple comment such as 'Good to see you back in class'. Even a factual statement such as 'You're back' would have been preferable to nothing. As it was, Sharon felt unvalued by some teachers. Others took time to ask her to wait after class, wished her well and offered their support. Kerry also hinted at this feeling: on occasion she thought a few of the teachers didn't know she had been absent for a week.

Like Kerry, Sharon has not taken up any of the extra-curricular activities since her return. Team sports and competitive games are simply not for her and the non-sporting activities are not to her liking. She attends low impact aerobics with her mother and prefers that setting. Unlike Kerry, Sharon gives this matter little weight, but the school's definition of the curriculum as 'the totality of the learning experiences offered, in and out of the classroom' gives added importance to the inclusion of all pupils in the extra-curricular programme.

Sharon is more critical of the learning support, perhaps because her absences were of significantly longer duration or because the school made certain assumptions about the role of the ELB tutors. Despite the fatigue she was feeling, and her admittedly low motivation about school work or friendship over the course of several years, Sharon's major recollection of the time is of feeling 'cut off', in much the same way that Closs and Norris (1997) found that pupils could be 'forgotten' (p. 76). Sharon does praise the coordinating efforts of her Head of Year in terms of getting work to her, ensuring it was marked and returned to her, but her criticism is well put: 'There was bound to be separation . . . I was at home, but I'd have liked more contact.' Sharon has a family connection with the school and yet she still felt apart. Had it not been for that connection, and for the visits of a few of her teachers from time to time, Sharon admits she would have felt completely cut off, and the return to school, physically and emotionally difficult as it was, would have become even more daunting. Such small acts of recognition and attribution have an importance that goes far beyond any measurable gain in academic achievement. They may seem inconsequential but they are emblematic, not merely symbolic, and their significance lies in the affirmative messages sent to the absent pupil, and in their role in preserving a connection between pupil and school.

Reviewing provision for pupils with medical conditions

'People took a lot for granted', Sharon said, giving this chapter its title. In the context of a successful and caring school, which is concerned with the good of all its pupils and which has made honest efforts to keep them at the top of its priorities, there are five areas in which things have been taken somewhat for granted about pupils whose attendance and/or progress are disrupted by illness, and which will now receive careful reconsideration:

Caring in action

- The way in which the Pastoral Care Policy is implemented and the mediation of the school's caring ethos into the daily realities of these pupils will be reconsidered.
- There will be clearer policy and practical guidance on promoting the learning of these pupils.
- Many of the pupils may be unable or unwilling to take part in extra-curricular activities but they should be encouraged and enabled to do so. The range of activities is already under review, with a view to giving as much access as possible.

'Splashdown' procedures

- Formulating and implementing effective 're-entry strategies' for pupils after extended or intermittent absences is now high on our 'To Do' list.
- Teachers of major subjects such as English and Mathematics, with a greater number of timetabled classes, are in a better position to establish a working relationship with pupils than others who see them only once a week; if that day is a holiday or coincides with illness of teacher or pupil, even longer may elapse between classes. Little wonder some teachers were unfamiliar with Kerry's and Sharon's comings and goings. Some tactics to get around this difficulty will be introduced.

Keeping in touch

- This does take place, but contact with pupils on long-term absence needs to be structured; certain 'trigger points' will elicit action by the school, including arrangements, if needed, to keep contact with peers.
- There will also be parental contact on a regular basis. Even if there is nothing new to report, simply registering continued awareness of, and interest in, an absent pupil is a significant act.

- Liaising with ELB-based home tutors has not been a strong point and there will be agreed steps to improve it.

Supporting learning

- Current arrangements, focusing on the Heads of Year as coordinators of work provided by individual subject staff, will be augmented by Code of Practice requirements, especially IEPs.
- It is important to improve measures for promoting and monitoring the learning of these pupils. Laptop computers – and e-mail – have been mooted as a way of facilitating 'distance learning'. How the technology might be obtained and made available to pupils is under consideration.
- Structured involvement of the SENCO, departmental heads and parents, as well as Heads of Year and subject teachers in all of this is essential.

Staff development and in-service training

- Time will be found to focus on the needs of these young people and on how staff can be supported as they strive to meet those needs.
- This will begin with whole staff decisions and move into the arena of the different subjects.

Conclusion

If we are to improve the actual, as opposed to the intended, ways in which we support and encourage pupils with special needs, particularly those related to chronic illness and other medical conditions, we would do well to heed Fullan's (1991) words, 'Educational change depends on what teachers do and think' (p. 27). Hopkins (1991), who distinguishes between 'root' and 'branch' innovations, is adamant that this is more than telling people what to do and letting them get on with it: 'We need implementation-friendly policies that devote attention to the process as well as the content of change'. He adds two points of particular significance for our school:

> The first is that in times of innovation overload, it is even more essential to prioritise, and not to dilute precious energies and resources by trying to do too much. It is imperative to do a few things as well as we can, and the rest as well as we would have done anyway. The second is to pay attention to the roots, to the management arrangements, in order to build a culture and infrastructure for change. (p. 61)

The School Development Plan, now at the end of its natural life, is being replaced through a collaborative effort designed to involve staff and to give wide 'ownership'. In this school, the staff, like our colleagues elsewhere, have had much to contend with in recent years but there have been very considerable improvements in terms of pupil achievement. The overall 'corporate concern' has been with the well-being, happiness and success of the young people who 'sign up' for this school; it is now timely to look into ways of ensuring greater inclusion of a group of pupils, two of whom have, in this chapter, articulated feelings of 'otherness' and of being 'cut off'. It may well be that some level of such feelings is inevitable, and if so, the aim will be to lessen their impact on individual pupils. A school-wide audit has already begun, and it will provide the kind of information necessary for compiling a 'route map' that is always appreciated when embarking on a journey into new or unfamiliar territory.

CHAPTER 11

Towards quality educational services for children out of school for reasons of health

Peter Feeley and Carolyn Skilling

The views of a head of hospital and home teaching service in Scotland

Introduction

Scottish education is deeply involved in raising educational standards and evaluating provision in schools and education services. We have debated the feasibility of 'measuring the unmeasurable and intangible' such as ethos and inter-personal factors but, both nationally and locally, we have opted for criterion-referenced systems of evaluation with the proviso that special circumstances should be recognised within the systems. But how do we recognise quality? How do we measure it; and surely it is more than just a feeling, an intuition built on professional experience? What standards do we have by which to gauge the success and effectiveness of education? This is particularly problematic in out-of-school services which are, by their very nature, geared towards individual pupils in non-standard situations.

Means of evaluating quality

In Scotland the 5–14 programme offers schools and teachers guidelines rather than the more rigid standards of the National Curriculum in England and Wales but it does, nevertheless, give us a clear basis on which to plan educational programmes. It offers advice on how to achieve breadth of educational experiences, consistency of approach and a means to ensure continuity and progression. Standard Grades and Highers, and now Higher

Still, involve highly structured educational programmes with inbuilt indicators of achievement.

Various means are available to assist schools and services to ensure a high quality of provision. Schools and support services are able to identify areas of particular strength and those in need of improvement by using the processes outlined, and performance indicators provided for all areas of schools' provision, including ethos, in *How Good is our School?* (HMIs Audit Unit 1996) and in a supplementary document *Taking a Closer Look at Specialist Services* (HMIs Audit Unit 1997). In Scotland Her Majesty's Inspectors' (HMIs) function as a national quality development and assurance force for education, with both general and specialist functions.

Many areas of Scotland also produce their own self-evaluation measures. Schools and services are encouraged to conduct surveys of users of their service, that is, pupils, parents and the wider school community, and teachers themselves. Currently, local authorities are undergoing 'best-value reviews' designed to ensure that high standards are aspired to and achieved and this will undoubtedly include provision for children with medical needs. Just as schools are using target-setting (HMIs Audit Unit 1993 and 1999) to identify curriculum targets to work towards, so all who are involved in providing for this group of children and young people need to scrutinise the effectiveness of their work and ensure that they are 'making a difference'. Similar expectations should exist regarding the education of children when they are unable to attend schools for reasons of health as apply in schools.

Acknowledging reality

Clearly, we have to recognise that there are likely to be obstacles to teaching and learning in out-of-school circumstances. These may arise from the child's own state of health. If in pain or undergoing treatment a child may not be receptive to teaching and indeed it may be counter-productive. However, we should recognise the therapeutic effect of education. If small achievable goals are set within the framework of their own educational programme, the opportunity to experience success will do a great deal to enhance the pupil's well-being. The benefits go beyond educational attainment.

The task for educators is to acknowledge 'immovable' barriers to educational progress and to find ways of eliminating, reducing or working round others. One of the difficulties concerns the availability of time. When a child is in hospital there are often many demands on his or her time for treatment and therapy. Teachers must ensure that time spent with pupils is as productive as possible. Flexibility and adaptability are essential in such circumstances. When a child is at home requiring home tuition, efficient use must be made of teacher time to ensure that valuable educational opportunities are not wasted. Timetable planning must ensure that more time is not spent driving than teaching!

Other factors in educational progress centre around the range of subject specialisms available, particularly in small services, the service's ability to recognise and meet special educational needs, the level of professional development of teachers and the extent of access to suitable resources and facilities. However, the greatest barrier to achievement may well be diminished expectations and aspirations. It is essential that all concerned set standards which are both realistic and challenging. This involves a partnership across hospital education services, 'home' schools, parents, young people themselves, and hospitals. Each has a vital role to play if we are to achieve quality.

Hospital and home education services

All educational services must start from a clear philosophical basis. There must be policy statements which set out the principles upon which it is based and which illustrate the means by which education will be delivered and supported. This 'foundation' must be understood and agreed by all staff and should be available for scrutiny. Without this, decisions may be made on an *ad hoc* basis, and may lack consistency and focus; individual staff members will have no corporate basis on which to form their own judgements, and assessment of children's progress and evaluation of the service as a whole will be invalid and unreliable. Clear principles will also help reduce the possibility of misunderstanding between providers and 'customers' – our pupils and their parents – in relation to what may be attempted and achieved.

Policies should cover the breadth and range of subjects to be covered and meeting the individual needs of the pupils. The varied needs which pupils may have must be addressed. Provision of a stimulating and appropriate curriculum will do much to enhance the pupil's emotional state as well as minimising the disruption to progress. Teachers must work closely with other disciplines, and policy statements should offer guidance on collaboration to ensure that a holistic approach to the child is achieved. Advice on resources, especially the effective use of information technology, must be given.

Policy statements should require close liaison with the pupils' home schools to ensure cross-establishment consistency. Familiar school work and the assurance that they are 'keeping up' as far as possible will do much to encourage and reassure pupils and parents. Policy statements or related practice guides should offer practical suggestions about how parents may play a positive role in their children's education in hospital and following discharge. Because we see parents on a daily basis in hospital, we may be better able than schools to develop practical partnerships with parents and involve them actively. This really helps children, but parents may also find it gives them a constructive outlet when they may be feeling helpless and frustrated. It may enable parents to continue their educational involvement after their children's discharge, having seen its importance in hospital.

Hospital and home education teachers have, arguably, greater professional development needs than others. Not only are they required to deliver the curriculum as fully as possible, but they must do so in a hospital or home setting, working at the bedside, competing with the demands of other professionals, visitors and families and assorted distractions, and taking account of the physical and emotional state of the young person involved. Secondary specialist teachers may have sole responsibility for ensuring that educational programmes are in line with the many developments and initiatives emanating from local authorities and the Scottish Parliament. Careful planning is essential to ensure that opportunities for professional development are utilised as effectively as possible. A careful balance should be maintained which ensures that staff are familiar with developments in both educational and medical fields relevant to their pupils' progress and treatment.

Appropriate personal and professional support must also be offered to staff working with young people who do not always thrive and recover, as soon as the situation is recognised and parents have consented to some information being given to key staff. While this is not 'staff development' as commonly understood, it is an important aspect of keeping staff morale and effectiveness high; they must retain their sensitivity towards pupils and families without 'burn out'.

Hospital and home education services must transmit information about work achieved to pupils' home schools so that there is a shared awareness of progress and gaps. Young people must be credited with the work they have put in while in hospital and schools' support of hospital and home teaching must be fully acknowledged. Reporting back to schools should take place regularly while pupils are in hospital, more fully at discharge and when home tuition is concluded. This assists the progress of pupils and will also do much to raise awareness of the service.

When children are discharged from hospital but are not immediately able to return to school, arrangements must be made for home tuition. The details of such policies and plans will vary according to the length of recuperation or ongoing illness, the nature of the condition, the geography of the area concerned, family circumstances and, in Scotland, the way individual authorities interpret the legislation which permits but does not legally require provision to be made. This has been discussed in Chapter 1 of this book. A Ministerial address following the SOEID (1998) Discussion Paper promises that national guidance will be addressed urgently but, in the interim, education authority advice should be readily available to teachers, pupils and parents alike.

Schools

Home schools must play their role to the full if we are to ensure continuity and progression for our 'shared' pupils. Their own policies address the reality that on a regular basis some of their pupils will be absent for reasons of health and that for a few pupils this will be a long-term situation. Schools should sustain their responsibility for their pupils' education during these times and should seek flexible and imaginative ways to offer support. Social as well as educational contact between home school and the absent pupil is important.

With increasing public scrutiny of standards of achievement in schools it is in everyone's interest that all pupils are given the necessary support and opportunities to attain their highest levels of success. Schools can contribute to this by ensuring that detailed and accurate information is available to hospital and home tuition services about educational programmes being followed and materials being used. There should be a named person within each school responsible for this, with sufficient authority to ensure that it takes place effectively. Within the primary sector this could be an assistant head teacher or head teacher, while at secondary level it might be an assistant head teacher or principal teacher of guidance. Learning support teachers may also have a critical role. The more diffused responsibility for supporting learning in Scottish schools, whereby all teachers must play their part with learning support specialists, can assist whole school approaches but may make contact by external agencies more problematic than the SENCO 'single stop' contact elsewhere in the UK. This is particularly true for large secondary schools with extremely busy head teachers.

Schools should make materials and resources available to young people and to hospital services when they cannot otherwise be provided. Communication is the key to good joint working and technology has a vital function in supporting the education of such pupils. The humble telephone or fax machine offers the opportunity for immediate and detailed exchange of information, but with more schools using the Internet and the development of video-conferencing the opportunities are increasing exponentially. It should be possible to lend equipment to pupils in hospitals or at home, particularly as laptop computers are becoming less expensive. Schools should consider explicit reference to young people with health difficulties in their information technology policies to ensure that they are not 'out of sight, out of mind', educationally or socially.

In certain circumstances schools themselves may be expected to provide home tuition while pupils are at home. Information as to how this can be arranged and what can be reasonably expected by parents should be readily available to all parents from schools and local authorities. As with education in hospital, parents must be aware of what they are entitled to expect, if indeed they are aware that such services exist, and should not be faced with the additional stress of trying to uncover information about educational support for their children at a time of considerable anxiety.

Children and young people

Every good school or educational service takes account of the views, interests, needs, attitudes and aptitudes of its pupils when planning its curriculum. This is established good practice and is now given greater force by the Children (Scotland) Act 1995 and equivalent Acts elsewhere in the UK. This is even more important for pupils who are unable to attend school for reasons of health. They should be consulted on areas of priority particularly at critical stages such as transition from primary to secondary and at presentation for external exams. Their views should be sought about content of programmes and also on preferred means and styles of delivery. As teachers, we must not be afraid to ask pupils for their opinions on the effectiveness of our work, as our key purpose is to help pupils learn.

Pupils have responsibilities in learning as well and they should be encouraged to make the best possible use of the educational support available and to cooperate with teachers and parents.

Parents

Parents are increasingly involved at all levels in Scottish education, from policy-making to the classroom. They should be aware not only of their rights and what they can reasonably expect but should be encouraged to consider how they can support the education of their children. They can do much to offer encouragement and to ensure that work left for their children is carried out. They are often able to act as go-betweens with schools and hospital services and this function should be valued, although parents' goodwill and stretched energies should not be abused. Their involvement in the communication process will help all involved in the education of their children to be as aware and informed as possible and will also encourage a smooth transition from hospital to home and then to school. They are the common thread to this process, but parents of these children, as with all other parents, will vary in their ability and willingness to fill this role.

Local authorities

The arrangements that local authorities make for the education of young people unable to attend school vary widely. However, they should all be encouraged to describe the nature and extent of their provision in published policies and should offer advice and guidance to schools and parents as to access and procedures. Equity of access is important – it should not be left to individual parents or schools to struggle in a policy and information vacuum from which assertive and informed parents may access services unknown to others.

Children with chronic and recurring serious and/or rare conditions may be treated and educated in hospitals or hospices out of their own local authority area. This raises the issue of inter-authority payment for education, a new situation in Scotland but already in place in other parts of the UK. Local authorities should enter willingly into discussions with their counterparts across the country to ensure that such administrative considerations do not hinder educational provision being made or add to parents' and children's worries. Again, having statutory out-of-school provision should reinforce such agreements. The new Scottish Parliament could do much to raise the profile of pupils in these circumstances and to offer a clear legislative framework, guidance – including indications of standards – and encouragement to local authorities and schools to ensure that they have clearly-stated policies and effective practices.

Conclusion

With these elements in place and those involved working in close cooperation, the educational well-being of young people with health problems should be greatly improved.

The perspective of a former English education authority officer, responsible for quality assurance, now Director of PRESENT/NAESC

Introduction

Approximately 100,000 children are estimated to lose ten million hours of education every year in England and Wales because they are unable to attend school on the grounds of health (NAESC 1996). Every school will have some pupils who are missing out on their educational entitlement for this reason.

Education is a right for all children, including those unable to attend school for reasons of health or exclusion, in England, Wales and Northern Ireland, although children out of school in Scotland are, as indicated in the first half of this chapter, dependent on discretionary provision from the local authority. Quality educational services, however, will not be a reality for sick children anywhere in the UK until this absence deficit is made up. Sick children need more education, more easily available, and more support in returning to school.

Although most sick children return to school and enter adult society, they do so with fewer qualifications than their peers and less chance of obtaining satisfying work. Too many remain at home and never achieve employment. Their leaving qualifications do not match their ability, contact is lost with friends, they lack confidence to continue their education, and consequently have poorer life-chances. As Kennedy (1997), discussing wider access to continuing education, put it succinctly, 'If at first you don't succeed, you don't succeed'. Education itself is a strong incentive for recovery but even for those who do not recover, continuing education improves the quality of life (see Chapter 12).

The Government's vision of excellence of education for all children (DfEE 1997) must apply equally to sick children. But, despite sterling efforts by many teachers, the truth is that the quality of education for sick children remains patchy and inconsistent.

Bolton's (1997) report provided compelling evidence that education for sick children is a way of retrieving normal life, a confidence booster, a distraction from pain, fear and loneliness and a support in coming to terms with life-threatening illness and altered futures. Without maintenance of educational and social continuity with their 'home' schools, sick children are at risk, at least as much as other children who also experience educational discontinuity – excludees, homeless children, looked-after children, Romany travellers, Forces children, young carers, and refugees. Sick children are doubly disadvantaged – first by ill health and then by the loss of their full educational entitlement. Flexible quality education for sick children may provide models for others experiencing discontinuity in learning.

Children who have experienced illness during their primary education may need to make up basic skills during secondary education. They may also have had little science, technology and other subjects in which hospital teachers and home tutors lack the knowledge, skills, and appropriate resources and contexts for teaching. Those who become ill in their adolescent years can miss units of work which may preclude them from assessment for recognised qualifications or they may under-perform, damaging their future educational and employment prospects and self-confidence. Good quality, well-supported distance or tutored open learning would improve their achievements and opportunities.

Entitlement to education for sick children

The Education Acts (1981), England and Wales and (1980) Scotland, related special educational needs to the learning difficulties experienced by children of the same age and to disabilities. Chapter 1 of this book sets out children's entitlements to education and argues strongly that children with medical needs do indeed have learning difficulties and that some are additionally disabled so should be covered by arrangements for pupils with special educational needs.

Some teachers make allowances for 'struggling' sick children affected by absence or fatigue by lowering performance expectations. This 'benevolence' is actually a hazard because education missed is rarely made up without specific intervention. Other pupils appear to cope, but actually are struggling with problems, often associated with previous discontinuity in learning.

The vast and increasing majority of children with medical needs attend mainstream schools, with some who have more pronounced, specific and complex difficulties attending special schools or units. When they are absent, their education ideally will be addressed by their usual school in flexible collaboration with hospital or home tuition services to provide an appropriate, continuous and differentiated educational programme in hospital, at home, or at school.

Inclusion of sick children in the statutory duty imposed on local education authorities by the Education Act (1993) England and Wales, to provide 'suitable education' for all children who are not attending school (see Chapter 1), was a step forward. However, although the law defined 'suitable education' as 'efficient education suitable to (the child's) age, ability and aptitude and to any special educational needs he may have', there is no definition in the law or in the official guidance in *Circular 12/94* (DfE 1994), or *Circular 14/96* (DfEE 1996b), or the *Good Practice Guide: Supporting Pupils with Medical Needs* (DfEE 1996a), as to what actually constitutes adequate discharge of this duty. How much education is 'adequate and efficient'? What are the starting time margins for teaching during absence? What qualifications should teachers have, particularly for secondary age pupils? What, in short, can be offered as standards for high quality appropriate out-of-school education?

Education remains at risk for approximately 10 per cent of children (BPA 1995) who have medical conditions which affect their everyday functioning and, by implication, aspects of their education. Schools, therefore, need to be sure that their special educational needs/Support for Learning policy specifically addresses the health-related learning needs of affected pupils. The policy needs associated administrative procedures to track pupils' education in school and when absent, to identify curricular shortfall and to outline a plan to make good lost time as far as possible. One of the duties of the SENCO in England and Wales is to maintain a register of pupils with special educational needs and to draw the attention of school managers and governors to their specific requirements. The SENCO and the school policies are therefore key to quality education for children with medical needs.

Education Authority provision in England and Wales includes hospital schools for in-patients, hospital classes, tuition centres outside hospitals and schools, and peripatetic home tuition services. Such provision for sick children may be part of an authority-wide service for all children who are out of school, or outreach services from an integrated hospital/home education service, or simply teachers employed on an hourly basis as need arises. Provision costs vary according to pupil numbers and the policies of education and health authorities. However, all such expenditure is additional to that provided to mainstream schools. Since the duty is the authority's, ensuring that budgets are adequate to meet it should also be the authority's concern. In practice, busy and relatively powerless teachers may find they have to be the budgetary defenders and agitators.

Recently, the concept of 'integration' has evolved to become Government-endorsed 'inclusion' (DfEE 1997). This impacts directly on pupils with medical needs, wherever educated. Schools in England and Wales are now explicitly required to consider the learning needs of sick children on their rolls, whether present or absent. Advice and training has increasingly been made available to many, but not all, teachers through a combination of voluntary and statutory sector resources. Many schools are ready to draft supportive policies to meet the needs of sick children.

Quality provision for sick children

The problems experienced by sick children are known to families, hospital teachers and home tutors. Less known is what actually constitutes quality educational provision for sick children. One role of NAESC (see Tait, Chapter 6) has been to investigate practice and disseminate this information throughout the system. Good services must be planned and delivered to reflect our beliefs about rights and opportunities for pupils with medical needs. NAESC sets out ten principles to guide all educational services for sick children.

A quality service is one which:

1. values the child as an individual with a full entitlement to a broad, balanced, differentiated curriculum;
2. aims to develop the skills and abilities that underpin effective learning for the child in the contexts of home, school and hospital;
3. aims to design, deliver and assess a learning programme which is based on the unique needs of each individual (IEP);
4. aims to help the individual child use a variety of services and resources available in the community to support their individual learning programme, e.g. the media, health, social, library, careers, recreational and welfare services;
5. aims to meet special needs arising from disabilities by means of locally coordinated, multidisciplinary specialist services delivered in the home, school or community by appropriately trained staff;

6. is easily accessible without the complexity of a Statement of Special Educational Needs/Record of Needs and delivered conveniently when the child can make most effective use of it;

7. plans actively for young people to return from a period of hospitalisation to timely and appropriate provision at home or at school;

8. is delivered to a child's home or school as required by the IEP and with account taken of the medical needs of the child;

9. uses modern information and communications technology and encourages sharing of curriculum information with the child, the family and the hospital and mainstream school;

10. is staffed by locally-based teachers who are available to visit children and young people in their own home, in hospital or at school;

Given these principles, quality services for sick children take shape more clearly. This is important. If the aims of education authorities, schools and hospital services are not explicit they cannot evaluate effectiveness. Consideration of existing provision in the light of the ten principles is enabling the NAESC to identify worthwhile and interesting practice to act as exemplars for education providers.

Aspects of quality evaluation

How can we evaluate the quality of services in order to sustain and develop further what is good and improve what is not? Quality assurance is not a new concept. Registered hospital schools in England and Wales are subject to inspection by the Office for Standards in Education (OFSTED), as are all mainstream and special schools. One immediate improvement would be to extend the OFSTED inspection framework to include local authority tuition units and services currently outside their remit, and to ensure that equivalent processes are in place in other parts of the UK. There should be performance criteria relevant to services for sick children, as recommended at NAESC's conference on inspection issues and standards setting (NAESC 1997b).

The important role of hospital schools and hospital-based teaching, and the specialist knowledge of teachers working in them, must be safeguarded. However, with fewer children actually becoming in-patients and hospital stays reducing in length for many children, there is increasing emphasis on home and sometimes special centre teaching. Services for out-of-school and peripatetic teaching are increasingly being reorganised into larger generic services, in theory offering greater flexibility and range of skills in staff and opportunities for mutual support and staff development. However, authorities need to be aware of the risk that specialist knowledge and in-depth understanding of children in specific situations may be dissipated and devalued unless well managed and supported.

Availability is an aspect of quality. Some authorities and schools provide an excellent hospital education and home tuition service but, intentionally or otherwise, limit its accessibility, or widen its accessibility by reducing contact hours. Nationally, the picture illustrated in the NAESC *Directory of Current Provision* (NAESC 1995, 1997a, 1998) is one of patchy teaching provision with marked inconsistency in procedures, costs, and level and length of time of tuition. These inconsistencies are a product of inadequate management and resourcing at authority level, emphatically not because of tailoring provision to individual pupils.

Teaching time lost to children through significant absence must be quantified and missed content detailed. Subjects taught and evidence of pupil learning in education contexts outside the 'home school' must be recorded and communicated to the school. A named person in the home school should be responsible for ensuring the continuity of education for every sick child. Plainly, this means collaborative planning, not simply transferring information.

Hospital and home teaching services need to use a consistent method for registering sick children. Statistics on sick children, including those from Health Authorities, are, at best, estimates. If records of absence through ill-health at children's home schools were to be collected and combined with the records of alternative services a clearer picture of provision and the gaps in it may emerge. National education census systems could also address this on at least an occasional basis.

To be effective, learning programmes must harmonise with the country-relevant curriculum framework and every sick pupil must be subject to the same assessment arrangements as their peers. Arrangements made by examining bodies already incorporate procedures for non-standard entrants and those with special requirements. These should be reviewed in the context of the needs of young people with medical needs. A strategy for students working at home to submit coursework and examination entries electronically should be developed.

The introduction of individual learning accounts in England and Wales, proposed by the National Campaign for Lifelong Learning, may be one way to make sick children eligible for home tuition and further and higher education, and to provide essential information technology equipment and distance learning courses.

The educational content of provision for young people 16–19 and beyond is of the greatest importance, but of even greater importance is the issue of educational entitlement for these young people (see Tait, Chapter 6). Second chance post-school education is a necessity for these students to catch up on missed learning. New communication technologies are set now in a revolution of learning to offer a second chance to these students. The National Grid for Learning and associated developments should rapidly open up the horizons for young people with special learning needs. Continuity for individual students can be maintained and missed education can be made up at a later date at home, at college or even in the workplace.

To take advantage of new communication technologies, hospital teaching and home tuition services must also move quickly to establish policies and plans for managing an integrated virtual learning environment. Educational excellence in these services is more likely to depend on effective innovation in the provision and management of new technology than any other factor.

Conclusion

Putting these ideas into practice is, of course, a significant challenge for educators at all service levels. There could be considerable advantage in interested professionals piloting an approach within their own areas of concern and responsibility. Starting in small ways and learning from experience it is possible to build up a powerful and widespread commitment to quality and entitlement and access for all sick children.

A period of serious illness may be frightening, debilitating and lonely, but it can also be an opportunity to continue learning and to develop new interests and skills, provided quality education services are available.

CHAPTER 12

More like a friend: case studies of working in wards and at home with children with a poor prognosis

Ann Burnett

Counselling has its beginnings, both historically as an emerging discipline and daily as a popular activity, in many different professions. It fills the gap between psychotherapy and friendship, and it has become a recognised extension of the work of almost everyone whose business touches upon the personal, social, occupational, medical, educational and spiritual aspects of people. Because, like Topsy, it just grew, because it falls as much within the province of bringing on the already well-functioning as that of diminishing distress, and because it refers to people who are counsellors and others who apply counselling skills as they deem appropriate, there is no unified concept of its work.

(Noonan 1983, p. vii)

Introduction

I am employed as the senior teacher for a city Hospital and Home Teaching Service. The children I work with come mainly under the Oncology, Haematology and Neurology specialities in the hospital. Children in the Oncology and Haematology wards have usually been diagnosed with cancer, leukaemia or other blood disorders. Children with brain tumours, epilepsy or brain injury are admitted to the Neurology ward.

When I came into this job eight years ago I came from a background of primary teaching followed by learning support. While this background went some way to prepare me for my role as a hospital and home teacher for ill children, by far the most important experience I brought to the job was that of being the mother of a child who for most of her childhood years was chronically ill. This did not automatically make me an expert but it gave me valuable insights into the dynamics of families with chronically ill children, the main one being that nothing can be taken for granted and that one should never presume to understand the depth of feelings involved in these situations.

I quickly realised that, as an institution, a hospital is not geared to creating a learning environment for children. Overall, the focus is on the physical or mental health of the patient and the educational dimension is of secondary importance. As a result of this overall strategy, education is generally quite low on the priority scale. Despite this I have found that when my contribution is recognised to be part of the overall treatment and care of the child, others concerned with his or her treatment will make an effort to cooperate and are willing to be flexible and where possible draw up a timetable. When working with children in the home environment, which has its own stresses and strains, I found the setting to be much more conducive to learning and less distracting.

My primary role within the hospital and home is that of teacher. This can be understood as being largely the same as that of any teacher in mainstream or special school, primary and secondary. Within this role it has always been part of my professional understanding that there is an element of counselling. Good teachers acknowledge that they are trying to develop the whole person and in so doing need to respond to the needs of the whole person. Any child who is upset or anxious is clearly not in a learning frame of mind and it is important that these other issues are dealt with adequately. Within the hospital context the 'other issues' can be of crucial importance to the sick child's total well-being.

In this regard it is important that I know something of their medical details and treatment and, in particular, any side effects. Often the child that I meet is behaving in ways that are alien to him or her and that are caused by the drugs he or she is receiving. Clearly this can be a source of much distress to the child and to her or his parents and it is essential that I do not compound the situation because of a lack of information. It is also important to acknowledge that, while all the children I work with are either in hospital for a specific medical condition or at home because of their health, and the priority is to treat this condition, treatment is not always possible:

> there is still a limit to what can be achieved by even the most skilled and dedicated doctors and nurses. Counsellors who work with sick children need to be aware of this, and able to offer help on the basis of reality, rather than through false hopes and false expectations.
> (Campion 1991, p. 72)

My initial approach to child and parents can be difficult because parents of a newly-diagnosed child may often be very protective and even hostile. This can be one of the most challenging aspects of my work. In later discussion with parents many have said they did not want anyone other than medical or nursing staff near their child but only as time progressed, and the initial shock wore off, did they realise the value of what they saw as non-medical agencies. I have to be able to gauge when it is right to introduce schoolwork and for weeks it may be a case of just popping in for a chat until I feel we have a relationship based on trust.

This hostility is juxtaposed with the fact that parents and patients often perceive me, 'the teacher', as the sign of hope – the link with that world to which the child and family belonged before the child became ill, and the bridge to that world should the child once again become 'normal' and return to mainstream schooling.

The following case studies are listed in chronological order. This chronology is an important factor in my development as a hospital/home teacher as each child that I dealt with added to my knowledge and highlighted areas within my personal and professional life that I needed to develop.

Case studies

Sam

Sam was one of my first pupils with a life-threatening disease and it would be true to say I learnt more from Sam and his family than Sam ever learnt from me. I first met Sam in a busy medical ward where he was beginning to require more frequent admissions to hospital to treat his cystic fibrosis. His attendance at school had been erratic for a while and he had little interest in pursuing his schoolwork while in hospital. Each day brought a strengthening of his resolve not to cooperate and I was perplexed. What had happened to my teacher's authority? Here was I, confronted by a small seven-year-old boy who managed with stubborn resistance to confound any approaches I made. Eventually I came to realise that, in order to pursue my educational aim, I had to enter his world; I could not presume on the 'normal' teacher–pupil relationship. For any professional, to be stripped of all conventional roles is to be left feeling very exposed and vulnerable. Initially, I found it difficult to allow myself time just to be with Sam. I worried how this would be perceived by others; was I trying to justify time-wasting? This was my first lesson.

During these sessions I began to see Sam as a child, a human being in his own right, learning not to define him in terms of his illness. Gradually, Sam and his mum and dad came to trust me and we were able to start schoolwork. At this point it was very important that I liaised closely with his school. It was important to Sam that he was doing the same as his friends in school, although he loved it when I was able to tell him we were actually ahead in some areas of the curriculum. It became clear Sam would not be returning to school and would have to receive teaching at home. I knew then I could not rest on my laurels if I was to be Sam's sole teacher on a long-term basis. I was Sam's home teacher for two and a half years and during this time I became one of the few professionals who had sustained contact with the whole family. I became quite simply more like a friend, while still remaining, if not a teacher, then an educator. At some indefinable point our sessions changed from being curriculum-led to child-led; English became the time when we worked on Sam's autobiography and this also crossed over into using information technology.

Through our chats I discovered Sam had some questions he wanted answered. These questions became the vehicle by which we pursued environmental studies. One of our last projects before Sam's death was to find out how a local biscuit factory managed to get chocolate in the middle of an enclosed biscuit. We organised a visit to the factory; the execution of this visit entailed detailed planning. A nurse had to be organised, portable oxygen ordered, and a car big enough had to be found which could accommodate his electric wheelchair. The day the visit was to be made, Sam developed a severe chest infection and the visit had to be cancelled. His disappointment was crushing and it was hard to know what to say to him. As I was trying to distract him, the managing director and personnel manager of the factory arrived with assorted biscuits and proceeded to explain to a delighted Sam exactly how their biscuits were made.

I don't think these people really realised what they had done for us all. They had acknowledged a child's right to learn no matter what his condition. For his parents these people's presence in their home meant that, even though Sam was approaching death, other people also valued their son and thought it important that he continue in the learning process. As a teacher, I felt affirmed in the importance of my work with chronically ill children. Sam died ten days later.

James

James was a five-year-old boy with a life-threatening illness. His treatment was severe, painful and prolonged. He was in hospital for 18 months with rare visits home. James' problems were compounded by his behaviour as an elective mute. When anyone entered his cubicle he adopted a closed tense position. To work with James I had to begin to take on board what he was going through, to try and feel empathy with his dilemma and to understand what had brought him to this point. I was helped in this respect by an article by Buck (1988) in which she looked at the likely causes of 'elective mutism'. She quoted Gemelli (1983) who said that 'every child has a threshold of how much tension and anxiety the child can tolerate and still be able to speak', and Halpern (1971) who said 'it is not so much the power of speech as the power of silence or retention with which the affected child controls an unfamiliar world'.

In this case I had a three-fold strategy:

- to gain his and his mother's trust
- to help the child explore and make sense of his environment
- to encourage speech in all situations, bearing in mind that I could help him whether he talked or not, by establishing other means of contact and communication.

Working with his mother proved to be easier than I thought it would be as she was grateful that I felt it was important that her son continue with his education despite his poor prognosis. From a more practical point of view, she appreciated the break she could take from the pressurised environment of the isolation cubicle when I arrived.

Initially, making contact with James was hard going. I had to enter into his world and try to listen attentively to all his messages while being very careful not to impose my own viewpoint. I had to learn to interpret minimal inclinations of the head and slight gestures and eventually after many sessions I was rewarded with 'yes' or 'no'. To arrive at this stage, all sorts of media were used, including storybooks, pictures and computer. In this particular case my computer provided the vehicle by which he decided to communicate. As he was often too ill to sit up, we would both lie on his bed with my laptop perched precariously on a box between us.

Initially, we looked at Disney characters with a wide range of facial expressions, angry, happy, sad, and so on. In response to my asking which one did he feel like today, he would point one out, usually angry, sad or frightened. From there we would write a short story under the characters' pictures such as 'All doctors watch out, I feel really mad today!' After printing out several copies James would give one to his mum, stick one up on his window and give one out with a contemptuous look to any medic who annoyed him that day. These pictures and stories became the vehicles through which James re-engaged with the world, setting up a dialogue as nurses, doctors and physiotherapists would comment on them. James would respond usually monosyllabically but this was still a giant leap for him and as time went on he progressed to reading his stories to people.

Sadly, James' condition did not improve and he was given months to live. His mother still wanted me to visit, feeling that my visits gave a structure to his day that was not purely orientated towards medical care. Physically, James was able to do less and less but he was very mentally alert. I had kept a record of all his work in a folder and he loved to look through it and show it to visitors. As he deteriorated we would look through his favourite categories of clipart on the computer, usually cars, lorries and buses. He would indicate his favourite picture of the day. I would print it out and James would tell me whom it was for and, if he was able, he would write 'from James' on the bottom. If James had been able to rationalise it I am sure he would have said he was giving a gift to those who loved him so they would have something to remember him by.

After James' funeral his mum said she found having a record of James' work a great comfort. It was proof that James had existed and had left something of himself behind.

Robert

Not all children express their anxiety as forcibly as James. In my next case study the child presented as a sociable boy who seemed to have become accustomed to illness and treatment. He had had several months of chemotherapy followed by a bone marrow transplant and whole-body radiation (Faulkner *et al.* 1995).

Always classed as a 'good boy' by staff, very compliant, no arguments, he would settle down to schoolwork with no grumbles. His parents expressed fears that he was 'not the same child as before'; they referred to his previous liveliness and sense of humour. They had mentioned their concern to the medical staff but did not pursue it as their immediate concern was for his possible recovery. In some ways he was easier to deal with while more subdued. I covered nearly the whole range of the curriculum and introduced the idea of a Hospital Diary to chronicle what was happening to him and how he felt about it. While respecting his right to privacy, I felt as Campion (1991):

> One of the most difficult aspects of working with children who are living in situations from which they cannot escape is that of respecting the child's privacy and his own efforts to cope with a situation he cannot change. On the one hand, we are aware of the value of talking about one's fears and anxieties; on the other it may be more comfortable not to talk, or to even think, about certain painful realities. (pp. 72–3)

He began to communicate his fears through the diary. Initially, the stories were about a friend who was always in trouble and who became very ill. As we talked about his stories it transpired that he believed that if he was good and did as he was told he would get well again and treatment would stop. This idea was constantly being reinforced by others describing him as a 'good little boy'. Within his frame of reference he equated 'being good' with adopting a passive and accepting role.

Through his diary we were able to explore his fears and anxieties (Varma 1984). As we developed, using his diary, his stories became direct and pointed about his feelings. He was adamant he would never go back to school while bald, as he worried about other children's reactions. Using the computer, we kept up a regular correspondence with his class. Initially, he was fearful of discussing aspects of his illness, especially his hair loss. As he began to regain his sense of humour he would tell them in graphic detail how many times he had been sick, where he had been sick and on whom he had been sick.

Eventually, he described his hair loss, enclosing a drawing of himself. The responses came by return of post: What had he done with his hair? Was his head cold? Would he get a wig? One child wanted some for a collage he was making. After this response he decided he would go on a short visit with me, but he would wear his hat and not take it off. As we approached the classroom I was struck by this small boy's courage in facing up to his greatest fear. He was in the classroom for two minutes when the hat came off, prompting a barrage of questions from his classmates. He declared that he could only answer one question at a time, so would they please put their hands up. On our return to hospital he couldn't wait to tell the staff that, since his class knew nothing about leukaemia, he would have to write a leaflet for them. He was doubly pleased to find out he was ahead in his maths and that none of his class could match his skills in computing. From this point things went smoothly; I continued teaching him at hospital and at home until, after completion of his treatment, he was successfully reintegrated into his class.

Sarah

Sarah was a five-year-old girl with leukaemia still on treatment when she started school. Three months after starting school there were some cases of chickenpox in the school. This meant Sarah had to stay at home as the effect of chickenpox on a suppressed immune system can have very serious consequences. When the school was eventually clear of infection Sarah had been off school for four months. Her mum took her back to school and Sarah became extremely distressed, screaming and clinging onto her mum. This went on for three weeks with no improvement of the situation. The oncology liaison nurse asked if Sarah could meanwhile have home teaching in the hope that eventually we could persuade her back into the class.

Whatever was wrong did not affect Sarah's attitude to learning and she was a keen and diligent pupil. We formed a relaxed and friendly relationship. She looked forward to my visits almost as much as I did to making them. Her mum and dad were very young and the family unit was loving and supportive, but the school situation was causing a great deal of anxiety. In an effort to understand Sarah's perspective I visited the class teacher. I found her to be enthusiastic and willing to make any effort to welcome Sarah back into the class. As time went by I worked closely with the class teacher. Sarah and I worked along the same lines as her class, involving her in special events such as Red Nose Day. When the class went on outings, Sarah and I went too and had lots of fun. The only place we couldn't get her was back into the classroom. Once again a child was confounding me. We had long chats about the class, about her feelings, about how it was time to return to school, but when the time came the same behaviour presented itself. I decided to take time out from 'talking about' the problem and each visit now took the form of schoolwork followed by little gossip sessions. I shared a little of my life and told her tales about my children, and Sarah in turn talked about the baby her mum was expecting, her cousins and various family escapades.

What became clear was that Sarah loved to chat but never in these chats did the subject of her illness or treatment arise. It did not seem to be a 'block', for when I brought it up it was acknowledged but she would soon move on to other topics. This little girl was trying to tell me she was more than her illness, she had a life other than her treatment. But what bearing did this have on her extreme reluctance to return to school? I began to wonder if perhaps she felt regarded as 'the leukaemia girl', 'the bald girl' in her class, when all she wanted to be was 'an ordinary girl'.

With her parents' agreement I decided to broach the subject of changing school and repeating her first year. To everyone's astonishment Sarah thought it was a wonderful idea. After consulting with her class teacher we decided to go ahead with finding her a new school. Within a fortnight she was settled successfully in a new class. The whole process took nine months.

Again the lesson was reinforced that children and their lives need to be regarded in their own right and not be defined merely by their illness.

Saima

My next case study shows the importance of the school maintaining contact and encouraging peer contact for a child with a prolonged illness.

Saima was a fourteen-year-old Asian girl admitted to the Neurology ward. Her symptoms proved difficult to diagnose but it became clear that her hospital stay would be a prolonged one. I passed her on to my secondary colleagues but maintained daily contact.

Saima made few demands on staff and was always pleasant and uncomplaining. My colleagues informed me that she was working well, work had been sent in from school and she was enjoying the stimulation. Homework was always done and the ward staff would often help in the evenings. I had mentioned to the school that it would be positive if they could organise some sort of correspondence and perhaps a visit or two to Saima, but the end of term was approaching and, with one thing or another, nothing materialised, nobody came.

On our return after the summer holidays we discovered Saima's condition had worsened to the point where she could only move the fingers on her right hand. She communicated via a keyboard; my secondary colleagues continued to work with her, adapting their approach to suit her physical condition. Again we contacted her school, but it was the beginning of a new session and things were hectic. Before anything was organised Saima died very suddenly. The last piece of personal writing she had done on the keyboard with her English teacher three days before read, 'I am very afraid I may die but what upsets me the most is that no-one from my school has written or been to visit me, I feel I don't matter'.

Perceptions and conflicts

My experience in my work situation has led me to an awareness of conflict within my dual role, that of teacher–counsellor. A teacher is often perceived as having an authoritative role by herself, child, parents, and other professionals. A counsellor must, as Wolff (1976) states, be willing to be open to all possibilities:

> empathic understanding of the child, is . . . sometimes hard to grasp for people such as teachers and nurses who are accustomed to an authoritative role in relation to children. It means that in a treatment setting the adult gives up the notion that he knows better than the child what the matter is and how it must be put right. (pp. 227–8)

Consequently, I feel I have developed a child-centred approach to my work, beginning with the view as expressed by Crompton (1992), 'A childist counsellor would begin with the idea of a child of whatever age being a complete person rather than an immature version of the adult he/she would become.' (p. 5)

I do not, of course, deal with a child in isolation – parents and family, medical and nursing staff are also part of the package. Nursing staff react differently, many believing that I should be fulfilling the traditional authoritative role, telling children, for example, 'Here comes the teacher, she'll soon sort you out', while others are happy to be involved in the educational process. Both staff and parents bring to this encounter their own perceptions of the teacher based on their own personal history.

I have to take into account the differing expectations of all those above and also take on board the expectations of my employer. It took a long time to come to terms with the 'guilt' of not spending every moment teaching and to realise the necessity of my counselling approach.

Conclusion

From my experience I have been confirmed in my belief that, as an educationalist, I must also fulfil the role of counsellor. Within my work situation I am continually faced with the need to seek strategies which enable the child to re-engage in the learning process. To engage with the child one must engage with the family.

Adults often believe that it is in 'the child's best interest' to withhold information or to pretend that everything is normal. This can generate mistrust, shame, fear or feelings of being out of control or of not being valued as he or she actually is. Throughout childhood, communication skills are being developed and expanded but it is difficult for some children to find words adequate to express their feelings in particular. This inability of children sometimes to express their feelings is taken to indicate indifference, acceptance or a lack of need to talk about what has happened to them. This can be compounded in the hospital context by all the stresses and strains that being outside their normal environment brings, but I believe as Wolff (1976) expresses:

> We have been afraid to look in case what we see is more than we can bear. Yet our fears may be to a large extent irrational. Human beings, especially children, are resilient. They have capacities for coping with adversity that often surprise us. But unless we look, we shall not know what these strengths are nor how best to help children to make the most effective use of them. (p. 70)

CHAPTER 13

Schools and death

Oliver Leaman

Introduction

This chapter is divided into four sections: death and loss within the curriculum, teaching children who have life-threatening or terminal conditions (this section also touches on cultural and religious issues), responding to classroom questions and challenges about death, and coping with the death of a pupil. I hope that it offers a reflective progression of ideas which will help teachers in particular to cope sensitively with death in relation to their pupils and their families, and to their colleagues and themselves.

Death and loss within the curriculum

It is often said that we are a death-denying society. When I started researching how teachers deal with death in schools (Leaman 1995), I was told that this was a topic of little interest. Often when I told the head teacher about my interest, he or she would say this was not a concern in that school. Yet, after a short time in most schools, teachers would talk at length about death, as though it did really interest and concern them. This is hardly surprising. Death and loss are inevitable facts of life, and issues relating to them will constantly arise in a direct way in every school, whether it takes the form of friends leaving school, parents divorcing and unsurprising deaths of pupils' grandparents or ageing pets, or in traumatic incidents of accidental or 'premature' deaths of public figures. Even if teachers and pupils have no very close experience of death, they do know loss, and recognise death as an essential aspect of human life, and they will have formulated some concepts.

Before we discuss the curriculum appropriate to children with life-threatening conditions, let us look briefly at the curriculum for children in general in Britain. Actually, there is really no such thing as 'British' education, since the constituent countries of the UK have significant differences in their schooling processes. With respect to death, though, there is commonality in the countrywide tendency for death not to feature significantly in the curricula. Researchers exploring this issue expect that in Northern Ireland this might be different, given the long history of violence and murder there. Yet there is nothing specifically done on the topic in most Northern Irish schools. For one thing, most of these schools are denominational, i.e. either Roman Catholic or Church of Ireland – and so find scope within their religious education framework to refer to and make sense of death and loss as they occur in pupils' experience. Secondly, and importantly for our further discussion, there is a feeling in Northern Ireland that education should be as 'normal' as possible despite, or perhaps because of, the unusual conditions under which many people live. Third, there is a common perception that death is essentially a private matter confined to the boundaries of the family concerned and their closest friends.

There is then very little mention of death in the curricula of the UK. I have argued that this is because teachers feel uncomfortable discussing the topic, since teachers, as an occupational group, base their working practices around the idea of life following a regular pattern, preferably an upward incline of aspiration and achievement, so that physical or cognitive deterioration, or early death, are anomalies or contraflows with which it is difficult to deal. Also, middle-class teachers tend to be more risk-averse than their working-class pupils, and so they may also find it more difficult to connect with and communicate about the beliefs and attitudes of their pupils around smoking, substance abuse and dangerous physical pursuits which may lead to death. Teachers, in common with a large proportion of the population, find illness and death troubling, not only to face in their own lives, but to think about in any depth at all. As topics, they present human beings with huge moral, intellectual and practical challenges. Finally, death as a topic does not find a clear single locus in the curriculum.

Looking at the curriculum, death could variously be included in the sciences – especially biology – religious and moral education, and the social subjects – especially history and literature. Most often, if addressed at all, it may be consigned to Personal and Social Education, quite appropriately if treated in a child-centred and individually sensitive and exploratory manner. Activities which build 'classroom communities,' such as circle time, may also provide a framework. In theory at least, it could be treated permeatively or opportunistically throughout the curriculum, yet there is no widespread developed strategy about how to deal with this topic, despite some very useful written guides (Ward 1989, Leaman 1995, Phillips 1996, Brown 1999, see also Chapter 15). One might think this strange, since the one thing that everyone will do is die, and children as well as adults may be able to live their lives more fully if they are able to acknowledge and address the reality of death and loss in their own lives and those of others. The existence of an already over-full curriculum only partly explains the absence of death and loss within it but cannot really excuse it. More needs to be done.

Teaching children who have life-threatening or terminal conditions

Working with children who have conditions which may reduce their life expectancy offers challenges to teachers, nowhere more obviously than in relation to death – both as it may appear within the formal or informal curriculum and in relation to the children's own deaths. Teachers need to be able to address these challenges positively and sensitively, to be able to listen to and work with *all* children in their classes, including those with life-threatening conditions and with their families. They need to be able to do this without distress or offence to anyone, including themselves, and to know how far their involvement in this area is helpful and how far it is not. Burnett (Chapter 12) writes about working as a teacher with children who are very seriously ill and being taught within the context of a hospital or at home. She also speaks about the merging of the roles of teacher and counsellor in these contexts. Such depth of contact is not feasible for most school teachers because of their responsibilities for teaching so many other children, and also because of insufficient training and time. This section of my chapter is more about children who are within mainstream and special schools.

A special curriculum for 'special pupils'?

Death is for most of us quite a frightening fact of being alive, and yet it is not expected to be imminent. Like the bill at the end of a meal, we can enjoy the meal while knowing that at some point it will have to be paid for. Some diners will find their enjoyment of the meal is spoiled by the thought of the bill, while others will ignore the bill until it is presented. Most will accept the fact of the eventual bill, but not allow it to interfere with the pleasure of eating. But there are some who are in the position of the apparently insolvent diner to whom the management constantly shows the bill. Children with life-threatening conditions are in this position: they are frequently reminded by things and events around them of the omnipresence of death.

Should death and loss be part of their curriculum, as I have argued for the general population of children? One might think not, since they have enough to put up with without such reminders. On the other hand, many will be very aware of death, of their own death. They may already perceive it in their own symptoms, serious episodes of illness and in discussions around them. Children, including very young children, are much more perceptive than many adults believe. They may be saddened, depressed, angry, frightened, resigned, or a combination of all these, because of their realisation.

We should not therefore devise a curriculum which disproportionately emphasises death, but neither should we avoid the topic because of a child or children in class with a life-threatening condition. Many of those involved with these youngsters (Eiser 1993, Closs and Burnett 1995) report that the best thing about education for them is its 'normalising' effect: it creates a space which can be outside their illness, in a sense, and offers some equity with their peers. This would suggest that the 'normal' curriculum should be followed.

However, an important difference between children with life-threatening conditions and other children is that the former have a life span which is likely to be limited by contrast with the norm. Education for them may not result in employment, graduation or the achievement of other societal expectations. For many teachers who plan and teach towards such ends this is difficult to accept, especially when some children may actually regress educationally, and achievements may be 'lost'.

We must, therefore, identify aims which do not require such ends if teachers are to feel as motivated in their work with these children. There is a lot of evidence that such children do get a lot out of education. They can enjoy the discipline attached to it, the fact that they feel connected to reality by the routine, the opportunity it affords for peer company, the achievement of tasks which are appropriate to their current abilities and which draw on the same range of subjects and topics as their peers. It is not just a matter of pleasure, but of effective learning. Through learning they satisfy many of the real purposes of education, one of which is to introduce children to some of the key ideas and practices of our culture. It is not relevant how long a child may live, or whether his cognitive and emotional achievements and skills go into decline at some point. 'Lost' achievements are still very real at the time they are achieved.

The right to a broad and balanced curriculum within the various frameworks in the UK is the right of each individual child. In so far, then, as death is introduced as a topic within the curriculum for other children, it should also be there for children with life-threatening conditions, but with no additional expectation on any pupil to make more contributions than they freely offer. Contributions made by any child must be listened to seriously and accorded respect – always easier in a class and school where a positive ethos of valuing diversity and the contributions of all is already established.

Teachers' needs

It is still difficult for many teachers to accept that for some children continual improvement will not take place. A teacher in a mainstream school showed me a series of videos which included a child with a deteriorating condition, and it was clear that over a period of time there had been significant regression in learning. This was particularly upsetting to the teacher since the pupil had progressed well in the first few years at school. It is easy for teachers to say that they must take one day at a time, accepting progress and regression, but it is not so easy to do. It may be particularly problematic to mainstream teachers for whom it may be an unexpected 'one-off' situation. They need support (see Chapters 8 and 15) if they are to remain confident and motivated.

Teachers in some special schools for children with complex learning difficulties or for children with physical and medical needs are more experienced in the difficulties involved. They understand better that what looks like a setback or 'plateau' may still really be a significant achievement for a particular child. Yet for them, too, it may be difficult to accept learning losses, lowered pupil and family morale, and their own feelings of impotence.

There may also be issues about children's motivation and questions of discipline. Children with serious conditions, like any others, may consciously or unconsciously behave in ways which are aimed at getting what they want. While this could be seen positively as assertive normality, teachers may feel torn between maintaining the class's behavioural norms and making special concessions – 'making it up to them' – because of the teachers' own feelings of sadness about the child's prognosis. Teachers must assert the class behavioural norms but must also make allowances for real individual differences in energy levels, learning capacity and emotional responses to stress by adjusting the nature of learning tasks and teaching strategies. Making 'unfair' disciplinary concessions can lead to peer rejection (Norris and Closs 1999).

Some well-motivated teachers may become depressed when children with advanced conditions themselves appear to give up. A teacher, Margaret, had in her class a pupil, John, with a virulent form of leukaemia. Although he was often absent in hospital for treatment, Margaret enjoyed working with him, watching him being as naughty as the other children. When his condition worsened and it seemed clear he would not be much longer in school, he became pliable and obedient. Margaret commented:

> It looked as though all the fight had been knocked out of him somehow. When I told the class what I wanted them to do he just picked up his books and sighed and got on with it. Now, if that had happened to the other pupils I would have thought, 'That's great, they are knuckling down to their work'. But I knew that was not the case with him; he'd just had enough and was going to agree with everything. It was a terrible moment.

Personal issues for children with life-threatening conditions

A range of quite personal issues may arise in special or mainstream schools.

Identity

Children with serious medical conditions may often be confused about aspects of their identity. Any child may be confused, of course, but their points of confusion may be less complex and sensitive. For most children there are role models, of how people change and what they become, available through the media, their relatives and all those adults and older children who are 'significant others' for the child. There are very few role models for seriously ill children, and those which exist are often stereotypical or 'unreal'. This is also true of literature. Phillips (1996) provides some helpful advice on reading for children in general.

There are apparently relevant incidents in UK and Australian soap operas, watched by children widely, yet there is something inherently 'unreal' and sensational in much of what is shown. In programmes such as *Grange Hill,* characters with illness and disability do feature, and this is helpful, more so than series such as *Children's Hospital* and *Children's Ward. Children's Hospital* tends towards sentimentality, emphasising the sudden changes in children's medical conditions in hospital, but does not show the more tedious and normal interludes. *Children's Ward* is more successful in portraying ill children as not entirely powerless and dependent on others but actually quite able to be manipulative and naughty. This programme is quite useful in helping ill children find an image of their condition in the media, although they comment on how the most unpleasant and boring aspects of life in hospital or at home recuperating are missing.

However, as one fourteen-year-old with heart disease said to me when I was discussing this:

> It does not matter that there are not children with my sort of illness on the telly, since there are not many ordinary children on the telly anyway; they are all so good-looking and have such interesting lives that even well children must find them unrealistic. In the same way that ordinary children must enjoy watching perfect and interesting lives, so do I. I don't want to see children who are like me all the time. We deserve a bit of fantasy also. Actually, perhaps we deserve it more.

Culture and religion

The multiple layers of influences on culture, especially as we move from the national to regional, local and family contexts and consider the diversity of the population within the UK, can create uncertainty of thought and action in teachers, however great their wish to promote and value diversity. Death as a topic within the curriculum and the presence of children with life-threatening conditions may, indeed should, raise sensitivity to the children's and families' values systems and religious beliefs and practices, especially in relation to death.

Some teachers have a deep religious faith, and are understandably worried about talking about religion or issues such as death, which have cultural and religious overtones, with children who come from different backgrounds. When Joan, a Catholic teacher working in hospital with seriously ill children, was working with a refugee child of a Muslim background, she was hesitant about discussing her faith with him, even in the context of comparative religion. She recognised that, while he was so ill and cut off from his background, he was especially dependent and vulnerable to the influence of those around him. She knew that teachers have no right to proselytise or indeed to impose in any way their personal belief systems on children. What Joan's pupil probably needed most, apart from his parents, was a warm accepting person, preferably someone who spoke his first language and understood the culture of his home childhood, to listen to him. Education staff may wish to read about how death and loss are treated in some minority ethnic and religious communities in the UK (see Chapter 15).

While caution is critical where teacher and pupil and pupil's family do not share religious beliefs, sensitivity still needs to be exercised even when there is a common faith since there may still be substantial differences in the degree of religious observance, the detail of belief, and how death, illness and dying may be approached. Families who lay no claim to religious faith may also still have a family culture around living and death.

Home–school relationships

Schools can help children with life-threatening conditions and their families by being aware of what they believe and want, not so that teachers can intervene, but so that they can be quietly supportive. This is what matters. Values and religious views may not coincide; a Catholic teacher may worry about the soul of a child from an agnostic or atheistic family; a teacher may view the family's plans for a trip to Disneyland before the child dies as a needless extravagance for a family whose resources are already over-stretched; the family members who do not acknowledge the nature and extent of a child's condition and its likely outcome might be perceived by some teachers as self-deceiving. These matters are simply not teachers' business, whereas education and the general support of children and their families are.

It may be helpful if one member of staff who has already established a particularly good relationship with the family acts as a point of contact and information conduit between school and home on personal matters. While key people in schools' systems, such as the head teacher, class, guidance teacher or SENCO may have particular responsibilities which cannot be usurped, the choice of contact person might best be made by the family. This would allow other teachers to transmit any concerns or requests for information to the family in a sensitively mediated way. This contact person would himself or herself need support from school management and possibly additional training in interpersonal skills and the use of person-centred approaches (see Chapter 15). This would not make him or her a counsellor, but would enable them to be more effective in supporting the child and family.

Counselling, personal support and guidance needs

Where a child with a life-threatening condition either openly asks questions or makes comments in class about death, or where behaviour becomes withdrawn, very anxious or angry, he or she may need to explore more deeply their concerns and ideas and to receive more support than can be delivered by that teacher in class at that time. It is not simply a question of time and place, but also a question of proper child counsellor or child psychotherapy training for the highly sensitive task of working with a child, and possibly the parents, to explore deep, personal and painful feelings. Such trained personnel are not readily available within schools, and any indication of need for this kind of support would probably be best referred using the school's official referral systems through the Child Health Service, or more rarely through the Educational Psychology Service. Some schools may be fortunate enough to be linked to properly accredited child-counselling services.

At all times, and especially in relation to younger children, schools need to be very careful to avoid interfering with family structures, arrangements and beliefs which will generally be most children's main source of support. Nor do all children with life-threatening conditions need counselling or want it. It may be enough that those around them simply listen to what they have to say and respect it. They may simply 'cope'.

Bullying and friendship

Bullying is a pervasive problem in most schools. It would be nice to think that wherever seriously ill children are educated there would invariably be an atmosphere of sympathy, cooperation and friendship between children who have disabilities or medical conditions and those who do not. The contrary is too often true. In special or mainstream schools, children may emphasise differences between each other, and be unpleasant to those most different, particularly those whose symptoms or treatment result in physical differences. If the life-threatening nature of a child's condition is known to others, he or she may be vulnerable to the most cruel of taunts (Eiser 1993).

There is no point in pretending that 'everyone is the same' when the differences are so evident. The task is to ensure a positive, mutually supportive and valuing ethos and to implement an effective anti-bullying policy (SCRE 1993) throughout each school. This improves the education of all but requires the sustained commitment of the whole school community. Children with very diverse profiles can learn a lot from each other, and can form close and significant relationships in school. Friendship at school (see Chapter 7) can be harder for children with serious and life-threatening health conditions to achieve. They may understandably also find it hard to distinguish between kindness, helpfulness, pity and genuine friendship. As teachers, we need to be aware of such confusion, be on hand to support potential friendships and very much on the alert for physical, verbal and 'excluding' forms of bullying, which the victims may be unwilling to report. The 'contact person' (see *Home–school relationships,* above) may have an important role for the child as a confidant in this respect.

Questions about death

Many questions, no absolute answers

Questions about death are going to arise in classrooms whether the school has addressed death and loss in the curriculum or not, so teachers need to be prepared. This becomes particularly salient when there is a child or children in the class with a life-threatening condition, but as I have already indicated, most children will become acquainted with death if not through family and close friends, then through the media.

What then should a teacher do when *any* child asks a question in class about death? There are no easy answers here, and I certainly do not wish to suggest that there are formulae that can be applied. On the other hand, there are some points which the teachers I have worked with in the past suggest should be held in mind. This guidance is geared to classrooms where a child has a life-threatening condition but where most pupils are not affected by such conditions and do not have substantial personal experience, knowledge and understanding. It also assumes that children with life-threatening conditions are assured of skilled additional one-to-one guidance and counselling if required.

Be honest

There are few things more unsatisfying or worrying for a child than a teacher who dithers, looks worried and shifty. Try to answer any questions about death, including your own views of it, if any, as clearly as possible if you have thought through your views. Be frank that this might not be a topic which you feel easy discussing. Children, whatever their own experience, will respect you more for acknowledging ignorance and uncertainty than for pretending knowledge and certainty. A teacher in a mainstream school was talking in a tutorial period to a thirteen-year-old girl with a terminal condition about her future, and the girl raised the issue of death quite bluntly. The teacher recounted how she was thrown into confusion because death was a topic about which she personally felt very anxious. Her pupil put her hand on the teacher's arm and said 'It's all right, Miss, you don't have to talk about it if you don't want to'. The tutorial ended well, the teacher thought, because the pupil felt that she had developed, out of necessity, a more mature attitude to death than had her teacher.

Refer back to pupils
It is perfectly acceptable, indeed sometimes preferable, to respond to questions by saying that you do not know for sure, that perhaps no one does, but that you would be interested in your pupils' views. It is a teacher's skill to enable children's thinking, learning and understanding, not just to transmit knowledge. This may apply particularly to questions which relate to religious issues, beliefs and death. There is no reason why you should not respond to a child's question on what your views on death are, although it is critical to remember the dangers of indoctrination and the special vulnerability of some children to the views of those in authority. Staff with strong religious views may need, as mentioned before, to be particularly restrained here, even when an older child or young person initiates such a discussion, since it is children's and their families' beliefs which matter most. This is where the hard work in preserving a distinct teacher role may pay dividends. Even if you have strong religious views on the nature and meaning of death, they must be presented as your views, in a way that shows that you accord the views of others as having equal validity, and those of the child or young person supremacy in his or her own life.

Be conscious of cognitive maturity as well as age of pupils asking questions
Pupils' ages may not be the only or best indication of what to say to them. We normally expect that children of around five or under have rather fluid views on death, especially its irreversibility, but this is not necessarily the case with children with medical conditions who have spent a lot of time within contexts such as hospitals where they learn a lot – deliberately or incidentally. They may well have friends who have died and will have a greater understanding of the topic than their healthy age-peers. Some older healthy children may, by contrast, have relatively immature views because of their lack of experience. It is difficult therefore for a teacher to align her approaches to suit all pupils within any context. All we can do is be as sensitive to individual children as possible.

Be frank about not being a medical practitioner

Questions about death which lead to further questions about specific conditions or general medical matters – their own or those of others – from healthy children or those with medical conditions should be handled with extreme caution. There is a tendency for children, particularly young children, to lump everyone together – doctors, nurses, paramedics and teachers – but this is something which you should avoid accepting. A clear demarcation of roles will make it easier for both you and the child to get on with more specifically educational matters. At the same time, it is important not to be dismissive of children's questions, especially if they indicate the need of a child with a medical condition who is seeking to further his or her understanding. In such a case an answer such as, 'That's a really interesting question. Maybe you should ask Dr (name school doctor or child health consultant) about it', would be appropriate.

Be clear about not being a 'parent'

Your work with the child is primarily as an educator; you are neither a parent nor a relation. You should always try to establish a professional boundary between yourself and the child emotionally – not always an easy process – but it is that distance which allows you to fulfil the teacher's unique and valuable role. It does not follow that being professional means being callous, or that caring for a child means being unprofessional. Your role is not primarily that of a carer. The child will have others whose role is primarily carer, and you may also care about him, but as a teacher and not as a relation. This sounds rather harsh, but it is not; it represents something which is valuable in your relationship with the child, the fact that you are there to represent education. If each such child affected you in the ways in which parents, carers and closest friends are affected, then it would be impossible for you to carry on and work with other children. You are not there only for that child.

Coping with the death of a pupil

At any time a school pupil may die as a result of an accident, an unexpected acute illness or other trauma. In schools where one or more pupils have life-threatening conditions the likelihood is higher, and in some special schools which cater for children with life-threatening conditions, death is all too frequent.

General principles to enable coping

Given the first statement of this paragraph it would make sense for all schools to have some contingency plans and to compile a 'contingency dossier'. Yule and Gould (1993) assert the need for schools to be prepared to cope with a range of crises, especially to reduce trauma to children, parents and staff. If a school is trained adequately for fire drills, then when a fire arises there is more chance that everyone will leave the building safely and calmly. If teachers and pupils have already spoken about death and loss, if staff have thought through some basic contingency plans in relation to the possible death of a member of the school community, the school will be in a far better position to cope with the reality (see Chapter 15).

News of the death of a child

Even when a premature death is seen to be inevitable by the family of a child and by professionals giving medical support, even though the child may have been very ill and absent from school over some time, and even though those closest to the child will have been encouraged to talk about the eventuality, those involved with him or her will still experience a sense of shock when the news comes. This will be most acute for those closest to the child – class teacher and 'contact person', school auxiliary helpers who may have been involved in giving school-based care, close peer friends and their parents. Even if the child has been absent for some time, it is likely and desirable that these people will have remained in contact with the child and his or her family and, where possible and if the family are in agreement, visited him or her. It is important that these key people are informed first and that they are offered support and a range of choices about what they want to do – to be together perhaps to comfort each other, or to be with other close friends, or to go home quietly if there is someone at home to be with them.

The shock may be even greater about children who, despite their condition, may have seemed relatively well and attending school. There may in such cases be a strong feeling of 'unfinished business' and of goodbyes not said, which can exacerbate grief.

Other staff and children should be informed as soon as possible after this with a carefully prepared warm and appreciative statement – not a eulogy (see Nelson, Chapter 14) – about the child and his or her place in school, some suggestions about what they might wish to do immediately to remember their fellow pupil, an assurance that those close to the child are being looked after and that the school community will be kept informed of further arrangements. Many schools now prefer this to be done more intimately in classes rather than in the more dramatic context of a whole-school assembly. If it is to be done in classes then it is important that the procedures can be handled warmly and supportively by all the teachers concerned. There are therefore implications for prior training, and it is important that staff who wish to opt out of such responsibilities for their own personal reasons are free to do so. Parents of young classmates, or of other children who might be less able to take the news home clearly, should also be informed.

Some children and, less commonly, some staff may respond to the news with overt demonstration of feelings which others may be tempted to judge as excessive, while some may appear on the surface to be totally unmoved. It is important simply to accept that shock and other emotions may be shown – or not – in widely diverse ways, and that children and staff will, with support and in their own time, come to terms with the death. There is no 'good' or 'bad' way to react.

Sometimes in the case of more traumatic deaths or where a very close friend or member of staff seems to be experiencing particularly stressful or prolonged symptoms of grief, calling on the services of a counsellor may be appropriate. Counsellors' names, addresses and telephone numbers should be part of a school's contingency plan dossier. When a child dies, siblings will need support that is practical and empathic over some years but, again, there should be no preconceived notions as to how the child feels or will respond. He or she will have to cope not only with the death of his or her brother or sister but also with all the repercussions on his or her parents and on family life.

Some practical matters are best left until some time later – it would be insensitive to package up the contents of a child's desk immediately to send home although in a few weeks or months this may be what the parents decide they want. Classmates would also not wish 'all evidence to be removed' immediately. Later they may need help to move on: 'I thought that when I cleared John's desk this weekend and rearranged the room, I would put up that nice photograph of you all around him when he visited the school so we can feel he still has a place here'.

Valuing the dead child

What matters most to parents, siblings and close friends in relation to school responses is that the dead child is acknowledged as having been a valuable member of their community, that he or she will continue to be remembered positively, and that their own loss and subsequent feelings are acknowledged, respected and supported, not just in the immediate period after the death and at the funeral, but for some time afterwards. It would not be unreasonable to think in terms of several years, although there will be areas of vulnerability which may never disappear, especially for parents. Parent support may come most appropriately from the home–school contact person but it is important to remember that he or she will also need support. Head teachers have an important representative role for schools, even though in large schools they may not know individual children well.

Ways of demonstrating that a child was valued and will continue to be remembered include:

- Staff members' and pupil friends' attendance at the funeral (if parents wish them to attend – this must be checked out tactfully).
- Flowers at the funeral or house (again if this is thought to be acceptable to parents).
- Letters of appreciation to the family from the head teacher and other staff closely involved with the pupil.

- At a later stage possibly some collation of appreciative notes, drawings, photographs from the child's class or close friends may be given to the family.
- A service of celebration of the child's life or some kind of planned memorial meeting may be held at a time agreed with parents, so that they and other family members may attend if they wish.
- Again at a later stage the school might offer parents a choice of ways of remembering the child within the school, which pupils may also discuss, for example, planting a small tree or special bulbs in the school garden, a picture of the child specially framed for hanging in the school hall, a framed picture drawn or painted by the child to be hung prominently somewhere in the school, a special book for the library, a prize to be offered in the child's name for something he or she was interested in.
- Remembering parents intermittently through the next few years by asking them to school events (and not being hurt if they choose not to attend), by making occasional warm, spontaneous telephone calls ('I thought of you today when I passed Mary's picture in the hall and I just thought I would telephone to find out how you are'), by remembering the anniversary of the child's death for three or four years with a letter or card.

Coping with death in a school community will always be a sad experience, but schools can do much to make it more bearable.

Acknowledgements

I should like to thank Jill Calderwood and Kerstin Phillips for very helpful comments on earlier drafts, and Alison Closs for contributions to the final section.

CHAPTER 14

Privileged witnesses? Siblings' views

Bernadette Kelly and Jeremy Nelson, with an introduction by Alison Closs

Introduction

Much research has been carried out into the effects that illness and disabilty have on healthy siblings, some of it of dubious validity and reliability. That children are affected by their sibling's conditions is undeniable but, as Eiser (1993) and Lobato *et al.* (1988) point out, much research has been conducted from a pathological perspective, seeking evidence of childhood and later adult psychological and behavioural maladjustment, academic 'failure' and poor relationships. Substantially less work has been done from a prosocial perspective. The multifactorial aspects of researching the lives and responses of diverse people in diverse, dynamic and complex relationships such as families have often been underestimated. Meyer and Vadasey (1997), however, reviewing research findings about siblings of children with special educational needs, note that while siblings often have unmet information needs, and can experience isolation, guilt and resentment, pressures to achieve or to care, and many worry about their siblings' and their own future, they also have opportunities to develop valuable human qualities: appreciation of family and loyalty to them, pride in their siblings' struggles to cope, the development of sensitivity, human insight and maturity beyond their years.

Eiser (1993) suggests, as she does in relation to children with medical conditions themselves, that siblings' own voices should come through more strongly in research. Lobato *et al.* (1988) mention that siblings themselves talk most in interview about the importance of 'parents' and siblings' ability to communicate expectations and feelings openly, to flexibly adjust routines to meet individual members' needs, and to problem-solve effectively'. (p. 403)

School staff should have neither positive nor negative expectations of siblings in their responses to their brother or sister's illness or disability, but rather a heightened alertness to opportunities for constructive interventions in whatever arises, support for children's learning, ensuring clear lines of communications with both affected and healthy children and their parents, support for the family unit and positive encouragement of siblings' prosocial behaviour, but with no unrealistic expectation of sainthood!

Bernadette Kelly (elder sister) talks about John

John is the youngest member in our family of five – the 'baby of the family' and I am next to him, the fourth. We have one older brother and two older sisters. I don't really remember John's arrival. I was about eighteen months old when he was born. Like so many older siblings, I did indeed feel the normal emotion of jealousy. This was perhaps made worse by John needing more attention than other children. He was born with his heart the wrong way round and on the wrong side of his body. It had only one chamber and one outlet, where normally people have four. Of course, I did not understand the condition then, masked behind the big words that described it. All I saw was another child draining all my mum's and dad's attention. I felt I had been pushed aside and forgotten. I've been told many anecdotes about my attention-seeking antics and, even though I cannot remember them, I can laugh at them now. The day John was brought home from hospital one proper little madam curtly told her mother 'Put that baby down and take me'. Yes, that little madam was me – and she still is me. John shaped my personality. Had it not been for him I might have been a placid, content person but because I felt I needed to strive for attention it became a way of life. Today, to say I am assertive might be considered by some to be an understatement.

Growing up, everything seemed 'normal', whatever that means. I knew there was something wrong with John, but to me he seemed fine and I resented that he was, in my opinion, being pampered. Being told John was 'special' didn't help because I remember thinking, 'What? And I'm not?' I began to feel I was losing my identity, being introduced as John's sister, not Bernadette. I was crying out for attention, good or bad, I didn't mind, just to get noticed. This was not because I was badly neglected – I wasn't. I think it was just in case anybody forgot I was there, although they didn't get much of a chance for that. I liked people to feel sorry for me. I would rather that they were amazed by me but the sympathy vote is good enough and easier to obtain, particularly with a 'special' brother. Many of my tactics shamed mum and dad. Thankfully, we can laugh at them now. The worst was how I regularly knocked on the neighbours' doors to ask for a 'piece and jam' telling them my mum didn't feed me. Looking back, it seems unbelievable I would do that. Apart from my attention-seeking, I like to think I was quite a balanced child, even if the evidence I've presented seems to suggest the contrary.

John was in and out of hospital quite a lot but initially I paid little attention. Throughout primary school John seemed in many ways to be normal, like other boys of his age but lacking in energy, although not being able to play football never stood in his way. John always had a good time – he isn't and never was a moaner about things he can't do. Even though I wasn't paying too much attention to John's life at school I did notice the differences between John and myself. John had a woman with him all the time, his auxiliary. It was her job to look after John in case he became ill at school. John missed a lot of school and I moaned constantly about how this wasn't fair. All I saw was me being pushed off to school and John being left in bed, in comfort I thought, but actually dead tired. I was not with him when he had to spend days in hospital for check-ups and tests.

When visitors came to the house John enjoyed making them laugh and he could always get the laughs. But when I tried all I got was that half smile that says 'Very nice, dear'. Everybody who knew or met John marvelled at him and I thought sourly how he would have a new scar from an operation to show them, or even just the old ones. I was puzzled by John most of the time. John didn't really want to show people his scars or talk about his health, while I was there breaking my neck trying to achieve a slight gasp when I rolled up my sleeve to reveal a barely noticeable scratch I had acquired during a game of football.

John was sent down to London as he was now on the heart – lung transplant waiting list there, but I still never thought much about things. The first time I actually paid really serious attention to John's medical condition was two years ago, when we nearly lost him. He had an operation and serious post-operative complications. I was suddenly aware I didn't actually know what was wrong with him. I knew what to say when people asked me what was wrong with John. He had his heart on the wrong side, it was the wrong way round, he only had one chamber and one outlet. This was the rehearsed spiel that anybody who asked what was wrong with John got. It suddenly occurred to me that I didn't understand what I was saying. What did it all mean?

I gradually realised that what I really wanted to know was not all the medical things – but what it all really meant to me, to us as a family. I needed to ask questions like, 'Will John die?', 'When will John die?' 'Will he waste away or is he going to get this transplant?' I needed answers and, to be honest, I still don't have them. In a way, I want to go back to being the little girl who was filled with resentment because there was no real pain involved in that life, or not the pain I now recognise. I am too scared to ask my mum and dad for fear of what the answer will be. Or maybe even they don't know. And I'm tired of hearing the same answer to any question about John which is usually 'I don't know'. That is the thing which is the most frightening, the not knowing and only being able to watch John struggle on.

I had never really paid much attention to anything happening to John, in school anyway, until he reached High School age. I had always taken it for granted that John would be going to my secondary school. With John you have to remind yourself that he is in fact ill. In his appearance he looks healthy, if a little blue in colour, but underneath lurk John's many complicated problems and threats to his life.

It was suggested by the education authority that it might be better for John to attend another secondary school instead of the one the rest of us had all attended. Even though our head teacher wanted John to come to our school, it was not equipped to deal with John's physical disabilities such as not being able to climb the stairs. The proposed school already had a lift and other facilities which would benefit John. Practically, this was fine, but in reality it wasn't such a good idea. John was being expected to start at a strange school where he did not know anyone, beginning all over again, making new friends and so on. John was being deprived of a choice, a choice every other primary seven pupil had made – where did *he* want to go? I think John felt he was being penalised because of his health condition. He had always been emphatic that this did not affect or hold him back from anything he wanted to do but now it seemed it was about to do just that.

I felt angry because John was being put to another school simply for convenience. I felt that the school or authority should purchase any equipment John needed, not only for John but for the next child with a condition similar to his. I didn't think John would be the only person ever to use the equipment. In the end a chair that goes up and down stairs was bought and he was allowed to go to our school but I believe the only reason he is there today is because mum and dad were prepared to fight for John.

I have become more interested in John's health and more and more amazed at him every time I look at him. I was selfish before. How did everything affect me? What was *I* going to do? John had lived silently with all his own questions. I sometimes feel ashamed of my feelings. I'm always the first to describe myself as mature and like to think I'm grown up because of all I've had to deal with, but in reality John's the mature one. He doesn't resort to childish measures – he simply gets on with things. By studying John and other ill children like him there is much to be learnt. When you notice the persistent courage these children have you feel humbled that it takes a child to show you this. The family unit was supposed to be John's support, his life-line, but John has proved to be our support and our lifeline.

All I can say to any other family or school in this situation is to enjoy the time. Don't waste a moment. Marvel at this wonderful individual who is undoubtedly coping a thousand times better than you are. And don't be afraid to lean on your children when you need to, because, strange as it may sound, you won't get through any day without your child or children supporting you. Also, if there is a Bernadette in your family or class, try to help her understand but, failing that, just let her get on with it!

Jeremy Nelson (younger brother) talks about Matthew and Miriam

'Do you have brothers and sisters?' is a reasonable question, simple for most people to answer without thought, but tricky for me. It is difficult even to be completely honest, let alone give an informative answer which spares the questioner acute discomfort or embarrassment. I want to explain why this question is both difficult and important for me. I'll tell you a bit about myself and my family and will try to relate, without too much pontificating, why the reader interested in education might want to know about my family and our experiences.

First, some facts. I was the third child born to my parents and am now 26 years old: Matthew, Miriam and I were born respectively in 1969, 1971 and 1973. We lived a middle-class life in a firmly middle-class environment and were always, as I remember it, comfortable. My parents are educated and have professional jobs, my mother having retrained as a teacher when I was about 10. Our genes blessed all three of us with intelligence, and we grew up in a family in which educational success was a normal part of life.

Before I was born, first Matthew, then Miriam, received a diagnosis of cystic fibrosis (CF). Like my parents, I am only a carrier. There had been no apparent occurrence of CF in either branch of my family before my generation. My sister also developed diabetes when she was about 13 years old, and both my siblings' health deteriorated significantly during their teens, so that both, by the time they were 19, had been placed on the organ transplant list, Matthew for a heart – lung transplant and, a couple of years later, Miriam for a lungs-only transplant, which had only just become possible. Matthew received the heart-lung transplant and enjoyed a new lease of life for about six months, then died of a series of post-operative complications on 16 March 1991 – the day after my eighteenth birthday. Miriam died while still awaiting her transplant on 23 June 1993. Neither made their twenty-first birthday.

Those are the facts, but they don't tell all of what I know, or what I felt, only what can be easily summarised. The rest is harder, like the answer to the 'Do you have brothers and sisters?' question.

After consultation with the editor about what this chapter was really about, I noted down two phrases: 'privileged position, a unique viewpoint' and 'witness to siblings in and out of school'. Both of these may apply to me, but I think it worth saying that my opinions are no more objective than anyone else's; probably less so. However, it is these subjective views that cannot be gleaned from anyone else that are most valuable in contributing to an all-round perspective. I will try therefore to concentrate on the views I hold which differ perhaps from those of our parents, teachers and peers.

I had always known that I would outlive both my brother and sister. Always, from whatever age it was that I was capable of understanding, I knew. There was no single moment of realisation – not one that I remember anyway, in the way one remembers a first kiss or fumbling sexual encounter. 'How awful for you. I couldn't have lived with that knowledge,' is a common remark. Not so. Living with that knowledge was, for me, absolutely and utterly normal. Not 'awful' but normal. This does not mean it was pleasant or joyous, just that it was not something that I had to suddenly – and possibly with great difficulty – come to terms with.

The normality of accepting my siblings', and to some extent my own, mortality, and the certainty that I would see them both to the grave, may have been unusual for someone growing up in the affluent West in the late twentieth century. I am no child psychologist but I feel that this has truly shaped my attitudes to the deaths of my siblings, and to myself as an individual. Incidentally, the fact that Matthew's and Miriam's deaths were to come as no surprise did not make them any easier to deal with, only less unexpected.

The 'awful knowledge' has influenced me in many ways, but primarily it has made me a realist, and someone very honest – with myself, at least – about significant emotions, their causes and the best way to deal with them. Others – friends – have come to me for advice, help, or an ear when a close friend or relative of theirs has been diagnosed with some serious ailment. Whether I have been a real help is unproven, but it was important to me that they had come to me. I suppose that I am pleased that my experiences can benefit, if not myself, then others; others about whom I care.

I do not think for a moment that the knowledge I have lived with, and the experiences I have had, have made me into a better person. At most they have made me more down-to-earth, and possibly more grimly realistic. The idea that living with difficult knowledge and unpleasant experiences somehow makes one better or builds character is, I think, absolutely ludicrous. This also goes for the 'idealisation-of-the-dead' – the process by which when someone dies, their previous involvement with anything 'bad' is denied and they become the embodiment of all things good, through selective editing of personal histories and memories. This is taking the idea of 'not speaking ill of the dead' too far.

This idealisation is one of the more common responses I have found in others. I don't think that it ever helped me. When I encountered it from one of my teachers who had also taught Matthew, the only effect it had was to decrease my respect for the speaker. Teacher: 'He was good – perfect, even'. Me – in my head: 'No, he bloody well wasn't – he was my brother who used to beat me up, who lied to Mum, and who called you all sorts of things behind your back, just like any other kid, only possibly with more vitriol'. It's hard to respect someone when they talk in nonsensical platitudes, whatever the motivation.

This is an important point. If people – teachers, colleagues, friends, – want to help someone who has been bereaved, then they have to be able to contribute something useful, if respect for them is to be preserved. Sympathies and greetings-card messages, 'There, there. How terrible you must feel', were not what I needed or wanted. I think I am more grateful to those people who chose to say nothing, for whatever reason, than to those who came out with empty, trite phrases. Maybe I am being too hard, even cynical? Maybe not. Why is this important? Because, if respect is lost for someone in a position of authority, they will no longer be turned to for help or advice. Generally, I had a lot of respect for my teachers, the idealisers aside.

When I entered High School I found myself in a similar situation to many others: that of having to adjust to no longer being a big fish in a small pond, but a little fish in a big pond, and finding that you were expected to make the same ripples as your elders before you. There is nothing particularly special about that, except that I was following some pretty unusual ripples. Why unusual? Matthew and Miriam were very academic, enthusiastic and accomplished, flying the academic flag for the school, but untalented and uninterested in sport. I was not quite the same. I enjoyed a range of sports, representing my school at rugby and basketball. Although intelligent, I 'lacked application', being more interested in discovering the mysteries of girls and alcohol, preferably both at the same time, learning to drive, driving my parents up the wall, skiving school and messing with all things taboo. As I said – a very typical, under-achieving male teenager. This surprised the school, and my parents, a great deal. The physical education department was stunned that a Nelson could actually take part in the infamous five-mile Dump Run, let alone play for a school team. The mathematics department was, I suppose, disappointed that I had no interest in winning the Scottish schools mathematics prize, as both my siblings had.

All in all, I think I had a glorious time at school, getting away with murder on a regular basis. Whether this is because my academically achieving elder siblings cleared an easier way for my alternative choices, or because, by the time I got there, the school was well aware of the Nelson clan and its special needs, and made allowances. At the beginning of each year I did enough to reassure the teachers that I was able, before I settled back into a life of idleness and bent rules. In retrospect, I think that I had the absolute best of all possible worlds. I was able, yet was still given a lot of slack, to the chagrin of my peers.

I think that Matthew's and Miriam's academic success was not unrelated to their social failings; both found it hard to make and keep friends, certainly during High School. Matthew was studying computer sciences and Miriam medicine. I am told that they each had a small but close circle of friends during university but, in all fairness, I was not there to see for myself, being busy elsewhere. But I do know that they both had serious relationships that meant a lot to them. Simply put, they were different: CF, and to some extent diabetes, made them so. If you have CF you have to take vast amounts of drugs, you may have a cannula in your hand, you are in and out of hospital, later you cannot take part in physical education; you cough an awful lot and you mature more slowly. Do you need any more reasons not to be accepted socially at school? Sadly, I think not.

Although the school may have made provision for their physical needs, I really do not believe that any serious attempt was made to accommodate the problems of the social aspects of CF. If they had not been so able academically, then my siblings' school life might have been significantly different. They would have found the work harder, but would possibly have been more socially accepted.

This forms the most powerful memory that I have of Matthew's and Miriam's school life, that of contradiction. They wanted, like all teenagers, to be accepted, possibly to be the same as everyone else, but definitely to be treated the same as everyone else. But they were not the same and they were not treated the same – certainly not by the other pupils.

After Matthew died, when I was in my last year at school, I cannot recall any member of staff saying anything to me or doing anything out of the ordinary to 'help' me. To be fair, this does not mean that nothing was said or done: the whole period is very fuzzy in my memory and it is difficult to distinguish individual events. I can say only that I do not recall if anyone did anything. This strikes me as a serious failing if indeed nothing was done, almost to the point of being unprofessional. Some of my peers later admitted to having avoided me, having had no idea how to deal with the situation: this I can understand in a group of 17-year-olds. It makes me wonder whether the teachers knew how to deal with the situation at all.

At Edinburgh University, to which I had progressed after school, my Director of Studies was on sabbatical when my sister died and I had to co-opt another. He and the faculty as a whole were very understanding and extremely helpful and swift when I decided that I did not want to sit my finals, but resit the year, which I did. I completed university successfully in 1996, and became the only one of my parents' children to receive a degree that was not posthumously awarded. I spent a year and a half working as an academic in Edinburgh University's Artificial Intelligence Department, before moving to London, where I now live and work.

I feel that it is important to note that my relationship with my parents and the whole intra-family relationships have undoubtedly shaped the way I felt and feel about my brother's and sister's deaths, but the effect is wholly unquantifiable. I owe a great deal to the love, strength and, above all, the openness of my parents; and I knowingly fail to do them justice here.

With the benefit of hindsight, I realise that the way that I chose to run my life at school and, in particular, the way that it differed from the lifestyles of my siblings, has much to do with our differing aspirations. My attitude has always been: 'It's all going to be fine. Things will sort themselves out, eventually'. This presupposes that there is going to be enough time for things to sort themselves out. For me, there was and has been; but not for Matthew and Miriam. I can only guess as to what all their inner aspirations were and how they would be shaped by the shortened time-scale.

One of the most painful things for me now is that I never really got the chance to get to know Matthew and Miriam as adults. This means, among other things, that I can never ask them how they saw their education and whether it tallies with my memories and feelings; or what they actually aspired to, and whether they reached all their goals.

So how do I answer the 'Have you got any brothers or sisters?' question? For all my introspective analysis, criticism of others and painful track record in this field, I still cannot answer this question without distressing someone. I just try to make it someone else...

CHAPTER 15

Resources to support education staff working with children with medical conditions

Alison Closs

Introduction

This chapter comprises seven sections, each dealing with a different kind of support resource. *All titles, publishers, etc. of books recommended in this chapter are written out in full in the Reference list, as they are for all references throughout the book.*

Research findings (Eiser and Town 1987, Closs and Norris 1997, Leaman 1995, Bolton 1997) have persistently shown that many education staff – teachers in all kinds of provision, auxiliary helpers, school managers and educational psychologists – not only need support to work more effectively with children with medical conditions, but hey themselves recognise this need and want it met. Support needs vary among individuals and schools, according to previous training, experience and the pupil population.

Staff's existing knowledge and competencies owe more to previous life experiences than to any systematic professional development in this area. Some staff and schools have taken 'crash courses' when children with a particular condition arrive in school or an already enrolled pupil has become ill. This staff development may take the form of actual formal training inputs, often provided through the school medical team, or occasionally through the local authority, or they may simply involve going to the library or nearest book shop to find some relevant reading, or contacting 'umbrella' or condition-specific organisations for information and advice.

Parent, and some child, research participants (Bolton 1997, Closs and Norris 1997) thought teachers often needed more information about children's conditions and their educational implications. They wished that education professionals had more time to listen, but also that some staff knew *how* to listen better and to respond empathically. They appreciated staff who did have relevant prior experience, including personal, family experience of medical conditions, or who made efforts to learn about children's conditions and to respond with understanding.

Education authorities and teacher education institutions have failed in the past to ensure that both initial and continuing teacher education, and the equivalent for auxiliary helpers and educational psychologists, address the inclusion of children with medical conditions.

The suggested resources in this chapter are divided as follows:

- books to develop interpersonal skills and relationships – adults and children
- human resources
- 'umbrella' organisations
- general texts/research about children with medical conditions
- books for teachers about health matters and medical conditions
- books/resources about death and loss
- teaching resources/ideas to help absent pupils and their teachers.

It is not the purpose of this chapter to produce a guide to medical conditions. This has already been addressed by organisations and writers mentioned in later sections of this chapter. Some large organisations, generally those linked to more common or better known conditions such as diabetes, epilepsy, heart conditions, cancer, including leukaemia, HIV/AIDS and asthma, provide information covering most eventualities, including educational implications and guidance for schools and teachers. Some information from other organisations is not sufficiently relevant to education, being too medical in orientation, while others are too short and general, or too complex and impractical. The second part of Chapter 6 illustrates how one small condition-specific organisation 'gets it right'.

Resources to help education staff develop interpersonal skills

The communication between education staff and families of children with significant health problems go beyond the normal range of home–school liaison. This is particularly so if a child becomes ill suddenly, or is diagnosed with a life-threatening condition, or if a child has a crisis in his or her education or health or both. Parents may be tense or depressed, children may be tired, irritable and worried. Education personnel may find coping with the child and thinking about the condition and its educational implications very worrying. 'Will he keep up? Will she be off a lot? Will he be ill in class? Will her condition deteriorate? Will he die? What is expected of me and who will help me? Is it really my job when I have so much to do already with my class?' Strained relationships may be an outcome, but not a necessary one.

Some people may be 'naturally' more sensitive and responsive to the needs of others, while others acquire sensitivity through experience, sometimes a painful process for themselves and others. However, it is generally agreed that many people can learn in a planned way to be more perceptive about themselves and others, better listeners, more open to the views and experiences of others and generally to relate better and more easily, even when very difficult issues are involved.

The kind of knowledge, skills and attitudes required very often form the core content of counselling and interpersonal skills courses. This is *not* to suggest that education staff working with children with medical conditions should become counsellors. Teaching children, and counselling them and their families, are generally agreed to be mutually exclusive activities although exceptional circumstances and appropriate training may bring the two together (see Burnett, Chapter 12). Nor do these children or their parents necessarily want or need counselling. Families facing huge challenges and multiple stresses can be very resourceful and resilient and have their own resource networks of family and friends. However, some counselling *approaches* such as active listening and person-centred approaches (see Chapter 8) are invaluable in everyday working and communication and may be learned through experiential learning in an introductory interpersonal skills or counselling course.

Books are not a substitute for such active learning but there are several which address the kind of interpersonal skills that would be useful (Cowie and Pecherek 1997, Mearns and Thorne 1988). Some are specifically about school–parent relationships (Atkin and Bastiani 1988, Blamires *et al.* 1997, Carpenter 1997, Dale 1996, Davis 1993, Hornby 1994, Wolfendale 1992).

Another aspect of interpersonal skills which troubles teachers in relation to a far wider population of children is how far, and in what ways, they can make constructive interventions to enable friendships (Ramsey 1991, Roffey *et al.* 1994), prevent bullying (Duin 1997, Elliott 1992, SCRE 1993, Train 1995, Young 1998) and promote prosocial behaviour (Warden and Christie 1997). Ensuring companionship and advocacy by creating 'circles of friendship' (Jupp 1992 and 1994) will also be important for children with very severe and complex learning and communication difficulties.

Human resources

Direct contact with 'someone who knows' is a most useful resource:

- parents and children/young people themselves;
- child health services attached to schools and their specialist seniors, who can also access GPs and hospital consultants and relevant paramedical services;

- special educational needs advisers;
- staff of special schools or units for children with physical impairments and/or complex learning difficulties;
- professional workers or trained volunteers attached to associations/agencies linked to conditions.

Parents and children/young people themselves

Parents are often specialists in their child's condition and in the best approaches to dealing with their child. While the level of expertise in relation to the condition will vary from levels of competence comparable with some medical practitioners to the most basic understanding, *all* parents know their children in some ways which teachers cannot, and it is therefore worth spending time with parents to tap into the knowledge and understanding they have, especially when developing healthcare plans and IEPs. This knowledge can then be added to that of other professionals involved including medical and paramedical staff, and of education staff from their experience, observations and reading. It is particularly important that parents are encouraged to keep school staff up to date on their child's state of well-being. Chapter 8 looks at home–school partnerships and communication and how they can be enabled.

Children, too, can be knowledgeable about their condition as Eiser (1993) points out. Current medical practice is to educate and inform children, both to reduce their fears and to help them towards managing their own healthcare. They may know the boundaries of their own competence but this needs to be checked out with parents and medical personnel to ensure that reality does not become confused in younger or less able children (see Chapter 7).

Parents of other children with the same condition may also be a source of information but the health and handling of two children with the same named condition may still be very different. Confidentiality, family privacy and individual values need to be observed so this resource is one to view with great caution. However, another family may have already established good support and information networks which can be useful.

Child health services attached to schools and their specialist seniors

Key medical personnel, their roles and ways of working with children, families and schools are detailed in Chapter 7. Each education authority and school should compile its own medical contacts list and guidance on how and when to contact them.

Doctors and nurses working in mainstream schools may not have detailed knowledge of every possible condition but they do have access to specialist colleagues. Information briefings or formal inservice training for education staff can be arranged through these staff. Child health specialists will be involved in the kind of assessments and reviews which pupils with more pronounced, specific and complex special educational needs have. Such meetings are in themselves mutually developmental for all staff involved. Class and subject teachers, who are less likely to attend such meetings, should receive relevant information from staff who do attend.

Community paediatric nurses attached to Health Boards or NHS Trusts, their hospitals and specialist clinics, are an invaluable source of advice. In the past they have been perceived as working mostly with families but many, in common with paramedical professionals – or professions allied to medicine (PAMs) as they are now called – may be very helpful in interfacing educational and health matters and may also deliver some in-service training to education colleagues.

Special educational needs advisers/officers of the education authority

Some advisers and officers may have a relevant practitioner background in relation to these pupils. However, they all have an overview of provision and an extensive network of contacts as part of their work. They may therefore be able to put one school working with a child with a particular condition in touch with another school in a similar situation, or with staff from a variety of disciplines who have more extensive relevant experience.

Advisers may also be responsible for an authority's equipment and information resources. It would be useful if they could ensure that books recommended in this chapter were available for loan to schools, teachers, auxiliaries and educational psychologists, to augment those that individual establishments may buy for priority use.

Staff of special schools or units for children with physical impairments and/or complex learning difficulties

Most special schools are now part of neighbourhood or 'cluster' primary and secondary school groupings which offer shared understanding and support for the work of each member establishment. Some special schools may also reach supportively beyond their own group and indeed beyond their own authority.

While the populations of all schools, special and mainstream, have been found in recent research (Allan *et al.* 1995) to be more heterogeneous than before, schools which have mainly catered for children with physical disabilities, and for children with complex learning difficulties, have had more and wider experience of children with medical conditions of a complex and disabling kind than any mainstream school. Despite the differences in the learning contexts, experiential backgrounds and attitudes of staff in the two sectors, and of course the individuality of each pupil, the rich experience and very great knowledge of many special school staff *should* be tapped when a mainstream school has a child with such a condition on its roll. Special educational needs advisers or senior child health specialists may help make such links, or head teachers or other designated staff may make direct enquiries. Some special schools have taken the initiative in setting up advisory and liaison services, albeit often with limited resources.

Professional workers or trained volunteers attached to associations/agencies linked to conditions

There is a range of personnel employed by the larger voluntary organisations who are trained to support, advise, inform or educate professionals, families and the public. Some may be social workers or hold other professional qualifications. Their roles may be specific or generic. Some charitable funds may also pay for such workers within a health service context. Personnel of this kind are most common in relation to the more common or serious conditions, for example, epilepsy, diabetes, cystic fibrosis, liver disease and childhood cancers. Such professional workers may also extend their role to supporting the child in school and may see advice or in-service training as integral to this.

Some voluntary organisations train and employ volunteer non-professionals who have experience of the condition concerned, such as a parent or sibling for example, in a supportive role with families. Their support may be particularly insightful.

Local councils usually hold lists of voluntary organisations and their contact numbers, or some may be found through the Yellow Pages. Child health services are also generally aware of these organisations, and the umbrella organisations listed below are well-placed to help identify relevant agencies.

'Umbrella' organisations

There are several important organisations which have an 'umbrella' role in that other more specific organisations may relate to them administratively, or through information, referral or funding systems. The umbrella organisations may undertake political advocacy and networking while the other organisations are more 'hands on'. Among the most significant for children with medical conditions are:

NAESC/PRESENT, the National Association for the Education of Sick Children

St Margaret's House, 17 Old Ford Road, Bethnal Green, London E2 9PL, Tel. 0181 980 8523, Fax 0181 980 3447, Advice line Tel. 0115 981 8282, E-mail: naesc@ednsick.demon.co.uk

NAESC/PRESENT, founded in 1993, promotes the education of children whose education is at risk because of their health, whether they are at school, or absent in hospital or at home (see Chapter 6). They lobby, propagate information in, for example, their own quarterly newsletter, carry out research (see Chapter 4) and development work such as the creation of curriculum subject work packs to facilitate teaching and learning out of school, and community projects to involve young people with medical conditions with their healthy peers.

They have until now focused their energies mainly within England and Wales but are increasingly involved in Scotland and Northern Ireland. Recent editions of their *Directory of Current Provision* (NAESC/PRESENT 1997a, 1998) cover all four countries. They are currently campaigning for agreed national standards for out-of-school education.

SCENT: Sick Children's Educational Network for Teachers, e-mail: majordomo@ngfl.gov.uk

SCENT is one of a range of special educational needs and inclusion-focused mailing lists facilitated through the British Educational Communications and Technological Agency (Becta, Tel. 01203 416 994, Fax. 01203 411 418). It is an Internet mailing list set up to link teachers working with sick children, whether in school, at home, in hospital or elsewhere. SCENT is a forum for sharing questions and answers on many of the issues raised in this book and elsewhere. To join the list free of charge, teachers should send an e-mail message to the address given above with the following message: subscribe scent.

SKILL: the National Bureau for Students with Disabilities

Chapter House, 18-20 Crucifix Lane, London SE1 3JW, Tel. 0171 450 0620, Information service Tel. 0800 328 5050, e-mail: info@skill.org.uk, Worldwide web site: www.skill.org.uk

SKILL – Scotland, Norton Park, 57 Albion Road, Edinburgh EH7 5QY, Tel. 0131 475 2348, e-mail: SkillScotland@compuserve.com

While this book is primarily aimed at enabling the education of school-age children and young people, the educational issues facing school leavers with medical conditions, including gaps in learning and insufficient qualifications, mean that they will almost certainly need expert advice. The local specialist careers officer in Careers Companies is an obvious first stop but SKILL has multiple expert information and advice resources in relation to post-school education of all kinds, including further and higher education and distance learning across the UK, in addition to its lobbying and development roles.

Contact-a-Family (CaF)

170 Tottenham Court Road, London, W1P 0HA, Helpline 0171 383 3555, e-mail: info@cafamily.org.uk Worldwide web site: www.cafamily.org.uk
    Norton Park, 57 Albion Road, Edinburgh EH7 5QY, Tel. 0131 475 2608, e-mail: Scotland@cafamily.org.uk.
    Bridge Community Centre, 50 Railway Street, Lisburn, Belfast BT28 1XP, Tel. 01846 627 552.
    A Welsh office is currently being established.
    CaF is particularly concerned about children with conditions, whether inherited syndromes or other disabilities or illnesses, within the contexts of their families and a special interest in families of children with rare conditions. They aim to reduce the fear and isolation of families and to develop their knowledge and empowerment. They maintain a biannually updated directory of conditions and linked medical and support networks. It may be purchased in ring binder form and is also available on the CaF Website. Education authorities would find it a useful resource for access by all schools.
    CaF links families, answers queries through the national helpline or local office lines, runs conferences, supports parent groups associated with conditions, and puts families in touch with each other and with organisations or developments in other countries.

Action for Sick Children

29–31 Euston Road, London NW1 2SD, Tel. 0181 542 4848; Fax 0181 542 2424.
    15 Smith's Place, Edinburgh EH6 8NT, Tel. 0131 553 6553.
    4 Chestnut Avenue, West Cross, Swansea SA3 5NL. Tel. 01792 404232.
    Action for Sick Children is the campaigning name of the National Association for the Welfare of Children in Hospital and is primarily concerned with medical, nursing care and general well-being of children in hospital. It publishes a quarterly magazine, *Cascade*.

Association for Children with Life-threatening or Terminal Conditions and their Families (ACT).

Orchard House, Orchard Lane, Bristol, BS1 5DT, Tel. (Administration/Fax), 0117 930 4707, Information Line 0117 922 1556.

ACT is particularly concerned about palliative care of children with the most serious conditions and about those who provide the care, whether parents or professionals. It does, however, see education as an aspect of care and normality for children whatever their prognosis and therefore supports the provision of education for all children wherever they may be located. They publish a quarterly review, *Act-Now*, and their Hospice ACTPACK contains regularly updated information sheets about all the existing and proposed children's hospices in the UK.

The Association of Children's Hospices

c/o Hope House, Nant Lane, Morda, near Oswestry, Shropshire SY10 9BX, Tel. 01691 679 679, Fax 01691 679 465.

The Association brings together all independent and voluntary organisations – currently there are 18 hospices countrywide and 12 at the preparation level – which exist to provide:

- care and support for children with a short life expectancy and their families, in whichever way most suits their needs, in separate and specially designed accommodation, and in their own homes;
- terminal care when and where appropriate;
- bereavement support.

Full members fulfil all three criteria and have local authority registration. There are also associate member organisations which provide some but not all the specified services or which have not yet achieved registration. The Association's key interests are care, fund-raising and administration. Hospices exist to enable children with life-threatening and terminal conditions and their families to live their lives as fully and happily as possible. They provide medical and respite care and act as safe and nurturing environments for the whole family.

The hospice movement encourages families to maintain positive links to 'normal' life. It therefore encourages children to continue with their education as far as possible and welcomes teachers to visit children or stay in touch with them by whatever means seem suitable and in line with family wishes. Teachers are affected by their pupils' serious illnesses. Hospices' support teams recognise this and will try to support teachers' needs as far as possible. The Association produces a useful fact sheet about children's hospices (ACH no date).

Children's Hospice Association Scotland (CHAS)

18 Hanover Street, Edinburgh 2, Tel. 0131 226 4933, Fax 0131 220 1626.

While the Scottish hospice belongs to the UK-wide Association of Children's Hospices, CHAS was established to raise funds to build and support the first Scottish hospice at Rachel House, Avenue Road, Kinross, Fife, KY13 7EP, Tel. 01577 865 777. A second hospice service is envisaged in the west of Scotland.

The Northern Ireland Hospice Children's Service, 525 Antrim Road, Belfast BT15 3BS, Tel. 01232 777635.

Fund-raising and planning for a children's hospice in Northern Ireland are currently under way.

National Children's Bureau

8 Wakley Street, London, EC1 V7QE, Tel. 0171 843 6000, Fax 0171 278 9512.

The Bureau is a major political and public force in all issues which relate to the well-being of children, including legal rights, social, medical and educational issues. It is both proactive and reactive to such issues, producing its own publications and commentaries and organising seminars and conferences. It has an extensive library of books and journals, which may be accessed by professional and other concerned people by appointment. As part of its role as an information resource the Bureau has a CD-ROM, *Childdata,* listing relevant articles, legislation, etc., which may be purchased or accessed at some larger libraries. However, the well-being and education of children with medical conditions is only one of its multitudes of concerns. It does not generally answer individual enquiries.

Children in Scotland

Princes House, Shandwick Place, Edinburgh EH2, Tel. 0131 228 8484, has a similar role within Scotland to the National Children's Bureau, albeit on a smaller scale. Its work is almost entirely concerned with its umbrella role in relation to other organisations and to addressing issues of national importance in the ways which seem most appropriate, for example by producing readily understood commentaries on relevant legislation, running conferences and advising the Scottish parliament. It employs a Special Educational Needs Development Officer.

Its role does not include undertaking individual casework, although it is the managing organisation and base for Scotland's national SEN Helpline (see below).

Special Educational Needs (SEN) Helplines

The Scottish Office Education and Industry Department (now the Scottish Executive) set up and funded a helpline service in 1999, managed by Children in Scotland. It provides information and advice but does not take on casework, referring on to alternative organisations as appropriate. The Helpline number is 0131 222 2400, but it can also be contacted through Children in Scotland, Tel. 0131 228 8484.

In England and Wales many education authorities have appointed parent liaison/advisory officers who may be contacted through education authority offices.

Throughout the UK in less populated areas, where 'specialisation' may not be numerically viable, there are also many small local generic special needs support groups which can be particularly useful for families and other agencies and professionals. Local organisations of this kind may be contacted through local authorities' social services or through some of the 'umbrella' organisations already named.

General and research texts about children with medical conditions

Christine Eiser (see Chapter 3) has written extensively about children with chronic illness, mainly from a psychological perspective. Her books (Eiser 1990 and 1993) are particularly relevant for teachers and educational psychologists, enabling reflection on their own practices and letting them understand the impact of illness on the lives of children and their families. Of particular interest to teachers who have had pupils who have been hospitalised is Larcombe's book (1995), based on research into problems experienced by children returning to school after treatment for cancer, other chronic disorders and a range of orthopaedic conditions.

Further insights into the impact on families of illness and of medical conditions which are at the interface with severe and complex disability, and of the views of parents themselves on services needed and on parents' ways of coping, can be gained from three research reports, the first focusing on severe disability and the second and third on children with life-threatening and terminal conditions (Beresford 1994, While *et al.* 1996a and 1996b).

Research into the education of children with medical conditions has produced three recent reports (NAESC 1996, Bolton 1997, Closs and Norris 1997, see also Chapter 4).

Books for teachers about health matters and medical conditions

The comprehensive *CaF Directory of Specific Conditions and Rare Syndromes* has already been mentioned and is available through CaF's web site. Gilbert (1993) describes the nature and implications of the seventy most common syndromes and inherited disorders.

Some texts are specifically aimed at teachers working directly with children (Homan 1997, Irvine 1997) and all schools should have a copy of one of these. They give factual information about the most common medical conditions and their treatments, the policy framework in which health issues are addressed in schools, the practical implications for families and schools and, in some cases, implications for children's learning. Homan provides the structures relevant for England and Wales, Irvine for Scotland. Although Irvine's book focuses on primary schools, much of its contents are equally appropriate for secondary schools. These publications also list the main agencies/voluntary organisations associated with various medical conditions, their contact addresses and recommended further reading. In turn, some of these more specific organisations produce their own resource lists for professionals, parents, affected children and other children.

Books/resources about death and loss

Death and loss are facts of school life, sometimes in a natural and expected way, however sad for those affected, as with the illness and death of elderly grandparents of pupils. However, it is much more painful and potentially traumatic when the illness or death is that of a younger adult or a child. Chapter 13 of this book deals with 'schools and death' at some length, strongly recommending that every school should be prepared, in terms of resources, human responses and systematic approaches, to deal with unexpected trauma, whether the death of a pupil or some other happening. Yule and Gould (1993) is a useful text to help schools build up a working level of preparedness. Comprehensive, practical and sensitive cover is given to loss and the changes of all kinds that affect children and other members of the school community, including death, illness and divorce, in Brown (1999).

Ward (1989) helps school staff introduce the topics of death and loss to primary and secondary age children so that they have a 'coping foundation' in the eventuality of loss and death. Cruse Bereavement Care (Cruse House, 126 Sheen Road, Richmond TW9 1UR, Tel. 020 8332 7227, and local offices in telephone directories) have counsellors trained to work with bereaved children or with staff working with children. Support may be made available to schools. (Many children and adults, however, cope with death and loss through their own personal resourcefulness and family and friendship networks rather than through counselling.) Cruse also publish and stock a number of books specifically for young people and children themselves (Steffes 1997a) and for school staff helping bereaved pupils (Steffes 1997b). An annotated list of publications specifically for children and young people is also available from Cruse.

Another invaluable publication for all schools is Phillips (1996) which comprises an annotated list of books – fact and fiction – to use with children in relation to illness, loss and death, with a supportive introduction explaining and offering advice to the adult reader which should be read before embarking on reading with children or recommending books to them. Immense care has to be taken in the choice of book for any child or children.

Leaman (1995) explores how school staff and pupils think and behave in relation to death and loss, while Dyregrov (1990) provides explanations and guidance for adults about grief in children, how it may make itself evident and how children may be supported. Sarnoff Schiff (1979) and Wilkinson (1991) both talk about the death of a child from the perspectives of being parents, although both also consider the needs of siblings, with the second part of Wilkinson's book being a story for children about the death of a little boy's brother.

Multiculturalism should be addressed in death as in life. Schools should be sensitive and respectful towards different religious and cultural perspectives around death, dying and funerals. Very many books available, particularly the more detailed ones, are written from an assumption of either Christianity or secularism. Henley (1982, 1983a and 1983b) has written three very useful booklets about religious aspects of care, including dying, death and funerals, in relation to Muslims, Sikhs and Hindus. A book edited by Cole (1991) examines aspects of five world faiths – Hinduism, Judaism, Christianity, Islam and Sikhism – including customs and support around death. Brown (1999), again with sensitivity and practicality, also addresses issues which concern the diversity of faiths and cultures present in schools in the UK.

Learning resources/ideas to help absent pupils and their teachers

In Chapter 1, the willingness and flexibility evident in some teachers and schools developing inclusive approaches was recognised, but alongside that was regret and frustration that this could not be described as very widespread or uniform. Problematic issues around educational and social continuity for children with medical conditions are explored in Chapters 8 and 11. This section of this chapter discusses resources which have been insufficiently considered and under-used or simply not used at all. These divide broadly into resource processes and resource products.

Resource processes

When school work is sent to absent pupils, often after considerable delay and persistent parental requests, a courier system is the normal means of transfer. The main couriers are often the already very over-pressed mothers of the absent pupils but sometimes siblings, neighbouring children, or home and hospital teachers if they are involved, may take on this role. While this may offer a useful opportunity for liaison and social contact, in reality much of the time used is unproductive.

The postal service and telephone are often little used for tutoring purposes or for maintaining all-important social contact with absent pupils. The use of fax, e-mail, video and the Internet in relation to absent pupils is largely unexplored in many schools and education authorities, despite the burgeoning of equipment in schools and at home and in opportunities for equipment rental, and despite evidence of its effectiveness in distance learning with adults. Younger, less well-motivated or less well-supported children would find unsupported distance-learning problematic but, as asserted in Chapters 8 and 11, the challenge of supporting learning through communication technology needs to be taken up on behalf of absent pupils.

The Open School Trust, a non-profit-making charitable trust, has been a pioneer in distance learning approaches for children and has published advice on this (Open School Trust 1994). (See References for their address.) NAESC/PRESENT also argues strongly for better and more resources and better management of them and is linked to several ICT initiatives (see contact address and numbers above).

Resource products

Most curricular subject materials are designed to be used in class with teacher support. There is a need to examine existing resources to see whether any lend themselves more to use by children in hospital or at home with parents, or by children and teachers working through telephone, e-mail or fax.

Tutor-supported distance learning packages have been developed within the further education sector by a number of colleges, very often focused on academic or vocational awards. Education authorities in some areas have allowed or even encouraged schools to buy such packages to widen their curriculum choices. Some home and hospital teachers have used these packs with absent pupils, either providing the support themselves or liaising with college staff to provide a joint support network. Good tutoring partnerships and prior assessment of the suitability of open learning for individuals are both important. Once again, communication technology could play a useful part in this form of learning.

NAESC is developing curricular packs with sick children in mind and to date has produced a set of chemistry worksheets and a virtual chemistry laboratory on

CD-ROM, entitled *Go: Chemistry.* Technology and the sciences are problematic for absent children in terms of physical access and also sometimes because of the limited range of subject specialisms offered by out-of-school staff. Two other packs are planned: *Go: Health* and *Go: Space.* NAESC also offers training courses in the use of SIMS Curriculum Planner software to help record achievement and to bring coherence and continuity to children's learning experiences when their place and providers of education change.

Finally, NAESC has developed an INSET Pack for Secondary Schools to help school managers and SENCOs/Support for Learning staff develop positive whole-school policies and practices in relation to children with medical conditions.

Conclusion

It seems that, rather belatedly, education providers and resource producers are waking up to the challenge of supporting learners with medical conditions that are associated with debilitation and absence. They are also beginning to see it more as a rights issue than as one of mere benevolence, and are following a lead established by voluntary organisations. However, the process is neither sufficiently widespread nor consistent – plainly, the current situation is a case of 'could still do better', and 'must learn to work together'.

References

Acheson Report (1998) *Independent Inquiry into Inequalities in Health Report.* London: The Stationery Office.

Alderson, P. (1995) *Listening to Children: Children, Ethics and Social Research.* Ilford: Barnardo's.

Allan, J., Brown, S. and Riddell, S. (1995) *Special Educational Needs Provision in Mainstream and Special Schools in Scotland.* Stirling: University of Stirling.

Anderson, B. J. (1990) 'Diabetes and adaptations in family systems', in Holmes, C. S. (ed.) *Neuropsychological and Behavioural Aspects of Diabetes.* New York: Springer-Verlag.

Asher, S. and Coie, J. (eds) (1990) *Peer Rejection in Childhood.* Cambridge: Cambridge University Press.

Association for Children's Hospices (ACH) (undated) *What is a Children's Hospice?* (Factsheet). Oswestry: ACH.

Association for Children with Life-threatening or Terminal Conditions (ACT) (1999) 'First of the Diana Nursing Teams begins their work', and 'Exciting times for children's health', *Act-Now,* Spring, 1–2.

Ataxia Telangiectasia Society (1998) *Ataxia Telangiectasia: A Guide for Teachers.* Harpenden: A-T Society, 33 Tufnells Way, Harpenden AL5 3HA.

Atkin, J. and Bastiani, J. (1988) *Listening to Parents: An Approach to Home–School Relations.* London: Croom Helm.

Barnes, C. and Mercer, G. (eds) (1996) *Exploring the Divide: Illness and Disability.* Leeds: Disability Press.

Beresford, B. (1994) *Positively Parents: Caring for a Severely Disabled Child.* London: HMSO.

Blamires, M., Robertson, C. and Blamires, J. (1997) *Parent–Teacher Partnership: Practical Approaches to Meet Special Educational Needs.* London: David Fulton Publishers.

Blount, R. L. *et al.* (1989) 'The relationship between adults' behaviour and child coping and distress during BMA/LP procedures: a sequential analysis', *Behaviour Therapy* **20**(4), 585–601.

Bolton, A. (1997) *Losing the Thread: Pupils' and Parents' Voices about Education for Sick Children.* London: NAESC/PRESENT.

Bone, M. and Meltzer, H. (1989) *The Prevalence of Disability Among Children.* London: OPCS/HMSO.

Booth, T. (1998) 'England: inclusion and exclusion in a competitive system', in Booth, T. and Ainscow, M. (eds) *From Them to Us: An International Study of Inclusion in Education,* 193–225. London: Routledge.

British Paediatric Association (BPA) (1995) *Health Needs of School Age Children.* London: BPA.

Brown, E. (1999) *Loss, Change and Grief: An Educational Perspective.* London: David Fulton Publishers.

Buck, M. (1988) 'The silent children', *Special Children* **22**, 12–15.

Bull, B. A. and Drotar, D. (1991) 'Coping with cancer in remission: Stressors and strategies reported by children and adolescents', *Journal of Pediatric Psychology* **16**(6), 767–82.

Campion, J. (1991) *Counselling Children.* London: Whiting and Birch.

Carpenter, B. (ed.) (1997) *Families in Context.* London: David Fulton Publishers.

Chadwick, A. (1994) *Living with Grief in School.* Biggin Hill: Family Reading Centre.

Charlton, A. *et al.* (1991) 'Absence from school related to cancer and other chronic conditions', *Archives of Disease in Childhood* **66**, 1217–22.

Chesler, M. A. and Barbarin, O. A. (1987) *Childhood Cancer and the Family: Meeting the Challenge of Stress and Support.* New York: Brunner/Mazel Inc.

Clark, C., Dyson, A. and Millward, A. (1995) *Towards Inclusive Schools?* London: David Fulton Publishers.

Clayton, T. (1993) 'Welfare assistants in the classroom – problems and solutions', *Educational Psychology in Practice* **8**(4), 191–7.

Closs, A. (1998) 'Quality of life of children and young people with serious medical conditions', in Robinson, C. and Stalker, K. (eds) *Growing Up with Disability,* 111–28. London: Jessica Kingsley Publishers.

Closs, A. and Burnett, A. (1995) 'Education for children with a poor prognosis: Reflections on parental wishes and on an appropriate curriculum', *Child: Care, Health and Development* **21**(6), 387–94.

Closs, A. and Norris, C. (1997) *Outlook Uncertain: Enabling the Education of Children with Chronic and/or Deteriorating Conditions.* Edinburgh: Moray House Institute of Education.

Cole, W. O. (ed.) (1991) *Five World Faiths.* London: Open University/Cassell.

Contact-a-Family (undated, biannually updated) *The CaF Directory of Specific Conditions and Rare Syndromes in Children with their Family Support Networks.* London: CaF.

Cowie, H. and Pecherek, A. (1997) *Counselling: Approaches and Issues in Education.* London: David Fulton Publishers.

Crompton, M. (1992) *Children And Counselling.* London: Edward Arnold.

Dale, N. (1996) *Working with Families of Children with Special Needs: Partnership and Practice.* London: Routledge.

Davis, H. (1993) *Counselling Parents of Children with Chronic Illness or Disability.* Leicester: British Psychological Society.

Deegan, J. (1996) *Children's Friendships in Culturally Diverse Classrooms.* London: Falmer Press.

Department for Education (England and Wales) (DfE) (1994) *Code of Practice on the Identification and Assessment of Special Educational Needs.* London: DfE.

Department for Education and Employment/Department of Health/NHS Executive (DfEE/DoH) (1994) *Circular 12/94: The Education of Sick Children.* London: DfEE.

Department for Education and Employment/Department of Health (DfEE/DoH) (1996a) *A Good Practice Guide: Supporting Pupils with Medical Needs.* London: DfEE.

Department for Education and Employment/Department of Health (DfEE/DoH) (1996b) *Circular 14/96: Supporting Pupils with Medical Needs in School.* London: DfEE.

Department for Education and Employment (DfEE) (1997) *Excellence for All Children: Meeting Special Educational Needs.* London: DfEE.

Department of Education (Northern Ireland) (DENI) (1998) *Code of Practice on the Identification and Assessment of Special Educational Needs.* Belfast: DENI.

Department of Health (DoH) (1996) *Child Health in the Community: A Guide to Good Practice.* London: HMSO.

Dew-Hughes, D., Brayton, H. and Blandford, S. (1998) 'A survey of training and professional development for learning support assistants', *Support for Learning* **13**(4), 179–83.

Duin, N. (1997) *Bullying: A Survival Guide.* (Booklet to accompany the *Bully* series). London: BBC Learning Support.

Dyregrov, A. (1990) *Grief in Children: A Handbook for Adults.* London: Jessica Kingsley Publishers.

Educational Institute of Scotland – Alloa Branch (EIS) (1996) *The Administration of Drugs in Schools.* Alloa: E.I.S.

Eiser, C. (1990) *Chronic Childhood Disease: An Introduction to Psychological Theory and Research.* Cambridge: Cambridge University Press.

Eiser, C. (1991) 'Cognitive deficits in children treated for leukemia', *Archives of Disease in Childhood* **66**, 164–8.

Eiser, C. (1993) *Growing Up with a Chronic Disease: The Impact on Children and their Families*. London: Jessica Kingsley Publishers.

Eiser, C. (1994) 'Making sense of chronic disease. The eleventh Jack Tizard Memorial Lecture', *Journal of Child Psychology and Psychiatry* **35**(8), 1373–89.

Eiser, C. and Town, C. (1987) 'Teachers' concerns about chronically sick children: Implications for paediatricians', *Developmental Medicine and Child Neurology* **29**, 56–63.

Elliott, M. (1992) *Bullying: A Practical Guide to Coping for Schools*. Harlow: Longman.

Erikson, E. H. (1959) 'Identity and the life-cycle', *Psychological Issues* **1**, 18–164.

Evans, S. E. and Radford, M. (1995) 'Current lifestyle of young adults treated for cancer in childhood', *Archives of Disease in Childhood* **72**, 423–6.

Faulkner, A., Peace, G. and O'Keeffe, S. (1995) *When a child has cancer*. London: Chapman and Hall.

Fowler, M., Johnson, R. and Atkinson, S. (1985) 'School achievement and absence in children with chronic health conditions', *The Journal of Pediatrics* **106**(4), 683–7.

French, S. (1993) 'Disability, impairment or something in between?', in Swain, J. *et al.* (eds) *Disabling Barriers, Enabling Environments*, 17–25. Buckingham: Open University Press.

Fullan, M. (1991) *The New Meaning of Educational Change*. London: Cassell.

Gemelli, R. J. (1983) 'Understanding and helping children who do not talk in school', *Pointer* **27**(3), 18–23.

Gilbert, P. (1993) *The A–Z Reference Book of Syndromes*. London: Chapman and Hall.

Hall, D. (1996) *Health for All Children*, 3rd edn. Oxford: Oxford University Press.

Halpern, W. J. *et al.* (1971) 'A therapeutic approach to speech phobia: elective mutism re-examined', *Journal of the American Academy of Child Psychiatry* **10**(1), 94–107.

Hartup, W. W. (1983) 'Peer relations', in Mussen, P. H. and Hetherington, E. M. (eds), 'Socialisation, personality and social development', *Handbook of Child Psychology* **4**, 103–96. New York: Wiley.

Hazel, N. (1996) 'Elicitation techniques with young people', *Social Research Update*, **12** (Spring). University of Surrey.

Henley, A. (1982) *Asians in Britain – Caring for Sikhs: Religious Aspects of Care*. Cambridge: National Extension College/DHSS/King Edward's Hospital Fund.

Henley, A. (1983a) *Asians in Britain – Caring for Muslims: Religious Aspects of Care*. Cambridge: National Extension College/DHSS/King Edward's Hospital Fund.

Henley, A. (1983b) *Asians in Britain – Caring for Hindus: Religious Aspects of Care.* Cambridge: National Extension College/DHSS/King Edward's Hospital Fund.

Hergenrather, J. R. and Rabinowitz, M. (1991) 'Age-related differences in the organisation of children's knowledge of illness', *Developmental Psychology* **27**(6), 952–9.

HMIs Audit Unit (1993) *Quality Assurance in Education: Plans, Targets and Performance Indicators: Current Issues.* Edinburgh: Scottish Office.

HMIs Audit Unit (1996) *How Good is Our School?* Edinburgh: Scottish Office.

HMIs Audit Unit (1997) *Taking a Closer Look at Specialist Services.* Edinburgh: Scottish Office.

HMIs Audit Unit (1999) *Raising Standards – Setting Targets: Targets for Pupils with Special Educational Needs.* Edinburgh: Scottish Office.

Hobfoll, S. E. (1991) 'Gender differences in stress reactions: Women filling the gaps', *Psychology and Health* **5**, 95–110.

Holmes, C. S., O'Brien, B. and Greer, T. (1995) 'Cognitive functioning and academic achievement in children with insulin dependent diabetes mellitus', *School Psychology Quarterly* **10**, 329–45.

Homan, J. (1997) *Spotlight on Special Educational Needs: Medical Conditions.* Tamworth: NASEN.

Hopkins, D. (1991) 'Changing school culture through development planning', in Riddell, S. and Brown, S. (eds) *School Effectiveness Research: Its Message for School Improvement.* Edinburgh: HMSO.

Hornby, G. (1994) *Counselling in Child Disability: Skills for Working with Parents.* London: Chapman and Hall.

Hornby, G. (1995) *Working with Parents: Children with Special Needs.* London: Cassell.

Hymel, S., Rubin, K. H., Rowden, L. and LeMare, L. (1990) 'Children's peer relationships: Longitudinal prediction of internalising and externalising problems from middle childhood', *Child Development* **61**(6), 2004–21.

Irvine, S. (1997) *A Guide to Child Health in the Primary School.* Edinburgh: Health Education Board Scotland.

James, A. (1993) *Childhood Identities: Self and Social Relationships in the Experience of the Child.* Edinburgh: Edinburgh University Press.

Jupp, K. (1992) *Everyone Belongs.* London: Souvenir Press.

Jupp, K. (1994) *Living a Full Life with Learning Disabilities.* London: Souvenir Press.

Kagan, C., Lewis, S. and Heaton, P. (1998) *Caring to Work: Accounts of Working Parents of Disabled Children.* London: Family Policy Studies Centre/Joseph Rowntree Foundation.

Katz, E. R., Rubinstein, C. L. and Hubert, N. C. (1988) 'School and social reintegration of children with cancer', *Journal of Psychosocial Oncology* **6**, 123–40.

Kennedy, H. (1997) *Learning Works: Widening Participation in Further Education.* Coventry: Further Education Funding Council.

LaGreca, A. M. (1990) 'Social consequences of pediatric conditions: A fertile area for future investigation and intervention?', *Journal of Paediatric Psychology* **15**(3), 285-307.

Lansky, S. B. *et al.* (1975) 'School phobia in children with malignant neoplasms', *American Journal of Diseases of Children* **129**, 42–6.

Larcombe, I. (1995) *Reintegration to School after Hospital Treatment.* Aldershot: Avebury.

Lazarus, R. S. and Folkman, S. (1984) *Stress, Appraisal and Coping.* New York: Springer.

Leaman, O. (1995) *Death and Loss: Compassionate Approaches in the Classroom.* London: Cassell.

Lee, R. (1993) *Doing Research on Sensitive Topics.* London: Sage.

Lobato, D., Faust, D. and Spirito, A. (1988) 'Examining the effects of chronic disease and disability on children's sibling relationships', *Journal of Pediatric Psychology* **13**(3), 389–407.

Malcolm, H., Thorpe, G. and Lowden, K. (1996) *Understanding Truancy: Links between Attendance, Truancy and Performance.* Edinburgh: SCRE.

Masten, A. S., Morison, P. and Pellegrini, D. S. (1985) 'A revised class play method of peer assessment', *Developmental Psychology* **21**(3), 523–33.

Mayall, B. (1996) *Children, Health and the Social Order.* Buckingham and Philadelphia: Open University Press.

Mearns, D. and Thorne, B. (1988) *Person Centred Counselling in Action.* London: Sage.

Meyer, D. and Vadasy, P. (1997) 'Meeting the unique concerns of brothers and sisters of children with special educational needs', in Carpenter, B. (ed.) *Families in Context*, 62–75. London: David Fulton Publishers.

Morris, J. (1991) *Pride against Prejudice.* London: Women's Press.

Morris, J. (1995) *Gone Missing: A Research and Policy Review of Disabled Children Living Away from their Families.* London: Who Cares? Trust.

National Association for the Education of Sick Children (NAESC) (1995) *Education for Sick Children: Directory of Current Provision in England and Wales with a Commentary on the Problems and Issues.* London: NAESC/PRESENT.

National Association for the Education of Sick Children (NAESC) (1996) *Research into the Provision of Education by Local Education Authorities to Children who are Out of School for Reasons of Sickness.* London: NAESC/PRESENT.

National Association for the Education of Sick Children (NAESC) (1997a) *Education for Sick Children: Directory of Current Provision in England, Scotland, Wales and Northern Ireland.* London: NAESC/PRESENT.

National Association for the Education of Sick Children (NAESC) (1997b) *Inspection Issues and Standards Setting Conference Report.* London: NAESC/PRESENT.

National Association for the Education of Sick Children (NAESC) (1998) *Education for Sick Children: Directory of Current Provision in England, Scotland, Wales and Northern Ireland.* London: NAESC/PRESENT.

National Association for the Education of Sick Children (NAESC) (quarterly) *Present Newsletter.* London: NAESC/PRESENT.

Noll, R. B. *et al.* (1990) 'Social interactions between children with cancer and their peers: teacher ratings', *Journal of Paediatric Psychology* **15**(1), 43–56.

Noll, R. B. *et al.* (1991) 'Peer relationships and adjustment in children with cancer', *Journal of Paediatric Psychology* **16**(3), 307–26.

Noonan, E. (1983) *Counselling Young People.* London: Methuen.

Norris, C. and Closs, A. (1999) 'Child and parent relationships with teachers in schools responsible for the education of children with serious medical conditions', *British Journal of Special Education* **26**(1), 29–35.

Oliver, M. (1996) 'Defining impairment and disability: issues at stake', in Barnes, C. and Mercer, G. (eds) *Exploring the Divide: Illness and Disability*, 39–54. Leeds: Disability Press.

Open School Trust (1994) *Teletutoring via Fax.* Park Road, Dartington, Totnes TQ9 6EQ: Open School.

Parker, J. G. and Asher, S. R. (1987) 'Peer relations and later personal adjustments: Are low accepted children at risk?', *Psychological Bulletin* **102**, 357–89.

Perrin, E. C. and Gerrity, B. S. (1981) 'There's a demon in your belly: Children's understanding of illness', *Paediatrics* **31**, 841–9.

Phillips, K. (1996) *What Do we Tell the Children? Books to Use with Children Affected by Illness and Bereavement.* Edinburgh: PARC, Dept of Child Life and Health, 20 Sylvan Place, Edinburgh EH9 1UW.

Piaget, J. (1952) *The Origins of Intelligence in Children.* New York: Harcourt Brace, Jovanovich.

Pinder, R. (1996) 'Sick-but-fit or fit-but-sick? Ambiguity and identity at the workplace', in Barnes, C. and Mercer, G. (eds) *Exploring the Divide: Illness and Disability*, 135–56. Leeds: Disability Press.

Pridmore, P. and Bendelow, G. (1995) 'Images of health: exploring beliefs of children using the 'draw and write' technique', *Health Education Journal* **54**(4), 473–88.

Professional Association of Teachers (PAT) (1996) *Fact Sheet: Medicines in Schools.* Derby: PAT.

Ramsey, P. (1991) *Making Friends in School.* New York: Teachers' College Press.

Ritchie, J. and Spencer, L. (1995) 'Qualitative data analysis for applied policy research', in Bryman, A. and Burgess, R. (eds) *Analysing Qualitative Data.* London: Routledge.

Robards, M. (1994) *Running a Team for Disabled Children and their Families.* London: MacKeith Press.

Roffey, S., Tarrent, T. and Major, K. (1994) *Young Friends: Schools and Friendship.* London: Cassell.

Royal College of Paediatrics and Child Health (RCPCH) (1997) *'The Essentials of Effective Community Health Services for Children and Young People'.* London: RCPCH.

Russell, P. (1994) *Short-term Care: A Parent's Perspective.* London: Council for Disabled Children.

Russell, P. (1995) *Good Practice in Risk Management in Social Care.* London: Council for Disabled Children.

Sarnoff Schiff, H. (1979) *The Bereaved Parent.* London: Souvenir Press.

Scottish Council for Research in Education (SCRE) (1993) *Supporting Schools against Bullying: The Second SCRE Anti-Bulllying Pack.* (This pack includes the 1997 revised pamphlet, Mellor, A., *Bullying at School: Advice for Families*). Edinburgh: SCRE.

Scottish Office Education and Industry Department (SOEID) (1996) *Circular 4/96: Children and Young People with Special Educational Needs: Assessment and Recording.* Edinburgh: SOEID.

Scottish Office Education and Industry Department (SOEID) (1998) *Special Educational Needs in Scotland: A Discussion Paper.* Edinburgh: Scottish Office.

Scottish Office Education and Industry Department (SOEID) (1999) *A Manual of Good Practice in Special Educational Needs.* Edinburgh: SOEID.

Sebba, J. and Sachdev, D. (1997) *What Works in Inclusive Education?* Barkingside: Barnardo's.

Shakespeare, T. and Watson, N. (1998) 'Theoretical perspectives on research with disabled children', in Robinson, C. and Stalker, K. (eds) *Growing Up with Disability*, 111–28. London: Jessica Kingsley Publishers.

Smith, P and Sharp, S. (1994) *School Bullying: Insights and Perspectives.* London: Routledge.

Spirito, A., Stark, L. J. and Tyc, V. (1989) 'Common coping strategies employed by children with chronic illness', *Newsletter of the Society of Paediatric Psychology* **13**, 3–8.

Steffes, D. (1997a) *When Someone Dies: Help for Young People Coping with Grief.* Richmond: Cruse Bereavement Care.

Steffes, D. (1997b) *When Someone Dies: How Schools Can Help Bereaved Students.* Richmond: Cruse Bereavement Care.

Stiller, C. A. (1994) 'Population based survival rates for childhood cancer in Britain, 1980–91', *British Medical Journal* **309**, 1612–16.

Stirling Council (1998) *Guidelines for the Administration of Medication*. Stirling: Stirling Council.

Tomlinson, S. (1982) *The Sociology of Special Education*. London: Routledge & Kegan Paul.

Train, A. (1995) *The Bullying Problem: How to Deal with Difficult Children*. London: Souvenir Press.

United Nations (1989) *The Convention on the Rights of the Child*. Geneva: United Nations' Children Fund.

van Veldhuizen, A. M. and Last, B. F. (1991) *Children with Cancer: Communication and Emotions*. Netherlands: Swets and Zeitlinger.

Varma, V. (1984) *Anxiety in Children*. London: Croom Helm.

Varni, J. W. and Setoguchi, Y. (1991) 'Correlates of perceived physical appearance in children with congenital/acquired limb deficiencies', *Journal of Developmental and Behavioural Pediatrics* **12**, 171–6.

Varni, J. W., Katz, E. R., Colegrove, R. and Dolgin, M. (1993) 'The impact of social skills training on the adjustment of children with newly diagnosed cancer', *Journal of Paediatric Psychology* **18**(6), 751–67.

Ward, B. (1989) *Good Grief 1: Exploring Feelings, Loss and Death with under 11s* and *Good Grief 2: Exploring Feelings, Loss and Death with over 11s and Adults*. Uxbridge: Cruse Bereavement Care.

Warden, D. and Christie, D. (1997) *Teaching Social Behaviour*. London: David Fulton Publishers.

Welsh Office (1994) *Circular 57/94: The Education of Sick Children*. Cardiff: Welsh Office.

Welsh Office (1997a) *Good Practice Guidance on Supporting Pupils with Medical Needs*. Cardiff: Welsh Office.

Welsh Office (1997b) *Circular 34/97: Supporting Pupils with Medical Needs*. Cardiff: Welsh Office.

Wetton, N. M. and McWhirter, J. (1998) 'Images and curriculum development in health education', in Prosser, J. (ed.) *Image-based Research: A Sourcebook for Qualitative Researchers*. London: Falmer Press.

While, A., Citrone, C. and Cornish, J. (1996a) *A Study of the Needs and Provisions for Families Caring for Children with Life-Limiting Incurable Disorders*. London: Department of Nursing Studies, Kings College.

While, A., Citrone, C. and Cornish, J. (1996b) *Bereaved Parents' Views of Caring for a Child with a Life-limiting Incurable Disorder*. London: Kings College Department of Nursing Studies.

Wilkinson, T. (1991) *The Death of a Child*. London: Julia MacRae Books.

Williams, T., Wetton, N. and Moon, A. (1989) *A Picture of Health*. London: Health Education Authority.

Wolfendale, S. (1992) *Empowering Parents and Teachers: Working for Children*. London: Cassell.

Wolff, S. (1976) *Children Under Stress*. Harmondsworth: Penguin Books.

Young, S. (1998) 'The support group approach to bullying in schools', *Educational Psychology in Practice*, **14**(1), 32–9.

Yule, W. and Gould, A. (1993) *Wise Before the Event*. London: Gulbenkian Foundation.

Index